RATCHETDEMIC

RATCHETDEMIC

REIMAGINING ACADEMIC SUCCESS

CHRISTOPHER EMDIN

BEACON PRESS
BOSTON

BEACON PRESS
Boston, Massachusetts
www.beacon.org

Beacon Press books
are published under the auspices of
the Unitarian Universalist Association of Congregations.

24 23 22 21   8 7 6 5 4 3 2 1

This book is printed on acid-free paper that meets the uncoated paper
ANSI/NISO specifications for permanence as revised in 1992.

Text design and composition by Kim Arney

Library of Congress Cataloging-in-Publication Data

Name: Emdin, Christopher, author.
Title: Ratchetdemic : reimagining academic success / Christopher Emdin.
Description: Boston : Beacon Press, [2021] | Includes bibliographical
    references and index.
Identifiers: LCCN 2021012706 (print) | LCCN 2021012707 (ebook) |
    ISBN 9780807089507 (hardcover) | ISBN 9780807089514 (ebook)
Subjects: LCSH: Academic achievement. | Self-actualization (Psychology)
Classification: LCC LB1062.6 .E63 2021 (print) | LCC LB1062.6 (ebook) |
    DDC 370.1—dc23
LC record available at https://lccn.loc.gov/2021012706
LC ebook record available at https://lccn.loc.gov/2021012707

*To all the students who taught me
to be me and my HipHopEd family*

CONTENTS

FOREWORD

I Am a Ratchetmom

I write these words in tears and in utter amazement at this monumental work by Chris Emdin.

Emdin writes,

> To be ratchetdemic is to have no role in starving part of the self
> in pursuit of "academic" knowledge. It is a recognition that any
> education that is disconnected from helping students understand
> themselves and the power structures that influence their worlds and
> how these structures operate to stifle or obfuscate young people's
> purpose is not education at all.

I am a proud ratchetmom. A ratchetpoet. A hip-hop-generation single parent of a self-aware, poetry-writing, hockey-playing, music-producing, question-asking fourteen-year-old son named King. My son, raised on poems and possibility on purpose. An Obama-era baby who grew up knowing an American president looked like an older version of himself.

While my son is a well-rounded, globally thinking teen, raising him inside the United States education system has been one of the most difficult, heartbreaking experiences of motherhood. Everything I poured into my son would be slowly devoured, poked at, carved into an unfamiliar place outside our home called the classroom. A lively, free-spirited boy would soon be forced to sit still at outdated square desks facing a grownup—usually a white woman—and having to regurgitate whatever knowledge they were ordained to deliver for the day.

What's worse is, I was paying for it!

With few choices at high-performing, art-focused elementary or junior high schools in the city of Detroit, I simply had to make a choice of school based on things most white affluent parents will never have to consider: safety. Will my son be "safe"? Somehow I thought my tuition dollars would give him smaller classrooms (and it did), but it did not lessen the Eurocentric lens of the teachers and the systemic racism they learned in the same system they now teach in.

By the time King was in first grade, I was completely over it. I would spend my days nervously pacing in front of his classroom at the trendy progressive school he attended because my son told me the boys were being treated differently than the girls. He said the teacher was mean.

We loved this school in preschool and kindergarten. I loved the comradery of the like-minded parents. Still, a bad hire would change everything. This afternoon, I would catch the young, blond white teacher from far north of Detroit talking to the Black boys in the class as if they were not human. There was one student I remember whom she found "disruptive," and she would just give him puzzles and refuse to teach him most of the day. On this particular day, King must have done something to upset her, and she told him to go stand and face a corner for several minutes. I happened to be in the hallway, and I saw her eyes lock mine with a fear that had her rethinking her morning commute to be in front of brown and Black babies in Detroit.

She was never fired, so I pulled him from the school, and five other students would follow suit, and we (the parents who left the progressive school and I) created the Aker School for Gifted Children in the living room of one of the parents who already had a strong homeschooling experience with elementary school–age children.

As King got older and outgrew Aker, the stress of finding a safe place for my son to attend school while I was on the road being a poet, and educating other people's kids, did not stop. It became years of systems stripping down the essence of who he was/is. Write-ups sounded like misdemeanor charges in fifth grade at his small private neighborhood school, and as he got older, I found that school had some strange need for him to have some compliance with authority.

I'm a ratchetmom, meaning, I am educated, but I am from the west side of Detroit and will get in the face of a racist teacher and threaten an administrator attempting to humiliate my son.

Education became the front line for me, whether I wanted it to be or not.

One morning his failure to "pledge allegiance to the flag" became a parent meeting. He was gently asked by his nice homeroom teacher to put his hand over his heart. His response was his head shaking from left to right in the "no" formation. His defense: "I stood up, so I wasn't being disrespectful," and "I should not have to pledge allegiance to a flag." My then ten-year-old told his principal he was a Muslim, something that forced me to laugh with pride on the inside. "Oh, he is? Okay, well, good to know." It was news to me.

My ten-year-old had to use religion to explain why he did not have to conform to the class rule. He was defiant, but he was a solid student academically, so not much could be done.

Test scores over character. Personality overrides academic performance.

Over the years I have been forced to have to "Jawanza Kunjufu" these MFA'd- and PhD'd-up educators consistently.

It's exhausting, and it wasn't solely because of white administrators. I found some Black academics to be jealous of my son and to simply not "like him" because of his free personality and sometimes because I was his mother. In hip-hop, we call these people "haters."

I decided to twist my son's hair when he was two years old. I knew he would eventually maybe chop off his locs when he was older, but this is the way I wanted King to approach the world. When he decided he wanted to go to a Jesuit high school for seventh grade, I supported him. The open house should have been a sign to run, but my son is a Virgo, and aesthetically the school had all the pretty rich kid resources while being in "the neighborhood." This is a school with 80 percent white students, generally busing in from the suburbs, and 20 percent Black or "Detroit" students. You have to test to get in, and I knew many of the cool alumni. It's not a bad look for the resume. I tried. We tried.

During open house one of the music teachers made a comment about my son's locs that were long brown ropes nearly touching his waist. King had already told me he was hearing rumors that he would have to cut his hair. I told him that was nonsense. Then I was hit with the sucker punch. "You know he's going to have to cut his hair," said the white teacher.

"No one mentioned that to me when I was registering him and paying my deposit," I replied.

"It's in the handbook." He actually said those words.

"Really, the handbook. Well the handbook is outdated."

He was correct though. The handbook clearly stated that all the boys would have to cut their hair. No braids or ponytails.

He also told me and my head full of long blue locs that they were preparing the boys for "professional jobs." I asked him if I looked like I didn't work, and then told him I was sending my son to the school to prepare him for college, not the workforce.

Why in the hell are we in this matrix, King? Because this is America, right in the middle of my predominantly Black city.

When King cut his locs, I cried. I felt as if this system had won, but it wasn't long before King, with his new conservative coif, would become a challenge for the administration at the school. I was asked by the vice principal less than a month after King had enrolled if I had ever tested my son for ADHD. He referred to me as a mom from a school of thought that probably didn't believe in testing. I told him he was spot-on and that, no, I had not tested my Knight Arts Award–winning son, who was mentoring younger poets by ten years old and opening for Dave Chappelle, for any type of learning disorder.

We lasted one year in this "prestigious," expensive school.

What I learned is that the way this ratchetmom and artist-educator had raised her son challenged the well-educated adults in the US education system. Control and obedience were at the core of this curriculum, not tapping into his genius, and my young son could absolutely feel it.

In his fifth and last private school, in eighth grade, he approached me in the school parking lot and simply asked, "Is this a prison or a school? I feel like I can't sneeze or turn my head."

This school, with hallways full of Black and brown Detroit kids, offered only the longtime Black male janitor as staff representation for the young men. When I offered to do an affirmation program for the boys, it was met with the blank stare of disconnect.

What does my personal story have to do with this incredible book in your hands?

Chris Emdin has found a way to articulate the collective pain of a community and raise the bar for what is possible for American children everywhere.

Chris Emdin's powerful assessment of the US education system and the tapestry of tools he offers inside these chapters are exactly what is needed and necessary for this country to finally flip the script of the failed mediocre classroom experiment that is destroying the minds of all students but being enforced strategically onto the minds, spirits, and bodies of brown and Black students.

This book was built for parents like me. This book is some necessary calm for the collective worry of loving mothers and fathers. Those of us who drop their children off at school early in the morning and hope the lesson won't attempt to steal their joy or devalue their humanity before 3:20 p.m.

This book is for the revolutionary teacher who dreams of a student like my son. Invaluable professors who value art and understand that young people seeing themselves in their education helps to develop self-confidence and self-worth, and gives birth to spectacular critical thinkers and future humanitarians.

This book is for those of us on the front line of education, who understand that inclusion and global thought leaders are needed ammunition against systemic white supremacist constructs.

This book is for those who want to be better educators. For those of us who have felt the affliction of feeling less than brilliant, less than possible. For those who fought for their children the best way they could, without any protection, support, or encouragement from community or academia.

Chris Emdin is offering not just the spotlight on the truthful pain of it all but also an unfiltered salve to heal our wounds so we can begin to elevate what we consider higher ed in this country and beyond.

This book is for those who have felt like the lone sword-wielding warrior parent who feels no empathy from family or administrators. This is our tool box for survival, complete with a map for lesson plans and intimate, thought-provoking questions.

This book is for those seeking passion and bright eyes lit up with ideas and ringing with promises. Those advocates of honoring spirit over the ability to score high on standardized unsanitized tests. For those who truly see the potential, the innate gifts that our young people offer and want to pour into that greatness, pushing their curiosity into the stratosphere!

We need ratchetdemics to come together to break down the silence of elitism, the dumbing down of culture, and the wiping out of Blackness to support white-identified norms in the US education system.

We need Chris Emdin and ratchetdemics now more than ever.

In Solidarity,

jessica Care moore
Poet, Author, *We Want Our Bodies Back*

INTRODUCTION

*The practice of a healer, therapist, teacher, or any helping pro-
fessional should be directed toward his or herself first, because
if the helper is unhappy, he or she cannot help many people.*

—THICH NHAT HANH[1]

*You have to decide who you are and force the world to deal
with you, not its idea of you.*

—JAMES BALDWIN[2]

To be ratchetdemic is to achieve a state of consciousness that allows
one to operate in the world having mind, body, and spirit activated,
validated, and whole without distortion or concession as one acquires
all essential knowledge—academic knowledge, knowledge of self,
knowledge of how to navigate one's immediate surroundings, knowledge of the systems in which one is embedded (particularly those that
are structured to disempower), and knowledge of the world. Achieving this state of consciousness is the true mark of being educated, and
both getting to that point and helping youth get to that point are the
chief responsibilities of the educator.

Imagine a school system that is designed for students' complete
self-actualization and how young people would emerge from their
time within such a school system—fully aware of their greatness and
infinite potential. Our nation's education system professes to improve the learning of the whole child, which includes mind, body,
and spirit, but it chiefly concerns itself with "educating" the mind.
It does so not by cultivating or elevating the mind but by attempting to control and manipulate it to maintain systems that devalue

1

certain people and their words, thoughts, actions, and behaviors and elevate others. Our schools, particularly for Black children, function to fill the mind, police the body, and cast away the spirit. To be ratchetdemic is to have no role in starving part of the self in pursuit of "academic" knowledge. It is a recognition that any education that is disconnected from helping students understand themselves and the power structures that influence their worlds and how these structures operate to stifle or obfuscate young people's purpose is not education at all. To hold ratchetdemic knowledge is to see the limits of institutional knowledge and recognize that true knowledge of self, society, and the world exists when we open our eyes to the genius that each and every student possesses.

The ratchetdemic educator understands that true knowledge is not given; it is discovered. By designing learning environments and curricula to awaken curiosity, hard work, and determination, the ratchetdemic educator creates conditions that allow young people to make their own discoveries. Ratchetdemic educators recognize that the best types of learning contexts vary from the norm in terms of how loud the classroom gets or how unstructured it may appear. The ideal learning environments reengage parts of the self that have been deactivated in the pursuit of "book knowledge." Most importantly, ratchetdemic educators recognize that they must pursue their own work toward freedom from the constraints of institutional structures and model this pursuit for students.

Students must see you struggle with the tension between what is expected of you and what is the right thing to do. This does not mean that ratchetdemic educators do not understand or teach academic content. In fact, they have to have more command of the content they are delivering than the educator who just teaches what they are given. Ratchetdemic educators are expert in content knowledge but are not constrained by it. They deliver content in a way that has contextual value and uplifts the student.

The concept behind being ratchetdemic has always existed. It has always been the hidden ingredient in the work of those in the field of education who challenge the status quo and reimagine the way that power is distributed in this country and across the world.

It is in the education theories of hundreds of scholars like Gloria Ladson-Billings and Paulo Freire. However, it is more than words and theory. It is in the embodiment of them. When you hear recordings of Freire speaking or see Ladson-Billings teach, there is a ratchetdemic quality or authenticity that only becomes evident in their presentation—their voice inflections, their rawness, their passion, their fervor, their taking up space and claiming power even in powerful places. Power, in its most simple form, is the ability to do something that one wants to do and having the agency to act upon it. For the ratchetdemic educator and student, being ratchetdemic means exercising power through the ability to act in the way that feels most comfortable and authentic in the pursuit and expression of the knowledge. Power is also the capacity and the ability to direct or influence the actions and behavior of self and others. Being ratchetdemic is about pushing the boundaries of what is normal within schools to reflect the needs of groups of people who have been denied power. It is claiming the right to develop and express one's true genius and live as one's true self. I suggest that formal education, at its core, is about the distribution of information, tools, and resources for the sake of gaining or maintaining power within a particular social structure. Some are able to translate what they have received in schools into false power in the form of positions of authority or control within institutions. Others are burdened by what they have received in school because it has taught them to hide and inevitably lose the power they innately possess.

This is the season for educators of all types and in all disciplines to claim power and teach youth to do the same. It is the season to be game shifters and norm shatterers. In an era in which schools perpetually assault those who society has pushed to the margins, the need for the philosophy of being ratchetdemic has become more urgent than ever before. We have not seen such blatant opposition to Black folks pursuing power and wholeness since Jim Crow laws mandated segregation and endorsed a state-sanctioned devaluing of Black life.

In that era, there was a fear of educated Black folks and a villainizing of those who taught them. People with power were simply not going to let Black kids in White schools and let them flourish. With the election of Barack Obama in 2008, American society got a taste of Blackness in (political) power. The aftertaste has left bitterness in the throat of the power structure across the country. In response, it has spit out the most egregious hate in speech, tweet, practice, and policy. The Obama-era model of gaining power with/through institutional position came with a required gentility that did not do much for the agency of marginalized folks. Civility and respectability did not distribute power to those rendered powerless across industries and institutions for generations. In fact, political institutional power blinded many people to the denial of full power to Black folks everywhere and Black youth in schools. This is not to say that the presence of a Black family in the White House did not provide inspiration and motivation to Black people. It is to acknowledge that under an administration of civility and appropriateness, there were certain norms around the denial of agency that were maintained. Teachers who signed up to change the lives of Black and other minoritized children were quietly being assaulted by accountability checklists, empty standards, and pressure to conform to the status quo. Folks who were presenting "alternative models" to existing schools that doubled down on the poor pedagogy that stifles the spirit of the ratchetdemic thrived. An agenda of imposing blind conformity to the norms of institutions and forcing segments of the population to accept a brokenness of self and spirit were hidden under calls for high academic expectations.

The youth pushed back against this agenda in classrooms every day. They told us the testing was too much and the strict adherence to curriculum that made no space for them was suffocating. Some educators stood with them. Those who stood and still stand in staunch opposition to this flawed notion of what it means to be academically successful remain under assault. Those who possess an intellect deep enough to see through the façade of academic success that masks the inadequacies of the current system to meet the needs of Black folks are made to feel like they are crazy. Because our youth hold power in their truth and inspire others when they share it, they are often silenced and their truth is denied. What they have to say about how this system doesn't work is erased from the conversation about schools. They are framed as less than, inadequate, not intellectual or academic because of the fervor with which they deliver their message and not the truth within it. They reclaim power by embodying a ratchetdemic identity, one in which there is no role to play other than being one's authentic self, because that is all one truly has. It is the season to have all of who one is on display. It is the time to be all the beautiful things that one is at once. It is the time to be loud and thoughtful and angry and loving and ratchet and academic with fire in the belly and a desire to push the world to reimagine how they see us and others like us. It is the time to create space for the people we rarely get the gift of hearing from within institutions like schools. If given the platforms they deserve or the room to breathe and fully be, the silenced could empower so many to reclaim power and embrace their full academic and intellectual selves.

In this book, I honor the traditions of Black women who have always understood the power of holding on to a core identity that is rooted in community while displaying an intellectual heft that matches that of anyone who is credentialed or degreed. I think of women who not only embody this phenomenon but also those who write and speak about this phenomenon. Evelyn Brooks Higginbotham's work has consistently highlighted Black folks who were not seen as having value or whose stories had been stripped of complexity but who exhibited excellence in fields that range from politics to medicine with a certain ratchetdemic approach to being in the world. When she writes of the "politics of respectability" adopted by Black women from the late 1800s to 1920, Higginbotham describes women who created certain rules of engagement for operating in a world that saw them as less than because of their gender and race.[3] She describes women who saw an erasure of certain parts of themselves as a necessary endeavor for gaining social and political change. She also writes about Black women like Septima Clark, who was the quintessential ratchetdemic educator.

Septima Clark's father was born into slavery. Her mother was raised in Haiti and moved to South Carolina when she married Septima's father. Her mother was insistent that her children have a good life and be accepted by society. Septima's mother wanted the best for her children and translated that desire, for them to be more than their circumstances would allow, into an obsession with respectability, especially for her daughters. This led her to focus on getting Septima the best education possible but also ensuring that neither Septima nor her siblings behaved in a way that could be construed as inappropriate. Speaking too loudly or eating in the street was barred. Her children had to always be well put together, and the girls had to be "ladylike" in all ways at all times. In response, Septima pushed back against her mother's requests for her to be subdued in her interactions with the world. She "married down" in terms of social status, "married up" in terms of love. She realized even then that down was where the soil was, and for anything to grow, you go first to the soil. I argue that the soil is where the ratchet is. The academic is where the book knowledge is. For the world to have any true meaning, both have to be taken care of.

Septima Clark's ratchetdemic educator identity is captured most powerfully in one of the quotes she is most recognized for: "I have a great belief in the fact that whenever there is chaos, it creates wonderful thinking. I consider chaos a gift."[4] The chaos that she speaks of is not just random confusion but a disruption of the norm or status quo. Septima Clark saw the power that comes with interrupting norms, particularly those that exist simply because they stifle creativity and self-expression. Septima Clark's life and work show us what it means to be a ratchetdemic educator. She was a teacher in the traditional sense of having a classroom and a role to teach students subjects and in her mission to transform the lives of her students by meeting them where they were and creating a context in which they felt compelled to become part of the political process. She taught them their rights and made them aware of how they had been robbed of them, even as they were taught how to become literate. Her citizenship schools for adult learners taught illiterate adults how to read and write, but as Katherine Charron describes, the schools Septima Clark started also "provided a space in which adult African Americans could begin to dismantle their internalized sense of White supremacy [and] the feeling that white is right."[5]

In the spirit of Septima Clark, the ratchetdemic educator asks, What piece of this system is doing violence to my mind, body, and spirit, and what chaos can I bring to this space so that my students do not have to undergo the same violence that I had grown accustomed to or adjusted to? Martin Luther King Jr., in a powerful speech at UCLA in 1965, describes the unfortunate reality that the world often adjusts itself to certain types of injustice. The ratchetdemic educator does not become adjusted. In fact, our work is to be what MLK described as the "creatively maladjusted."[6] At one point, MLK called for the start of a new organization called the International Association for the Advancement of Creative Maladjustment. The organization was intended to bring together a critical mass of people who refuse to be held captive by institutional norms or acquiesce to the whims of those who hold and wield power. Its mission was to ensure that the creativity and authenticity of marginalized folks were used to disrupt systems that force them to adjust to systems that enact violence on them. I suggest that a cadre of educators who recognize that schools are designed to foster the brokenness of Black folks and who respond to this reality by teaching and being ratchetdemic are the ones who can see this mission to fruition.

On the rare occasion that we see someone embody a ratchetdemic identity, even if we don't know how to name what we are seeing, we revere them. We look to them as heroes of sorts because of the manner in which they navigate multiple worlds with ease in a way that is beyond code switching and closer to just existing. I think of attorney and political commentator Angela Rye, who describes her approach to existing in the world as sophista-ratchet, and Professor Michael Eric Dyson, who assumes a down-home Black preacher identity as he waxes poetic about topics that range from politics to pop culture. I see those who use complex academic terms and urban vernacular interchangeably and effortlessly. We look at these folks as anomalies who happened to have stumbled into their brilliance. However, I suggest that they resonate with us because there are elements of their genius in all of us. Their methods of engagement are essential for all of us. Angela Rye and Michael Eric Dyson speak and operate with a certain conviction that is complemented by their academic credentials and professional position. The self that they present is one that all educators must embody and model for young people. They are ratchetdemic educators. They connect with their audiences, deliver new information, resonate authentically, and speak truth to power.

In this book, I extend the genius of Patricia Hill Collins on intersectionality and Black feminist thought and bring it to schools, schooling, and their flawed ideas about academic excellence.[7] I am inspired by Brittney Cooper's work on antirespectability as protest and Treva Lindsey's work articulating the lived experiences of New Negro womanhood in Washington, DC, in the late nineteenth century. I have learned from Professor Terri Watson from the City College of New York and her embracing of her Harlem identity in her studies of education and from the radical love expressed by Yolanda Sealey-Ruiz in her book *Love from the Vortex*. I offer that these works should be brought to teachers and young people as a means to model for them that there are different ways to exist in the world. The movements that these sisters spearhead and the ideas that they articulate must be brought to classrooms and be a part of teaching and learning. The work is directly inspired by a 1971 conversation between Nikki Giovanni and James Baldwin—both Black intellectual icons—and a dialogue they had in which they discuss everything from love to politics while exuding a certain Black cool that was as palpable as it was intangible.[8] The subtle use of slang, voices rising in disagreement, the brilliant analysis of the conditions within communities, overall high intellect, and love expressed throughout the conversation are what ratchetdemic educators do. Nikki Giovanni and James Baldwin were teaching. They were comfortable in their own skin, free in their critique of society and each other, and held each other to the highest expectations. Ratchetdemic educators in classrooms do the same. They hold young people to the highest of expectations academically while holding society to the highest of expectations in accepting the genius of young people in whatever form it comes.

To be ratchetdemic is to get to a place where we unapologetically love ourselves as educators, to love and accept young people however they show up to school, and to get young people to fully love themselves. The ratchetdemic educator is not poisoned by public opinion or the lack of value assigned to teaching. They recognize that for any human being to reach the height of their potential and tap into the pinnacle of their greatness, they must first become a K–12 educator. It is in this role that your inner genius is awakened and most accessible to you. For those who choose teaching as a career, their genius is awakened every day of their professional lives. The daily practice of ingenuity, flexibility, creativity, and patience is the formula for awakening genius. For those who once taught, even after they no longer work every day in classrooms, the recognition of and reverence for the genius of teaching allows them to access their genius in their present work. Teaching is about being in touch with the youth and the communities they are from and being humble enough to learn from them as you engage in your work. The ratchetdemic educator does this continually and develops a certain genius that is unparalleled as a result. With this being said, it is absolutely possible to take a job to teach and never activate your genius. The genius of teaching is reserved for those who don't hide behind the title or credential and instead take on the actions required to authentically connect with students and their communities.

This book is about an age-old sentiment/approach not yet fully brought to the fore in education, and yet, it is a capturing of the spirit of the times. While it was designed with the teacher and the student in mind, there are lessons here for anyone interested in how schools have robbed the gifted among us of faith, love, discernment, intuition, and power. It is about how we may restore these valuable gifts to those who were born into them but lost them on the course to being "educated." It is about the hidden flaws of the education system and how it has been designed to harm the most vulnerable young people. This book is built from the sensemaking of narratives that I have heard from those who have been most affected by schools and schooling. It is a way of looking at self and the world that creates a way forward for frustrated young people in classrooms and those who teach them. It is information that has come to me from dozens of everyday people from a variety of professions. I have gained insight from activists, artists, bus drivers, busboys, cabbies, and cleaners, who shared their truths about how they have been broken by a system that was marketed to them as the way out of their present conditions only to place them in even worse ones.

Engaging in and with these truths has been hard. As an education researcher who has been charged with bringing these truths to light, I've had to keep quiet, listen, and then prepare to be a vessel for words and emotions that are larger than myself. This book is for and from parents, pedagogues, principals, preachers, advocates, activists, and *academics*. I italicize the word *academics* because my conversations with people within communities who do not have the credentials or degrees that are perceived to be requirements for being an academic have provided me with more powerful insight on schools and the negative effects of contemporary schooling than any professor or pundit positioned or presented as an academic. This book is for the millions of folks who talk about education with passion and have learned to wield and swing (s)words like *equity, cultural relevance,* and even *anti-racism* at educational injustice without recognizing that their wild swinging often fans the flames of a hidden and more insidious injustice than what they profess to be against. Being ratchetdemic is allowing our swords to do what they were designed to do: to bring the culture of young people to the fore and allow them to leverage their natural genius to overcome the oppression perpetuated by schools and schooling. It is about us taking a critical look at ourselves and how we have been shaped by institutions that rob us of our joy and passion while selling us a version of education that doesn't awaken the soul. It is about uncovering and recovering. Uncovering truth and recovering soul. Uncovering the reality that what we blindly pursue is useless. Test scores matter but they don't matter more than joy. Curriculum matters but not if it erases the student and kills their passion. This work is about recovering the authentic self that reaches the authentic student.

DR. WHITE

> *In every moment, each individual part must be what it is, because all others are what they are and you could not remove a single grain of sand from its place, without thereby, although perhaps imperceptibly to you, altering something throughout all parts of the immeasurable whole.*
>
> —JOHANN G. FICHTE, THE VOCATION OF MAN[1]

> *I have a dream that one day this nation will rise up and live out the true meaning of its creed—we hold these truths to be self-evident: that all men are created equal.*
>
> —DR. MARTIN LUTHER KING JR.

> *And judgment is turned away backward, and justice standeth afar off: for truth is fallen in the street, and equity cannot enter.*
>
> —ISAIAH 59:14

The years 2020 and 2021 were filled with both profound challenge and divine revelation. Like many who work with Black folks, poor folks, and others who have been pushed to the margins of society, I emerged from these years deeply aware that what we, as a nation and as a world, are far from where MLK dreamed we could be. The pandemics of coronavirus and state-sanctioned violence fell squarely on the shoulders of Black folks—and, in particular, Black children. They witnessed death in multiple forms and experienced it in unimaginable ways. They saw people they knew succumb to a horrific disease. They saw videos of people with skin like theirs being assaulted and assassinated by people whom they were taught all their lives to trust. Most importantly, they experienced the death of their innocence as virtues they believed in, like justice and equity, devolved into hypocrisy and fallacy.

As all of this was happening, the world kept going. Schools went back and forth between in-person and online instruction with no true investment in young people or concern for their teachers. Institutions did not consider that some young people were trying to sort through death and destruction in ways that others could not even fathom. Schools moved along in a pursuit of "normal" without considering the trauma our children carried before the pandemic—let alone during and after it. The world continues to chase normal by ignoring the pain of many while justifying that callousness by highlighting the successes of a few. And here we are, reeling from a global pandemic, while aiming to teach like nothing ever happened. We are teaching like pain and death aren't things that warrant our attention in classrooms, hiding inequity and injustice under the cloak of normal.

If this world is to be what MLK dreamt it to be, where equality is accepted as truth, and difference and experience are both welcomed and embraced, we must look at sameness and uniformity as the chief enemy of any progressive society. If everybody is trying to be like somebody they are not, and if the system of education is hell-bent on making everyone into a version of excellence that is about sameness, we will remain as we are, swimming in inequity, struggling to make connections with young people and their communities, paying lip service to social justice and cultural relevance, and maintaining the status quo. To move forward, we must accept that schools have become the chief site for a failed experiment in the socialization of Black folks, whose entire existence in American integrated schools has been about learning to behave in ways that are acceptable to White societal norms, even at the expense of their healing and their humanity. Schooling has always been about the upholding of White middle-class ideals that even White folks, who largely benefit from the enterprise, cannot fully align themselves to. The chief goals for us all must be not only to highlight these unsaid truths about schools and reject them by saying out loud how we have been harmed by them and begin the movement toward healing by being our authentic selves.

Unfortunately, schools assault authenticity just as fervently as they embrace socialization. It's not just that everyone is being forced to look, act, talk, and move in similar ways through schools; it is that teachers and their students are being stigmatized for stepping out of roles that have been defined for them. In many urban schools, this process is overt. There are schools where teachers who don't follow the curriculum or who choose not to follow established scripts about how to teach are threatened. Letters are placed in files and warnings about firings are part of the everyday discourse. Students who interrupt instruction that stems from scripted teaching are also penalized. They are called "disruptive" and are threatened with failing grades and suspensions. In these schools, where there is no space for dialogue about the ineffectiveness of the curriculum in meeting the needs of students and no questioning of how expectations of sameness are embedded in the curriculum, there is often a narrative that is shared with the public about equity being the reason for the type of pedagogy that is being enacted. The public is somehow convinced that equity means teachers have to do the same thing at the same time for all young people. It is in these schools that lines from MLK's speeches and quotes about equality get weaponized against teachers and used as justifications for teaching that stifles creativity and undermines authenticity.

MLK's argument for equality, which is about empowerment and dignity, gets used to drive a pedagogy of sameness and uniformity that is hard to debate if one is not aware of the intention behind the rhetoric. We must be clear that "All men are created equal" does *not* mean that all students are to be taught or even engaged with in a uniform manner. Somehow, *equality* and *uniformity* have become interchangeable and are used to justify a pedagogy of sameness that is being framed as the pursuit of MLK's dream. The "I Have a Dream" speech that those in power use to silence and paralyze young people and their teachers specifically states that "we can never be satisfied as long as our children are stripped of their selfhood and robbed of their dignity." When we don't consider teaching for equality to be about restoring selfhood and dignity, signs that said "Whites only" during segregation get replaced by "Whites only" curriculum and continues the process of stripping the dignity from youth and from the teachers dedicated to seeing their true value. By denying authentic expressions of self and teaching youth that their purpose in life is to pursue "better" versions of themselves, they never learn that the skin they are in and the experiences of their ancestors that they hold in their genetic code make them innately brilliant and powerful. This is especially the case when this better version has been defined by society as being as close as possible to a White, middle-class American ideal— the attainment of which, for Black folks and all who have other lands of origin, is ridiculous to aspire to. Equity then becomes about putting people in places where they are forced to engage in the perpetual pursuit of a position and/or persona other than the one they hold within themselves: a gross distortion of MLK's dream.

To depart from this distortion, educators must be clear that MLK's dream is not about enduring a stripping of your selfhood for the sake of getting a "good job" or having a house with a white picket fence, 2.5 children, a degree, and a dog. It isn't about collecting accomplishments. None of these things are prerequisites to being whole. His dream was not about educators selling young people on the idea that the closer they get to arbitrary benchmarks, the closer they are to worthiness. It was not about training students that they should do well in school so they can have things when they are older. MLK's dream is about seeing genius and greatness in who you are and being comfortable in a state of consciousness that allows you to exist without any prerequisites to counting as a whole person or a full citizen. To know and be yourself, and to exist in that place unapologetically and still feel and be equal to anyone else, is the dream. To get to that state of consciousness, every person must be able to identify the qualities that he or she is defined by—not the things we have or the credentials we hold but the things that define us—the things we love about ourselves and the things that resonate with the people who know and love us. For the teacher, one of the main questions to always ask yourself is, *When I leave the school building and I am around the person or people whom I love the most, who am I? Am I loud? Silly? Funny? Quirky?* The work of the teacher is to find acceptance in that person and to operate as that person at all times, especially when teaching young people.

For far too many people in the field of education, the version of themselves that I am calling for is completely unfamiliar or tucked so far away from who the public sees that it is hard to retrieve when they are in the classroom. The preparation of administrators and teachers does not require what Yolanda Sealey-Ruiz calls an archaeology of the self and a finding or falling in love with the self. I argue that the absence of that part of preparation for teaching impacts what teachers value and how teachers teach. Folks who have not found their authentic selves or who have learned to tuck away their raw, pure, and expressive (ratchet) selves are easily convinced to teach young people that they're not good enough and that they need to chase better versions of themselves. Because these educators are running away from their true selves, they see their ratchet self within as undeserving of visibility or love. These people cannot teach young people to love their full selves because they do not love themselves. Their entire identity is wrapped up in the position they hold, the credential they have been given, or the things they have acquired as a result of their position. Their sense of self is so bound up in a fabricated persona that if the things they have gathered through it ceased to exist, they would not know who they are.

The fact that young people do not have the titles that adults define themselves by means that they are closer to a version of themselves that is authentic and pure. When Black youth first enter schools, they don't imagine that there is a "better" version of themselves that they must chase. It is not until they are thrust into institutions that convince them that the endless pursuit of better is the chief currency for being successful that they begin to question themselves. When students encounter educators who are convinced that the purpose of school and life is not learning for the sake of gathering information to use in the real world but learning to be seen as better by someone they don't know or see, students begin to internalize that philosophy and start to see themselves as less than. In schools, there is no honesty about the flaws in the "better self" model or about how it is a celebration of Whiteness. Rather than painting an honest and robust picture of the world and the people in it, young people get enculturated into the idea that schools and life are only about achieving, amassing, and gaining grades, titles, positions, and things at the expense of what is framed as their "lower self," which is actually their highest self—the more authentic, expressive, and ratchet self that they had before they got to school.

An honest and robust picture of the world recognizes that there is cultural wealth in communities that have historically been seen as less than and genius in those who may not have a formal education. A formal education without knowledge of self is dangerous and makes you a danger to yourself and your community because you become a pawn of the institutions that gave you the education. A formal education with knowledge of self allows you to concurrently operate within the institutions and beyond them. Students who attend schools where there is no value attached to knowing who they are or seeing the beauty in where they come from blindly pursue getting better grades, being better behaved, and being pushed to meet expectations that have been intentionally designed to be insurmountable. These are expectations that have nothing to do with actually learning or being mentally, emotionally, and spiritually motivated to pursue knowledge or find joy in doing so. In a system in which being academic or scholarly is about being closer to something foreign to you, schooling becomes training for not knowing or valuing self. When the model for teaching is always focused on being better than what you are—which is predicated on the concept that who you are (particularly if you are a Black child) is never good or good enough—both teaching and learning become an exercise in collecting endorsements or accolades that can easily be stripped from you if you fall out of favor with those who gave them to you. Grades for students and even satisfactory classroom observations for teachers are often about gaining acceptance from those with power. This is not to say that I do not believe in high expectations or good grades. I believe in both. However, it is important to deeply interrogate what the expectations are and what the grades are for. Are we compensating young people with good grades for being quiet, docile, and obedient and attaching those behaviors to intelligence or being academic? Are we showcasing how good we are at keeping students silent when folks come to observe our classes, or are we teaching to incite passion, excitement, and enthusiasm regardless of how we are being viewed?

It is a well-known narrative in Black and other communities of color that academically high-achieving students are always asked by their families about the points they missed, even when they do well on exams and assignments. "Mommy, I got a ninety-eight," is often followed by, "What happened to the other two points?" "The teacher said I did well in school today," is often followed by, "Well, make sure you do better tomorrow." These responses are built-in mechanisms for destroying self-confidence implanted in the consciousness and manifested in the narratives of folks who have been historically positioned as less than. The ultimate goal of schooling for them has become gaining acceptance in and from society by first having their child gain acceptance from their teachers—who are trying to gain acceptance from their superiors. This ladder of seeking acceptance goes all the way up through schools to governmental bodies and age-old systems that are designed to ensure that Black people are not whole. In fact, more often than not, we train students who don't yet know themselves to blindly follow teachers who have not learned to know themselves either. To know yourself is to engage in committed, conscientious self-reflection with the goals of stripping away what you are doing for validation from institutions or systems and recognizing who you are, as you are, in the contexts where you are; not a title, a role, or a job but a person who is loved and who deserves love.

When education is about becoming someone "better" without recognizing the excellence in who we already are, we alter the world as it should be and tilt it toward inequity. We give power to those we are emulating and remove power from ourselves and those who are like us. We become actors who perform for the acceptance of others, and instead of valuing ourselves for who we are, we act out roles that move us further and further away from our authentic selves. People literally move away from what shapes them. They follow phrases like "Make your way out of the neighborhood" and "Teach for a bit then make your way out of the classroom." They physically and psychologically move toward being different from who they are and act out roles that are played until they stop recognizing who they are. In the midst of this elaborate pretense, our true selves lie dormant but festering beneath the stifling veneer of being better. Consider the story of a young person I mentored who knew her entire life that she wanted to be a teacher. Growing up, she was an amazing poet. She would attend spoken-word events across the city and gained some popularity for being amazing at her craft. Her voice was loud and powerful and seemed to be able to fill any room. As a poet, she took on the persona of a teacher. Folks sat and listened intently. They hung on to her every word. When she performed, people joked that she had already developed her teacher voice. Teaching was her calling.

In college, she struggled a bit academically but found a way to navigate through it. Her biggest challenge came when she had to do her student teaching. She wanted to teach elementary school and had to study under an established teacher who had her own third-grade classroom. Each day, she walked into this teacher's classroom and served as an assistant of sorts. She handed out papers and got the students to sit in groups of four as the teacher requested. On certain days, she escorted students to the cafeteria. These walks were one of the few moments when she got to be alone with the students. She told them stories, and they sang songs together. One day, as they walked down the hallway, she recited a poem she had written for them. It was about how she saw herself in them. The students were inspired. They showed up to class the next day reciting poems. Over time, they started speaking like poets. Their voices were strong, and their stories were vivid. When the official teacher saw this, she was livid and reported to the university that the aspiring teacher was distracting students and a bad influence. As a result, her graduation from the teacher education program was put in jeopardy. The students were reprimanded for "behavior unbecoming of a scholar" in the school. This is the type of language that permeates urban schools where the chief goal is chasing appropriateness and policing expression. In this case, the aspiring teacher quickly learned that becoming a teacher meant not being herself. The students learned that being a scholar was being spoken at and not having a voice themselves. The aspiring teacher left the experience believing that if she wanted to teach, she would have to change who she was. The students left the experience learning that they could only be scholars if they were quiet and docile. This is a familiar story for far too many teachers and also for students who are reprimanded for finding joy and only rewarded when they accept the absence of joy as part of the process of teaching and learning.

Teachers who seek out the profession because they want to make a difference in the world quickly learn to become followers of a script composed of lesson plans and test prep materials, acting out roles that fit that script until they lose sight of the reason they wanted to teach in the first place.

In acting, performers will often go through a number of steps in preparation for a role that they have been cast to play. Sometimes, this involves getting into the mind and body of the character in order to convey what the scriptwriters envisioned. Once this happens, many actors find it challenging to return to who they were before reading the script. Their real and fictitious worlds can sometimes blur so much that they cannot discern the difference between them. In some cases, actors have needed therapists to help them transition back to the real world. A notable example of this process is actor Michael B. Jordan's disclosure of the challenging process of getting both into and out of character when playing the villain Killmonger in the movie *Black Panther*. In much the same way, many teachers and students lose who they are as they act out roles of a societally scripted better version of themselves. Their sense of what is right has been so skewed by the roles they play that they cannot exist without a script to tell them who they are and how to be. This is why well-intended teachers and "good people" are hyperaggressive with children who look like younger versions of themselves. It is why educators who claim to understand anti-racism in education and who graduate from universities having taken classes on urban and multicultural education make students lie on the ground for mock slavery auctions (which has actually happened more than once over the last decade). There are thousands of educators who understand the script and language of equity, social justice, and cultural relevance without doing the work to understand who they are and what they believe about young people. The truth is that if teachers truly believed that all students have genius and that teachers are in touch with that central belief, they could never accept and implement a script that doesn't see the full student. When these teachers are confronted with the racism in their "anti-racist" teaching and cultural ignorance in their "culturally relevant" teaching, when we ask them if they realize that all the students who failed their classes are Black or that all the students who are constantly in trouble in their school or classroom are from a particular demographic, they use the language of equity from their script to justify their racism. They become so defensive that all that is being triggered is a dangerous aggression that they end up taking out on their students. This type of aggression is worse than if this type of teacher was never introduced to the language of equity and anti-racism in the first place.

I was once told the story of a young Black professor who overcame incredible odds to graduate with her terminal degree and finally get a job at a university. When she arrived on campus, she was advised to find a more senior professor to serve as her advisor. The university had put a mentoring system in place to support new faculty as they navigated the delicate balance between teaching, research, and service that is at the core of academic life.

As a Black woman in a predominantly White institution, the professor struggled to find someone who would serve as her advisor. This is not to say that people were mean-spirited or blatantly unwelcoming. No one told her that they would not serve as her advisor. In fact, their friendliness was inclusive on the surface, even though it felt anything but welcoming to her. Everyone smiled, but no one connected with her. There was no one she felt comfortable being vulnerable with. This all changed one day when, during a faculty gathering, she saw a woman I'll call Dr. White. Dr. White was an older Black woman and even looked a bit like the young professor. Dr. White sat in front of the room in a suit and commanded an air of importance. The young professor envisioned that she could be like her one day. Excited to see another Black woman in the room and itching to fulfill the university's request that she find an advisor, she walked up to Dr. White and said hello. Her hands moved joyously as she introduced herself and mentioned her excitement at seeing another person of color at the institution, and she even mentioned her upbringing and an abridged version of her battle through academia to get to this point. She may have even touched Dr. White's shoulder as she asked her if she was willing to serve as her faculty advisor. As she completed the request, she extended her hand and heart while waiting for a response. Dr. White lifted her head, turned it away from her, and said nothing. The silence spoke volumes. Eventually, embarrassed and heartbroken, the young professor walked away.

As she walked out of the room, she immediately began to question herself about how the encounter went. Why was I so informal? Was I disrespectful? Why were my hands moving a million miles a minute? Why did I put her on the spot? Had I acted inappropriately? The questions got even more dizzying as the week progressed, and these ignited an immense bout of self-doubt. Eventually, the young professor settled on a reason why she was treated so poorly. She concluded that she was too loud, too informal, and not academic enough. She stood in the mirror and practiced a less wild smile. She recited a more formal introduction that she hoped would erase both her last experience with Dr. White and also the piece of herself or part of her background that she believed caused the reaction she received. She was upset at the version of herself who made the first introduction. That was her ratchet self. She wanted to be better so she could be more accepted by Dr. White and all that she represented.

A few weeks later, at the next faculty meeting, the young professor sat in the back of the room rehearsing her lines in preparation for a reintroduction to Dr. White. The information being shared from the podium about the upcoming academic year may have been valuable but, at this moment, meant very little to her. She half listened and fully focused on her potential mentor. As before, Dr. White sat up front and looked sharp and focused. When the meeting concluded, the faculty greeted each other with the usual pleasantries and smiles that only last till the person the smile is aimed at turns their head. That's how these faculty meetings are—cordial and pretty on the surface, callous and petty beneath. As people filed out of the room, the young professor made her way to the front and prepared to undo the awkward interaction from the first introduction. She had replaced her T-shirt and blazer with a pantsuit with pockets. She held a book in one hand to keep it from moving wildly after she began talking. She was going to reintroduce herself to her new advisor and do so properly this time. She had learned her lesson. She adjusted the pace of her speech to match what was expected in this new space. With book in hand, back straight, and words measured, she began, "Pardon me, perhaps we got off on the wrong foot during our initial introduction. My most sincere apologies if my excitement to engage with you was inappropriate."

She paused after this sentence long enough for an eyebrow to raise from Dr. White and then continued her speech. "I was charged with identifying a new faculty member advisor and was wondering if you would be willing to be my . . ." Before she could finish, she got a response. In a thick seemingly British accent came the words, "No, I'm quite busy this semester; don't think that would be possible." Crushed once again, the young professor managed to scrape up enough self-confidence to thank Dr. White for her time before making her way out of the room.

This time, despite being hurt, she recognized that the response she got from Dr. White was not solely her fault. However, the experience left her thinking that there was something about herself that was flawed. Those two experiences with Dr. White had impacted her deeply and influenced who she was going to be as an academic. She promised herself that she would become an amazing professor. She would prove to her colleague that she could thrive in academia. For months afterwards, she toiled quietly while figuring out the lay of the land of the institution. She wasn't being mentored by Dr. White, but she was learning from what she saw. She learned the fake smile and meaningless banter others seemed to have mastered.

Months into this process, the young professor was fumbling clumsily with her keys while attempting to open the door to her office when she heard someone call her name. She turned around and standing behind her was an older colleague who seemed to recognize that she was struggling with more than opening the door to her office. She quickly collected herself and responded with her new professor identity and the empty words she heard them all say to each other, "Good afternoon, how are you? How's the semester going so far?" Fake smile intact. Wild hand in pocket. Her colleague responded with words she had heard before but with much deeper meaning: "Good afternoon, how are you?" The way the professor asked the question was almost like she really wanted to know how she was feeling. The young professor responded with caution but honestly as she fiddled with her keys, "Just trying to figure this thing out." She was talking about the door but meant the whole experience at the university. She didn't expect the professor to make the connection, but she did. "Yes, it's tough figuring this place out, isn't it?" Then, the young professor received a response she wasn't expecting. "You know, some of these folks have been talking about you. All the other new faculty have been working with their advisors and apparently, you don't think you need one." She was informing her but asking a question at the same time. The young professor was unnerved. After being vulnerable enough to ask twice, getting denied each time, and working through bouts of self-doubt, she was being perceived as arrogant. She responded with, "Wow! That is so far from the truth, but thank you." That exchange led to a meeting in this colleague's off-campus office later that week.

As she sat with this senior colleague, the last person she would have ever imagined would be a mentor or advisor because of her age, race, and stature in not just the university but the world, something powerful happened. In the middle of a conversation about why the older professor asked if she thought she was too good for a mentor and mentioned her perceived unwillingness to connect with other faculty, the younger professor broke down. With tears streaming down her face, she spoke about the existential crises that she was undergoing as a young Black professor on a predominantly White campus. She described the doubt that came when she stood in front of students she knew were judging her intelligence based on her skin and age and the trauma of being denied mentorship by the one person she thought would be the right fit. The fact that she stayed to herself was simply the only way she knew to make it through, she said. As she talked about her struggle to deal with the particular pain of the mentorship debacle, she attempted to compose herself and broke down further. The professor who invited her to this meeting touched her shoulder and asked, "Who did that to you?" In a small moment of calm amidst deep breaths, she stated Dr. White's name. She mentioned her two attempts to connect, the questioning of self, and the thought that her gritty urban persona may have been perceived as rude by the stately old-school British professor. For a minute, the young professor felt safe to be honest and vulnerable. She turned to her colleague waiting for a response. As with her encounter with Dr. White, there was an awkward silence. She didn't know what to expect but continued to wait patiently for a response. And then, clearly and loudly, the older professor said, "That mother*ucker is from the Deep South!"

In that moment, the young professor's first response was confusion, followed by laughter. In the weeks that followed, she felt an overwhelming sadness, not for herself but for Dr. White, who, she learned, had spent close to forty years with an accent and a persona that wasn't truly her own. Even if it had become hers, it wasn't what she came into the world and to the university with. The young professor started to consider that the lack of response during the initial meeting may have been deeper than she thought. Dr. White certainly understood the need to be cordial. She played the academic game so well that she knew its rule around empty social politeness masked as appropriateness. Dr. White could have at least faked her way through an introduction during their first meeting. There was something else at play that caused her silence. The young professor began to consider that Dr. White's silence may have been a response to seeing a version of herself that she had previously rejected. In psychology, mirror theory states that what we disapprove of in others is actually what we disapprove of in ourselves.

I imagine that Dr. White never felt comfortable expressing her full Southern self when she entered that institution in the 1950s. She had to be better than that. Her true self (and accent) had to be silenced because, somehow, she felt it was wrong. Decades later, when she saw unbridled self-expression coming from a young Black professor, she was likely to see it the same way she had been taught to see it in herself. It was not even worth acknowledging. The more measured response from the second meeting was a response to being more appropriate (closer to what was expected and accepted). The younger professor's responses to each of her interactions with Dr. White were also a function of her experiences. She would not have blamed herself for Dr. White's responses if she did not somehow feel less than all along. She broke down because what she experienced highlighted her search for validation and acceptance. Both responses reflect deep issues within our society and our schools that colonize the minds, bodies, and even tongues of folks who would otherwise be better and stronger versions of themselves. It is because of these types of experiences that we all need a better sense of schools, the people within them, and how both shape our experiences of ourselves and the world.

The narrative above describes the interactions of two adults with powerful experiences and histories who have each "successfully" navigated schools—both K–12 and higher education. Their interactions with each other as adults were born from their experiences within schools throughout their lives that shaped their relationship to education and each other. When I go into schools today, I see the interactions that gave birth to both Dr. White and the younger professor. I see children who are met with silence from the adults they are attempting to connect with. Children who put together a new outfit, who spend hours on a new hairstyle, or walk into school loud and excited about learning and who don't get any acknowledgment for, or get silenced for, their outfit, hairstyle, or enthusiasm understand what it is like to interact with a Dr. White. From early on in life, they know the feeling of being dismissed like the younger professor. They go through a similar questioning of themselves and experience doubt about their sense of worth. Children need validation from the adults in their lives in order to develop a sense of worth. They learn to value what the adults in their lives find important. When they learn what schools/adults value most is being accepted by those in power and not being themselves, they grow up to be the young professor, full of promise but swimming in self-doubt.

The reality is that no young person is fully equipped to connect with adults who either fail to see them or dismiss them altogether. They are not equipped with the tools to orchestrate a plan for moving forward within schools where teachers are not equipped to depart from their script. It is because of this that we must teach students about the power they hold simply by virtue of being alive. This is work that must be done for the student and the teacher. The two subjects that the teacher needs to have the most expertise in is them-selves and their students. Your subject is not just your content area. The job of the teacher is to first work toward fully understanding the people and experiences that have shaped them, reconcile the tensions between who they are and who they profess to be, and then get as far away as possible from any script that doesn't align with who they are. This is especially the case for educators of color who, by virtue of "successfully" navigating the treacherous landscape of an education system not designed for them as students, will find them-selves replicating the same structures they experienced when they walked into a classroom as teachers if they do not work to deliber-ately disrupt them.

In order to break this cycle of dysfunction, teachers must first ask themselves if their feelings of preparedness to teach come from the degrees they hold and the teaching credentials they possess or from a belief in what they have to offer young people and their commu-nities. They must ask themselves if they truly enjoyed school when they were students. If they did, what are they doing to ensure that they are the type of teacher who sparks the light in their students instead of dimming it. In my work preparing aspiring teachers for the classroom, I found a majority were motivated by one of their own teachers to pursue a career in teaching. A good number were also mo-tivated to teach because of negative experiences they had in school and their desire not to have others undergo the same experiences they did. Somehow, on the path of getting their degree and teaching credential, many of these students forget that their job is to ensure that students are not having as challenging a time as they did. Be-fore asking themselves if they are meeting benchmarks or standards, teachers must ask themselves if they are creating a joy for learning and a curiosity for knowledge or if they are maintaining a status quo that is more concerned with being better than being whole. I (would) ask these teachers, Do you believe that academic rigor means the class has to be "under control" and look and feel lifeless? Have you learned to have a disdain for a livelier class? Despite popular belief, rigorous classrooms do not require students to experience rigor mortis. Good teaching doesn't mean stiffening the body and removing life. Academic rigor is a feeling that is induced by an ebb and flow of both the body and the mind and an affirmation of the spirit. Your mind and body must both move for your spirit to feel at ease within a place. Too many educators, particularly those who teach Black youth, have been conditioned to believe that sitting silently, quietly, and individually with finger to forehead while grappling with a challenging problem is a marker of academic rigor. On the contrary, that is often the performance of lifelessness. True rigor is a contracting and expansion of the body and mind. It is marked by moving and coming alive. It is allowing your ratchetness to be expressed in different ways but always accepted as you learn.

Rigor mortis is the stiffening of the body and a ceasing of its natural ebb and flow. It has been scientifically recognized as the phase of death in which the body stops making adenosine triphosphate (ATP). ATP is considered by biologists to be the molecule that stores the energy we need to carry out just about everything we do. When the natural ebb and flow of the body ceases, ATP is no longer produced. If we apply this biological mechanism to schools, then when the natural expressiveness and movement of young people are stifled in the classroom, the spirit is no longer fed, and rigor mortis ensues. Where there is rigor mortis, there is no rigor. To be an effective educator who creates academically rigorous instruction, one's teaching must be centered around the infusion of life and joy. Academic rigor is about being loud, proud, mobile, unpretentious, and challenged to take on whatever obstacles come one's way even if they offer some challenge. To learn is to be full of life, not devoid of it. Once that recognition happens for teachers and students, we can reimagine the field of education.

This recognition of what education is and what it could be cannot come until we unpack all that has brought us to where we are and made us into who we are. As a person who has always had a love for education but a contentious relationship with school, I had to rediscover who I was before I could be an effective educator. This was something I never knew was a thing to do before I first walked into a classroom to teach. The revelation that I had to understand myself before I could teach anyone effectively came after my discovery that I was teaching ineffectively. It was a tough thing to accept because my motivation to teach was so pure and altruistic. I chose to teach because I wanted to be a role model for young people who looked like me. My goal was to help them forge connections to academic subjects that were usually framed as being outside of their purview. I was determined to make Black youth love math and science. I had beautiful personal reasons and motivations. Yet, once I got in the classroom, I became a younger version of all the teachers I hated in an effort to be seen as being effective by my peers and administrators. I demanded order and control, I often raised my voice at students, and I gave them speeches about making their way out of the neighborhood that we all came from.

The realization of how ineffective I was came after having cogenerative dialogues with my students. The dialogues that brought me to this revelation, which I have written about extensively in other works, were conversations I had with my students outside the classroom about how they were experiencing my teaching.[2] It was in one of these meetings that students I thought I was doing right by said I was disconnected and elitist. One student described me as "thinking you're better than us" and "always making it seem like we're always bad." These were tough messages to receive. I immediately got defensive. They didn't know my story. I was from where they were from. I went through challenges that I knew would resonate with them. I was from the hood and had made it out. Unbeknownst to me, that narrative was the problem. I had internalized the "make your way out of the neighborhood" ideology that I wrote about earlier in this chapter and was following a script on how to be as a teacher that made me see those who were still in and of the hood as problematic. Instead of listening, I was attempting to defend myself to young people who were only speaking their truth.

As they continued to critique me, I slowly began to really listen to what they were saying. Memories of my own experiences in school flashed through my mind—the very experiences that led me to teach. I remembered the incredibly difficult time I had navigating high school. I remembered the fight in my senior year that caused me to miss prom, graduation, and all the senior year activities. I remember my mother describing the fight as a capstone for four years of rebellion. I remember feeling as a teenager that I chose to be anti-school because I knew that school didn't like me. After graduating from high school, I was sent to a military camp on an army base to "get my life together" and start over. When I returned to New York City, I found myself at a local commuter college in the Bronx that allowed me to enroll for classes weeks after the semester had started. There I was, at a local college campus in the birthplace of hip-hop, where local rappers would show up at the radio station to perform while high-level science research was being conducted just feet away. The campus was filled with teenagers who were recent high school graduates, many with stories like mine, who were on the same campus with older students who were making it back to college after decades away from school. I conducted research in a science lab where hip-hop music played in the background as we did our work. There were no dress codes or demands for "appropriate" behavior. There was a freedom to be yourself *and* be smart that I had never encountered before. This is where I experienced true education. In the end, I found myself with a couple of college degrees, a love for the beauty and wonder of science, and an insatiable desire to change the world. This was the narrative that I had constructed and that I thought was leading me to the classroom. How could this be elitism? I fought the students on their critique for quite a while but eventually decided to go deeper. What else had shaped me? Who else shaped the way I saw the world? I had to go back to my roots—back to the soil Septima Clark spoke of.

I remember my first time visiting Jamaica. Not dancehall reggae music Rastafarian Jamaica; I'm talking high tea at noon, love the British more than the British love themselves Jamaica. I was twenty-one years old and visiting relatives on my mother's side of the family whom I had never met before. My mother immigrated to the United States in the 1970s as a teenager from an island that was, and is still, reeling from centuries of British rule that left the country socioeconomically and politically unstable after gaining its independence in 1962. Despite its independence on paper, Jamaica remains shaped by its past as a "Crown colony" of the British empire. Nowhere is this more evident than in classrooms, where droves of Jamaican children in freshly starched uniforms are forced to erase any expressions of individuality or agency in schools hell-bent on teaching complicity at the expense of personal freedom. In one school I visited recently, a sign with the phrase "OBEY AT ONCE" in bold bright colors against an otherwise drab background greeted guests and students alike. That was the chief school rule.

British traditions are at the core of Jamaican life for the socioeconomically advantaged, and many on the island associate a closeness to whatever tradition the colonizers practiced as a sign of affluence and having arrived. For many Jamaicans, it is by being like the British that they become their better selves. Along with colonizing the island and taking advantage of its natural resources through an exertion of power on the political front, the most debilitating legacies of colonialism in Jamaica and beyond are the effects they have had on the psyche of the colonized. It is in the perception of self as less than, a view of the person with a higher title or position as superior and adherence to strict social hierarchies, that a culture that demonizes its own gets built. This is as true in Jamaican culture as it is in American education. It is how I came to believe that I was saving students and helping them when they were the ones helping me to retain some sense of what makes me who I am. By being a version of myself that was not me, I was giving up the natural expertise and intuitive knowledge I had about how to design and create powerful learning spaces. I was trading what felt right and true about how to engage with young people for the more established practices that were valued by the institution but ultimately less effective.

The notion that White is always right in looks, thought, and practice is still an unwritten rule of law among much of the Jamaican populace (and across the diaspora). It is evident in the trend of bleaching the skin to appear more white and in the white wigs still worn by Jamaican judges. However, it is also evident in teaching students to be more "appropriate" in their dress and ways of greeting and convincing them that erasing their natural accent makes them seem smarter or more academic. There is a psychological and emotional colonization that singer Bob Marley refers to as "mental slavery" in "Redemption Song" that we all must be free from in order to be ratchetdemic. Black folks need to emancipate themselves from mental slavery so that they no longer feel less than their colonizers. This mental slavery is what turns teachers, particularly teachers who have the same background as their students, to teach young folks to feel less than people they don't even see or have access to. The effect of this belief that one is perpetually less than is an inferiority complex that manifests itself in an unbridled desire to be as close as possible to the person who makes one feel less than. It is something everyone undergoes—a sort of educational Stockholm syndrome. Stockholm syndrome is a phenomenon in which a victim experiences positive feelings for or an emotional bond with a captor or kidnapper. Educational Stockholm syndrome is the process by which people who were emotionally and psychologically harmed in school as students pledge an allegiance to the same educational system and work within this system to uphold the same structures that harmed them in their youth. Teacher education and preparation that does not teach teachers to center and love their whole and ratchet selves will maintain a process in which teachers love the system that silenced and harmed the very essence of who they were as students and continues to silence and harm who they are as teachers. People fall in love with people who don't love them back all the time. It isn't far-fetched to imagine them falling in love with institutions and systems that are designed to break them.

For my mother, her allegiance to colonizing structures was manifested as she came to America as a teenager and became British smart.

This was evident in her using obscure words, having tea at noon, and eating fish and chips on Fridays. Unfortunately, it also meant masking and devaluing the magic of her Jamaicanness and seeing it and those who proudly expressed it as being less than. She never connected with the Jamaican immigrants in the neighborhood and the family members who proudly described themselves as "from yard" whom we would meet on occasion. Those folks were too loud, too expressive, and too unabashedly Jamaican to be a part of our proper American pseudo-British lives. This meant I only got the luxury of hearing her beautiful Jamaican patois when she was so livid that the societally constructed gates of respectability that held back her true self couldn't hold back the linguistic magic she held inside. On those rare occasions, I would hear her yell in equal parts British and Jamaican patois. This blurring of her selves was so magical that I would sometimes look forward to her being upset just so I could hear the real her.

I grew up in Brooklyn and then the Bronx among Caribbean and African immigrants and Black folks with Southern roots. At home, my parents created a different world from what was outside the doors of our apartment that would often collide with the real world. In response, I became adept at navigating multiple worlds that I thought could never coexist until I blurred them in the hood and they did. Outside our apartment, I was a celebrated rapper. I had developed a way of making words rhyme while shaping them into metaphors and analogies that gained me respect on the street corners where rappers gathered. At home, hip-hop was not allowed. It was lowbrow and only for "other" types of people. I had to sneak to play my favorite rap songs on a small radio that I hid in my pillowcase. I would go to sleep at night with hip-hop beats pouring into my ear and wake up in the morning to my mother's classical music and gospel hymns.

When I left our apartment building each day, my hip-hop persona became essential to feeling seen and alive in my neighborhood. In some powerful moments, I would pull from the very proper words my mother used at home and use them in the neighborhood. I made the obscure words that my mother used like *petrichor* and *colander* hold value. *Petrichor* was the smell right before or after the rain fell, and a *colander* was used to drain pasta or rinse vegetables. As a rapper, I could put holes in an MC's self-confidence like a colander and make it rain so much you could smell the petrichor. Somewhere in between learning to be British Jamaican proper, surviving the hood, and going to school, I had figured out who I was supposed to be in the neighborhood. In the hood, when I rapped, I had the freedom to construct an identity that allowed my multiple selves to not only coexist but to thrive.

In school, it was a completely different story. School taught me that none of my stories was acceptable. I was being trained to stop asking big questions, erase my hip-hop-ness, and do exactly what I was told. The more time I spent in the classroom, the more challenging it was to be academically successful, because school created conditions that highlighted the tensions between the identities I had learned could coexist in the neighborhood. My experiences in an urban American school had a striking parallel to the legacies of colonialism in Jamaican schools. I argue that this is because schooling across the world has become a process of asserting the power of a particular way of being in the world that is not about making Black folks whole. The institution marketed across the world as the great equalizer never lifted certain people up to gain equal footing. It flattened them to make them smaller versions of themselves, only equal to others who have either always been small or also shrunken by structures and pedagogies that never allowed them to grow into themselves.

It was in the midst of attempting to reconcile the internal tension between being a successful teacher as it was defined for me and connecting to young people in ways that centered our shared ratchet selves that I came to understand that although schools have the potential to positively transform lives, in their current form, they are designed to shrink them. They reduce beautifully complex beings into flat replicas of smartness. They had done this to my mother and tried to do it to me. Like Dr. White, my mother had learned to be something other than herself in order to be perceived as being part of the cultural elite. The erasing of the music and language of her youth in order for her to be seen as better than others who came from the same place was a symptom of the need to perform for acceptance. Suddenly, I began to see tons of people in schools and other professional settings navigating these same tensions. This tension between what was familiar and brought me joy and what was expected of me to be accepted by those who held power directly affected how I taught. As a teacher, I was being someone other than who I was and being a person without a spirit of joy and peace because I was determined to pay allegiance to systems that never brought me joy or peace but gave me a position, some power, and the promise of acceptance. I was performing for White acceptance in the classroom even when it wasn't physically there to acknowledge me or my students. This brought me back to the first time I heard someone called "OOOOOORRREEEEEEEEOOOOOOOO!!!!!!"

CHAPTER 2

OREO

Who am I first? I have to know who I am first to know how to navigate this thing. If I am navigating and I'm becoming something that I'm not supposed to become, then I'm in the wrong place. Whether I made it in other people's eyes or not.

—CHADWICK BOSEMAN[1]

Oreo—a brand of dessert that has chocolate wafers on either side of a sweet white paste—comes in an almost iconic blue and white packaging that can make mouths water. Within the package, identical cookies in neat and tightly packed rows rest snugly against each other. If one of them is moved the entire row slips out of place. An Oreo is brown on the outside and white on the inside. Twist the exterior and the whiteness reveals itself. "Oreo" is also a derogatory term for Black folks who are perceived as acting White.

Those who are unaware of its true meaning commonly co-opt the "acting White" concept to accuse the Black community of having a dislike or disdain for education. Folks will say Black kids who don't value education insult their friends who "speak well" because they are educated. This is far from the truth and is a narrative put in place to justify two false notions that too many have taken as fact without interrogating it more deeply. The first is that Black children have a disdain for education. The second is that speaking a certain way means one is more educated or intelligent than another. My decades of research in urban schools indicate that Black youth do not see being smart as acting White and do not demonize members of their community for pursuing academic success. They do see acting White or "being an Oreo" as having certain disdain for Blackness or having a flawed view of the Black experience that falsely associates anything connected to educational success to Whiteness. Signithia Fordham and, later, building on Fordham's work, John Ogbu wrote extensively about the perceived burden of betraying one's race by engaging in behaviors associated with Whiteness, including doing well in school.[2] This version of the concept of "acting White" simply doesn't reflect the cultural values of Black folks, who have historically demonstrated a persistent passion for education, even when they were barred from being fully educated by slave owners. The reality is that, in this country, we come from a tradition that only partially educates Black folks for the sake of maintaining the existing social order. This country weaponizes the folks it has partially educated, as well as the subliterate, to assault those who reject the complicity and respectability inherent in the master's teaching(s). *Partial education* here means being book smart from schooling but lacking knowledge of the self and street smarts, and being unable to apply either in real life. In her powerful article "We Slipped and Learned to Read," Janet Cornelius gives insight into slave accounts and shares that, during this heinous period, there was the common practice of teaching slaves to read just well enough so they could regurgitate certain biblical scriptures that supported and sustained the power of slave owners. Cornelius writes about how some slaves were "educated" by slaveholders who ensured that slaves did not have access to or the ability to read any text (including sections of the Bible that may be interpreted as a rebuke of slavery) or study anything about themselves that would indicate that they were anything other than subjects destined to serve their masters. The slaves who were literate read and memorized scriptures and were then positioned as more intelligent than their counterparts, even though they were not fully educated. In this process, many who were elevated above their peers developed greater allegiances to their masters than their peers.[3] These are the folks who in the contemporary world get labeled Oreo. They have gone through a process of education that is about being only knowledgeable enough to reinforce the power of those who currently hold it. They will use being called intelligent by those within the power structure as a license to identify others (with whom they may share a racial background but who exist outside the system of education) as lacking it.

In education, the process of teaching and learning has become so intent on attaching intelligence to behaviors or actions that have nothing to do with what you know or how you express it that the word *intelligent* has been flattened into something with no actual meaning. In communities with complex ways of engaging and communicating outside school, having a representative of the institution calling someone intelligent or saying someone isn't intelligent means nothing. In fact, school-defined intelligence has been revealed to be about being unexpressive, uncreative, and dispassionate. No one with any true intelligence wants to be that. In most classrooms, the teacher is identified as the most intelligent or smartest person in the room. However, if that teacher cannot express passion, creativity, and imagination in the sharing of that knowledge, I would argue that that person is not intelligent. True intelligence is the ability to gain information, develop knowledge, hone skills, and apply knowledge and skills to meeting individual or collective goals that emerge in the moment. Intelligence by an institutional definition polices creativity and self-expression. Again, being smart or academically inclined has never been seen as being an Oreo in the hood. Black folks who call other Black folks "Oreos," Brown folks who call other Brown folks "bananas," or folks of color from varying ethnicities who call each other "coconuts" don't use these terms to indicate that being intelligent is acting White or that being academically inclined is being White. The derogatory terms come from folks of color embedded in their cultural truth seeing folks who look like them and who are from where they are from performing or expressing an unrelenting allegiance to institutions and norms associated with Whiteness, even at the expense of losing themselves and acceptance by their community. Being an Oreo is not about being Black on the outside and White on the inside; it is about allowing White folks to determine which forms of Blackness are worthy or useful. Dr. White was a Black professor in a White school and was unable to connect with another Black faculty member who viscerally expressed her emotions because Dr. White had learned to be unaccepting of forms of Blackness that involved loud voices and moving hands. Dr. White may have even made assumptions about the intelligence, or lack thereof, of the young professor based on how she presented herself.

I suggest that being Black and navigating the world by developing a command of White codes in certain social spaces is not what makes one an Oreo or any other variation of the term. The world requires us all to code switch in order to connect with others from different backgrounds or experiences. I code switch as a favor or in reverence to someone or a culture I respect because I want to help them connect with me—not because I am aspiring to be them or be accepted by them. For example, if a person enters into a new space with strangers she has never met before and realizes that the people in that space greet each other by bowing their heads, she may elect to do the same in a greeting, even if shaking hands is her cultural norm. In this case, there is an honoring of another person's cultural codes, and there even may be an appreciation of the willingness to adopt foreign cultural codes by those from the culture whose norms another person takes up. This is different from cultural misappropriation and an adoption of a foreign persona for the sake of attention or some other benefit. Dolezaling (pretending to be Black for some social benefit) is different from honoring Blackness. The term Dolezaling comes from the story of Rachel Dolezal, a White woman who spent a significant part of her adult life not just passing as Black but taking up leadership positions within Black communities performing what she believed to be Blackness. Recently, White academic Jessica Krug also revealed that she had spent her life performing Black and Latinx identities while gaining positions that were created or earmarked for Black folks. The work I am calling for is not about performing something other than who you are in the tradition of Dolezaling. It is in finding and embracing truth. Our collective truth requires us to always switch back to ourselves and have ourselves as our benchmark and baseline for academic excellence. In a perfect world, we wouldn't have to switch at all. There would be endless forms of interaction that all are privy to and all would accept, respect, and protect. Since that is not the case, we must honor our own traditions, even when we momentarily concede for the benefit of others. Most importantly, educators must create classroom spaces where the codes of the young people are the norm.

The major problem educators have that inhibits them from being effective is that they, like the chocolate wafers of the Oreo, have a main purpose of surrounding and protecting Whiteness. Protecting Whiteness, in this context, is not just about keeping school the way it is but about identifying things that edify the mind as White, even though these things belong to all of us. Creating a narrative that education can only function well when it is enacted in non-Black ways is protecting Whiteness. Education isn't White. Learning isn't White. Deep thinking isn't White. Therapy isn't White. However, doing any of those things in a way that does not reflect the beauty of Blackness; doing any of those things while demonizing Blackness is. Demonizing the ways that Black folks have done these things for generations is upholding Whiteness. Consider, for example, the newly emerging focus on mindfulness and quiet meditation in urban schools and the ways that it is framed as a way to "help students manage their behavior" and be more present and self-aware in classrooms. Then consider that young folks in urban neighborhoods are incredibly self-aware, reflective, and present when they engage in practices like hip-hop cyphers that do not have the same structure, look, or sound as quiet meditation. In cyphers, participants gather in a circle, stand equidistant from each other, perform poetry over rhythms for each other, and continue performing in a cyclic turn-taking process until all have become engaged and a collective often loud and emotional pinnacle is reached. This is a mindfulness practice that requires noise, voice, chants, rhythm, and active participation. These are ratchet modes of expression not welcome in most schools. Instead, what is welcomed is a stripped down and obscenely disrespectful (because it erases its religious roots) Buddhist meditation practice that is solely about quiet and stillness. This is not a critique of meditation per se. It is a practice that I find powerful. However, I also find that there are alternate means to get to the point of reflection and being present. I also find that the type of meditation practices welcomed in school are not actually about reflecting but about policing expression.

As a teacher, I found myself justifying practices like meditation (in the form of sitting quietly and not moving) that gave no value to my experiences outside of school or those of my students. In my holding and demanding absolute silence as the ideal learning environment for students whose life experiences outside of school were filled with the sonic richness of urban America, there was an unwillingness to see who they truly were. That was, unbeknownst to me at the time, a protecting of a form of institutional Whiteness that just didn't work for many of my students. My students saw what I was protecting and attaching myself to and responded to that. I was a Brown cookie teaching them to be less than by protecting Whiteness from their critique. I was being an Oreo.

The metaphor of the Oreo I am presenting here is necessary for all educators to understand the complex relationship between who they are and what they are holding up in the classroom. It not only highlights the ways that Black folks surround and protect Whiteness or White supremacist ideologies but also highlights the ways the entire education system does it. The Oreo metaphor is especially necessary for educators of color, because it highlights a major flaw of education as it relates to them and students who look like them—like brown cookies holding up white filling, the education system lifts certain Black and Brown folks to positions of power in education only to have them support and protect White norms that could not stand on their own. One need only look at positions like dean of behavior and/or dean of culture at schools that serve youth of color, where

Black folks who are the minority in the teaching staff are the only ones charged with managing the students. I have spoken to dozens of educators of color who signed up to be educators and who ended up in positions of "leadership" in which their primary responsibilities became ensuring that students' hats were off, uniforms looked the same, voices were kept low, and self-expressions were managed. These tasks have nothing to do with learning and turn the position of dean or administrator into protector of White norms. This positioning of Black educators as behavior managers has roots in an American notion that Black folks were not supposed to be educated and think for themselves but were to be managed and controlled. In this country, the education of Black folks has always had strings attached. This was alluded to earlier in the way Janet Cornelius described Bible literacy for slaves being only about providing religious instruction to maintain subservience to slave masters. This type of literacy has evolved into contemporary urban education in which there is education for subservience that is named as academic excellence and involves convincing teachers that their chief responsibility is preparing young people not to challenge the status quo. It is only in the ratchetdemic approach to education, which welcomes the pursuit of content knowledge in whatever academic discipline *and* offers all teachers and students the freedom to both be themselves and challenge systems, that true learning happens.

If one critiques the job responsibilities of educators who are simply teaching academic content like slaveholders taught the Bible (where a textbook or curriculum becomes the text memorized, blindly followed and accepted without creating space for questioning, critiquing, and empowering), these teachers step into a defensive or Oreo mode and fiercely protect the white filling that gives them their identity. If you ask what wearing a hat, being silent for most of the day, or always having a solemn demeanor has to do with learning, you will hear everything from "It's just the rules" to "I am preparing them for real life." You will not get a legitimate answer because there is no legitimate answer. These responses are simply about the fact that these folks have their entire sense of self attached to how well they enforce the rules. It is as if the brown cookies feel like they would have no worth without attaching themselves to the flimsy white cream filling. In reality, the filling has no worth without the brown cookies holding it up. If the brown cookies were not holding it up, the filling could not stand on its own. It has no true shape or structure. Similarly, Whiteness has no intrinsic value other than what society and educators project onto it, and its strength is predicated on people of color holding it up.

Over time, the Oreo has evolved from being just a cookie to a globally recognized brand. It has continually reimagined and remarketed itself despite being largely unchanged since the early part of the last century. Its endorsers are the most popular people across a number of demographics and across different eras—from Donald Trump to Wiz Khalifa. The system of education operates in much the same way. It will garner endorsers from different demographics who will bring in their audiences to support a product that they may or may not actually use or benefit from. On a systemic level, problematic approaches to urban education are endorsed and celebrated by folks with popularity, who will keep pushing the narrative that the system is only working well when it retains its roots in demonizing Blackness. These are often Black folks who are given the platform to open schools that instead of focusing on empowering Black children, double down on flawed pedagogy rooted in sameness and uniformity while echoing the talking points of folks disinterested in the liberation of Black children. I call these folks the double-stuffed Oreos. These people keep certain ideologies (however flawed) prominent despite the harmful effects they have on the most vulnerable young people. Black folks become the face of schools through the roles of principal and/or executive director but are often endorsed by White philanthropists whose only concept of good schools for Black and Brown youth is school uniforms, no excuses, complicity, and test scores (no matter how they are achieved). It baffles the mind why we continue to blindly attach ourselves to these norms—to this empty white filling. At some point, we have to ask ourselves why. I suggest that it is mostly about the convincing ways that these norms have been packaged and marketed to us.

PACKAGING AND CREAM

When you ask people why they love the Oreo, they will likely tell you it's because of the cream filling. There is something about the sweet white stuffing between the wafers that folks can't get enough of. Folks will remind you that the Oreo is America's favorite cookie. For years, the phrase "America's favorite cookie" was used as a slogan by the company.[4] This wasn't supported by any research or polls, and eventually, in 2004, the company changed the slogan to "Milk's favorite cookie." However, even after they stopped using it as a slogan, Oreo continued being named as America's favorite cookie. Part of the appeal of the cookie is the power of the iconic blue and white packaging that the brown wafers stuck to the white filling are uniformly and snugly wrapped in. Somehow, the packaging renders the wafers and filling the same. This blue and white packaging is analogous to the red, white, and blue packaging that is Americana—that erases the fact that Black folks are holding up Whiteness being packaged for us all to blindly consume.

Politicians from different parties have touted the idea that our education system is the central pathway to Americanness. Barack Obama described it at the Democratic National Convention "the gateway to middle-class life," and Donald Trump, in his book *The America We Deserve*, said it doesn't just teach the three Rs but is "meant to teach citizenship."[5] The concepts of middle-class life and citizenship are both essential to the narrative of Americana, which also comes with preconceived ideas about the roles for folks of color in society. If the purpose of school is to usher you into middle-class life or full citizenship, and neither of these ideas is necessarily inclusive of you as you are, then school is training you to not be yourself. A pedagogy that erases conversations about how the middle class is constructed based on wealth and proximity to it, and that is absent of dialogue about why citizenship is not afforded to all people, doesn't prepare one for the middle class or full citizenship. It prepares one to support the *idea* of middle-class life and citizenship. People travel from across the world to go to school in this country because of the exporting of the narrative around upward mobility and full citizenship. Schooling has been marketed and sold like it is the great equalizer. In reality, it serves as an equalizer not by uplifting and magnifying all voices equally but by neutralizing voices within the system that offer a different model for how it could and should operate.

Education in the United States has always been framed as the cure for all of society's ills. It is supposed to even the playing field and create socioeconomic equality, but it has not been interested in allowing brown cookies to stand alone outside of their attachment to the white cream filling. In other words, the success of folks in the United States has often been predicated on their adoption of White middle-class norms and a rejection of more visceral forms of expression that are seen as unrespectable. For example, a *New York Times* article described the increased likelihood of career advancement for Afro-Caribbeans over African Americans in corporate America.[6] The article mentioned that "white people tend to prefer and give better opportunities to Afro-Caribbeans over African-Americans, and African-Americans are more likely than immigrants from Africa to say that colleagues have underestimated their intelligence."

I suggest this preference for particular forms of Blackness essentially boils down to the comfort of those in power—what they consider to be more acceptable versions of Blackness. In education, a similar phenomenon exists in which there is little to no acceptance for approaches to education that showcase the rawness of how certain folks engage in communities while there is support for approaches that are much more aligned to what folks think learning should look like. For example, a project I started a few years ago that focused on young people writing and performing academically rigorous and content-rich raps was challenged for its academic merit by teachers and principals in a school and then stopped in favor of more test prep for a state exam in science. This was the case even though there was no cost associated with the rap-based program and an exorbitant one related to the test prep. The critiques of the rap-based program were rooted more in how loud the students got and how "distracting" their enthusiasm was to other students without a consideration for the fact that young people were acquiring content knowledge at a level that surpassed what they had been getting prior to the program's implementation and through the test prep. The rap-based method of instruction was perceived as too ratchet to have academic value. At the end of the academic year, when students underperformed on the standardized exam despite the test prep, and the few who had just a few weeks of the rap-rooted instruction outperformed their peers, there was no disruption or interruption of the implementation of the flawed test prep drill and kill approach to teaching. There was no consideration for implementing what had proven itself to work. The idea that the test prep being held up by the Black school administrators could be flawed was unimaginable. No one could fathom that the filling of the Oreo that the brown cookies were holding up just wasn't any good for the students.

This is how our education system functions. It maintains its power and control over us by convincing us that it is the best. We follow norms that contradict what we know is right, not because of their merit but because of marketing and packaging. We start attaching worth to aspects of institutions and their practices because it is easier to hold them up than admit that we have been conditioned or brainwashed into valuing something not worth anything. In the case of the Oreo, folks who profess it is America's favorite cookie will believe that they made this decision on their own. They either forgot or never knew that the company that profits from the cookie sold the world on the idea that they were America's favorite cookie. They convinced the world that this was true. Now, they do not have to keep saying it. The phrase has been removed from the packaging, but it has been ingrained into the collective consciousness.

Folks will not only argue that the Oreo is America's favorite cookie; they will argue that it is good for you. They will even refer to the fact that it has a cream filling to justify why it is so good. Cream is the natural fat that rises from milk. If the Oreo filling is creamy, it conjures up all the connotations and associations we have about cream, which include that it is natural and healthy. After all, the "cream always rises to the top." When folks are licking the filling of the Oreo, they are not aware that while the filling has the consistency of cream, it is not cream at all. In fact, at one point, checking the Oreo packaging, one would find that what it is made of is not cream but something the company calls "creme." The two words sound the same but do not mean the same thing. By law, the Food and Drug Administration does not allow any company to say their product contains cream when it does not contain it. The Oreo filling is labeled *creme* simply because it sounds like *cream* and can keep folks who think that it is cream believing that it is. The current education system functions in much the same way. It has convinced a lot of people that it is cream when in fact it is really creme—a fake meant to fool people into believing it has substance and value.

Once we know that the filling is not cream, we must find out what is in the creme. Some insight into this emerged a few years ago when two men were arrested and convicted of stealing a formula for titanium dioxide—a mineral used as white pigment in paint, sunscreen, cosmetics, and food coloring—from chemical giant DuPont. The men had conspired to steal the formula and sell it to China. This formula was stolen because there was much value internationally for a product that could make objects into a particularly bright shade of white, which this formula was known to do. There are other formulas for titanium dioxide that exist across the world, but, apparently, there is a global market for this American-made Whiteness. This phenomenon (a desire for American Whiteness) resounds not just in industry but in education, where America's favorite system and its manufactured Whiteness is marketed and lusted after across the globe. Titanium dioxide is like White supremacy. It whitens everything it touches, it has global appeal, and it has been added to a lot of what we consume, even though it was never intended to be ingested. In fact, the European Chemicals Agency has stated that titanium dioxide is carcinogenic, meaning it just may make people sick and kill them if inhaled and ingested in large enough quantities. In education, that is all we do. We force White supremacy in the form of White creme pedagogy down the throats of children. White supremacy—and the concomitant belief that Blackness is problematic—is the titanium dioxide that whitewashes curriculum: erasing Black and Brown faces from textbooks and removing culture from instruction.

In school, young folks of color are taught to enact blind complicity to institutional norms that stifle self-expression while being forced to consume creme curriculum that erases Blackness and turns everything—including the examples and images used in teaching—white. In the imagination of those who establish these norms, what they are upholding is valuable and nutritious—the equivalent of cream. Educators will argue that they are preparing young people for the "real world" and that obedience to school rules and teacher demands will help youth to be "college and career ready." In reality, educators are achieving neither of these results, because upholding approaches to teaching that they think are *cream* is actually forcing young people to consume *creme*. Young people who go through schools that force-feed them creme in the form of obedience and complicity get into the real world and are only prepared to be employees and workers, not leaders and innovators. They get into college and don't have the agency to go to office hours, lead discussions, participate in group work, or demand services they are paying tuition for. We've got to watch out for cream philosophies that mask creme pedagogies, that erase individuality and free thought, demonize questioning, and stifle free expression. They only prepare young people for a "real world" where they uphold others' norms, and their college and career experiences may give them degrees but leave them doubting themselves.

Rap duo Dead Prez's first album, *Let's Get Free*, was released in 2000 and features a skit in which activist Omali Yeshitela describes the ways that hunters in the Arctic capture wolves. He talks about how in places where the Indigenous hunt, wolves are killed by blades covered in blood that are placed in the snow by hunters. Hungry wolves are attracted to the scent of the blood. They think it is food. The blood is as attractive to the wolf as the creme filling of the Oreo is to folk who are starving for validation and attention from those who have power. Thinking that they have stumbled upon a meal, the wolves lick the blades like people lick Oreo filling. They cut their tongues as they lick and, unable to distinguish between the blood on the blade and their own blood, keep licking till they eventually die. While the licking of the Oreo filling does not appear as gruesome as the licking of the blade, the process of being drawn to a trap of cream that is actually creme represents a reality for many in urban education. The creme is presented as providing some sustenance or educational benefit but actually functions to make one a willing participant in one's own demise. We must refuse to be or to continue to consume the creme masked as cream even when it is held up by brown cookies. We must detach ourselves from a system that we have become so attached to. The only way we can remove ourselves is with the help of a device or tool that can move us in another direction. The only thing that can save us is the ratchet.

CHAPTER 3

RATCHET AS TOOL

Ratchet (device): A mechanical device that allows movement in only one direction.

Ratchet (tool): Metonomic name for a socket wrench incorporating a ratcheting device.

Ratchet: The embodying of all "negative" characteristics associated with lowbrow culture. Characteristics thought to be possessed by backward people of particular ethnic, racial, or socioeconomic status. Identified by ways of talk, dress, and overall disposition outside of societally established norms.

After years of abuse from my toddler, whose favorite pastime was jumping vigorously on the mattress, our bed was in shambles, and my family and I decided it was time to purchase a new one. We had purchased the original one around the time my daughter was born. We had gone to a local furniture store that had recently opened in the neighborhood and had a glowing sign out front that advertised its large inventory. This was a chance to support a local business and take advantage of what at the time seemed like a new alternative to existing furniture stores. Besides, deciding what size and style of bed would work best for our family seemed to be a decision that required going somewhere and seeing the bed in person. Going online for a bed was possible but seemed like a less viable alternative. Somehow, I was convinced that we were going to be choosing from a wide variety of options in the new store and that we would learn more about our options from a live salesperson who could answer any questions we had. When we got to the store, the salesperson simply told us to look around a certain section of the store and walked away. As we walked around, I realized that we were limited to very few options in the store. I also realized that the options the store had available mostly boiled down to either poor style and decent quality or poor durability and decent style. Since we decided to shop at this store, we would have had to pick from what was available even if it wasn't what was best for us, and we would have had to be okay with it. We eventually found a decent-looking bed with what I would describe as just good-enough quality. We were not necessarily happy with the decision, but the store owners made us feel better about our choice because they said they would help bring the bed to our home and put it together. They told us that other options would not include this service. The next day, they showed up, brought the bed into the room where we wanted it, and put it together for us. At the end of the day, we were just happy to have our bed.

Years later, after creaking under every combination of stretch and yawn from whoever was lying on it, the bed completely fell apart. We were forced to get a new one. This time, we decided that going to the local furniture store would not be the best option. With our price range for a new bed remaining relatively the same from when we made our last purchase, we ventured online. Initially, we believed that our previous limited options were a function of our price range. As we searched a number of websites, and after looking at what they offered in our price range, we realized that our online options were endless. We could get a bed that looked good, was in the right color, and had good reviews for durability. With this new information came agency, and we eventually settled on a bed that provided our desired sturdiness and beauty. We ordered online and waited for its arrival. It was delivered to our doorstep a few days earlier than we had anticipated. This time, however, the bed arrived in a box and we had to put it together ourselves.

When the box arrived, I emptied its contents on the floor and prepared to put the bed together. There were long pieces of metal everywhere, screws of varying lengths taped to the metal pieces, and a little metal tool in a plastic bag. Preparing for the difficult task ahead, I arranged all the parts on the floor and opened the plastic bag. I knew I could do this, but I had not done it before. I looked around for instructions and saw a note attached to one of the small metal tools that read the following: "This is your ratchet. Hang on to this. It loosens, tightens, and makes life easier." This seemed like a silly note and too simple a tool to help with the arduous task I had ahead. The ratchet is mostly used to tighten screws that are hard to reach or loosen those that are stuck to something else. When compared to the power drill and other mechanical devices I had at my disposal, the small ratchet seemed too basic a device to be effective. It was simply a four-inch piece of metal with a circular piece attached at the top with some grooves on it. And yet, after using it, you come to realize that it is one of those tools that you don't know how essential it is until you begin using it.

Despite the note that assured me that the ratchet "makes life easier," my instinct was to go for the power tools in my arsenal. There seemed to be nothing that needed to be screwed or unscrewed that my electric drill couldn't quickly accomplish. After all, the electric drill is a much more complex device that can twist at various angles and rotate at varying speeds. When it got plugged in and spinning, before I even tested its utility for the task at hand, it made me feel like I was getting a lot accomplished. However, as I started putting the bed together, the larger and more powerful drill proved to be too obtuse. Eventually, I grabbed the ratchet I had initially tossed aside and found it more effective than the more "advanced" and "effective" tool I had previously used. The ratchet was less cumbersome, fit easily in my pocket as I moved large parts of the bed around, and was easy to use in reaching hard-to-reach corners. It felt like an extension of me. It worked so much better than the more powerful and imposing drill that used force to meet the same goals.

My experience assembling the bed frame and discovering the utility of the ratchet helped me to make sense of a number of realities around teaching and learning that we often do not consider, particularly in terms of the education of young folks in urban America. The pedagogy we use to meet the goals of getting young people engaged in learning is like the drill. It has power and uses force but is not designed to be effective for the hard to reach. In fact, when used for a task it was not designed for, it can cause permanent damage to the item it is being used on. The ratchet, on the other hand, is designed for the hard to reach. It is light, can easily become an extension of who you are, and makes the task easier to accomplish.

From the experience of buying a bed based on the limited options in my neighborhood and believing that was my only option, a powerful analogy that gave me insight into what exists in contemporary urban education was revealed. The choices I was given were not any good so I chose the newest option only to find what I truly wanted/ needed wasn't available there. What I needed was never available as a viable choice. Like the new store that took advantage of being in our neighborhood and advertised itself as providing a lot of choices in beds, charter schools within urban communities manipulate the concept of choice just to get students in their building only to provide them no real options other than new versions of the same flawed pedagogies that many traditional schools enact—which equates to no choice at all. Across urban America, "school choice" is a phrase that charter schools have championed to market/present their schools as an alternative to traditional urban public schools that historically have not served young people of color well. The argument for choosing a different option is compelling because it is wrapped in an element of truth. Many traditional urban schools are not engaging in pedagogies that meet the needs of young people. However, the alternatives being offered to communities of color are simply new and oftentimes more dangerous versions of the same teaching that is not right for young people. The new schools replace having no tools (like most traditional schools) with power drills, when all that is needed is the ratchet.

In a recent conversation with a parent who had originally sent her child to a local public school, she talked about how that school was "killing his spirit." The joy and enthusiasm he had at home was lost once he started going to school. At one point, even on weekends when he didn't have to attend, her son would start his day saying that he did not want to go to school. While there is the normal teenage disdain for getting up in the morning, it seemed too soon for a seven-year-old to have such a strong distaste for school. She described looking for alternatives to his public school and how she met a representative from a new charter school who was making the rounds in her neighborhood speaking to community members. He told them about a proposed new building, new materials, and wonderful resources that would be offered in the new school he was heading. The parent confided in this person about her child's dislike for school, and the charter school representative quickly diagnosed the problem as a lack of structure in the child's current school. He told her that "kids don't like the absence of structure" and, following the "school choice" marketing narrative, convinced her that the new charter school was her only viable alternative. Trusting in the advice of the expert, she made the only "choice" she could but found that all she had signed up for was a more intense version of the broken pedagogy her son was already experiencing.

Instead of the lack of value for her son's culture and community that was manifested in the curriculum and teaching in his previous school (the staff and curriculum did not look like him, and teachers taught content without any focus on culture), the new school deliberately assaulted any expression of culture. There was no space for the ratchet, and there were rules put in place that were designed to eliminate any expression of an authentic self. Her son was policed on how to dress, how to walk down the hallway, how to speak in class, and how to move in the cafeteria, and he hated it. Eventually, he rebelled against the confining structures of the new school by intentionally breaking as many rules as he could. He got suspended. After he returned to school following his suspension, he got pegged across the school as a rule breaker, and he slipped comfortably into the role. He then entered into a cycle of pushing against the rules and being punished that wore him down until he acquiesced. Eventually, he got tired of being punished for rejecting the structures of the school and became silent at home and at school. He barely spoke to his mother and just seemed depressed. His mother complained to the school about who he was becoming at home—an extension of who he had become at school—and they responded by talking about how improved his behavior had been since his suspensions. What happened here was that two poor options were framed as choice, and the student and his mother ended up moving from a school that ignored culture to a school that placed extreme force on any expression of it. Both places fell short. There were no real options even though there was choice.

When shopping for a bed, finally getting what I wanted and needed required my understanding that choice is only as good as the options I seek for myself. My in-person choices left me without real options. Eventually, after the bed I initially "chose" fell apart, I went online to get another one. What I realized once I got the bed I had ordered online (the one that wasn't presented as an option that I discovered on my own) is that I had to put it together myself. I started to realize that the store employees at the furniture store had volunteered to put my bed together for me as a way to make up for the false idea of choice that they presented to me. I also came to realize that this entire process was a lesson in the need to uncover our academic selves for and by ourselves without relying on institutions to manipulate us into a false notion of agency or choice. It is in this process of finding for ourselves that we find our ratchet and can begin using it to construct what we want and need.

When I exercised my option to shop online and assemble the bed myself, the ratchet came to me. I then needed to use it. This proved to be more challenging than getting the bed from the store that was close to me and having it put together for me; however, it was more fulfilling. In much the same way, in any learning, or even in the creation of curriculum, the students must choose what they want to study and then design their own learning. On that journey, what they will learn will cover academic subjects/topics beyond what they know. The school may decide what subjects are taught, but the youth should decide how they are taught, decide what themes they want to explore, and customize the instruction to their own needs. It is when young people have options in identifying what they want, and the agency to put together what works best for them, and the confidence to pursue their passions, that their academic selves get activated. In order to design what truly works best for them, the youth need their ratchet.

Eventually, in order to rediscover his passion for learning, that young man had to be taken out of the new school. His mother allowed him to pick the school that worked best for him. He ended up choosing the school that he first attended but came back to it with a demand for what he needed from the school. He showed up as himself, demanded with his mother that the teaching there value and respect him, and he supplemented what he learned in school with ardent studies in what mattered to him. He discovered a passion for hip-hop and performing. When he recited his raps, his performances seemed to conjure up all the energy he had been forced to remove in the charter school. He tapped into a particularly raw and powerful ratchet self that earned him a reputation as a well-respected poet and emcee. Eventually, he earned a college scholarship to the First Wave program at the University of Wisconsin–Madison—a program for artists—and was celebrated there and across the country for being a poet performer and scholar. He made his bed and, because he had used pieces of his ratchet self to create it, had no problem lying in it.

The perfect bed that young man put together could not have been created if he had not found and used his ratchet. His frustration with learning in both schools before he found his path could be traced to the fact that he had never had the conditions in a school setting in which he could find and use his ratchet. This was as much the case with this young man as it is the case in the science classrooms where I conduct much of my research. In these classrooms, I am most often charged with working with teachers to make a transition from scripted curriculum and "cookbook labs" to project-based science. This work involves helping teachers transition from classrooms where young folks are memorizing science facts and conducting experiments with expected outcomes to classrooms where students have opportunities to work on projects or assignments where they have more autonomy and discover science on their own. After I have helped teachers make these transitions, I start suggesting to administrators that there is still much more work to do, because even in these more autonomous classrooms, Black youth will still have challenges navigating the classroom and engaging in science if the autonomy they have is limited by the confines of what is seen as appropriate behavior and what is expected from them. If a child has the freedom to engage in a project or learn about a science concept in a nontraditional way but still gets reprimanded for being too loud or expressing self in a way that makes the teacher uncomfortable, even a progressive, project-based, diversity-focused curriculum can cause violence. If schools do not permit or welcome students' expressions of ratchetness, schools are implementing an incomplete pedagogy. If there is no recognition of how students have come to have a disdain for schools, there is no way we can create schools that they love and that love them.

FROM TOOL TO WEAPON: GETTING TO RATCHET

In the fall of 1984, a cartoon called *Transformers* made its television debut. The main narrative followed the battle between Optimus Prime's heroic Autobots and Megatron's evil Decepticons. They both hailed from the shiny and metallic homeworld of Cybertron, which they left in search of sources of energy that had become scarce on their home planet. On this journey away from home, they ended up on a planet rich with resources. That planet was Earth. On Earth, the Decepticons attempted to snatch up all the energy sources they could

find while the Autobots protected Earth and prevented the Decepticons from gaining any real footing. The cartoon, which appeared to
be youthful fantasy disconnected from the realities of urban America,
quickly developed a cult following across the country but had a particularly strong following among urban youth of color. In the hood,
Transformers toys were collected by five- and six-year-olds as well as
fifteen- and sixteen-year-olds. Phrases from the cartoon became used
in everyday life. Energon, which was the fuel the transformers used,
became a word for money. In the streets of Brooklyn in the mid-'80s,
young people would sing the theme song from the show like they
were reciting lyrics from the latest rap song.

The reason that the Transformers had such appeal among urban
youth of color (particularly Black youth) is rooted in the stories of its
main characters: Autobots were the good guys who protected Earth
and humans, and the Decepticons were the bad guys. In the cartoon,
the Autobots were always framed as superior to the Decepticons. No
matter how hard they tried, the Decepticons were always reminded
that they could not escape being the enemy, no matter how valiant
their efforts were. Episode after episode showed them as the perpetual
losers. Not being seen as anything other than the bad guys and never
being heroes no matter how hard they tried resonated with Black
youth in the hood. This cartoon took on special meaning for Black
students in a school for academically gifted youth in Brooklyn in the
late 1980s and early 1990s. At Brooklyn Technical High School,
identified as one of the best public schools in the country, students of
color were consistently undergoing severe bouts of self-doubt despite
passing a rigorous exam to gain admission to the school.

Originally, it was an all-White boys' school for those who were
smart enough to pursue a rigorous education in science and mathematics. Over time, girls and folks of color were admitted. By the
late 1980s, the number of Black youth who attended the school had
increased to outpace the number of Whites. Despite this fact, the
soil and roots of the school remained the same. It was built for smart
White boys, and they had a strong legacy within the building. The

children and grandchildren of these White boys also had a special connection to the school and attended at the same time that new populations came in. We can think of the White students who had roots to the school as the Autobots. They were the heroes who had connections to the school and were there to protect its legacy. The Black and Brown youth who found themselves in the school had different experiences than their counterparts from other backgrounds. Despite the fact that they were intelligent enough to pass the test that got them in this special school, the way they were spoken to and the expectations placed on them made them feel like they did not belong. In recent conversations with Black students who attended the school in that era, many of them mentioned the struggle of being seen as not smart enough or being made to feel like they didn't deserve to be at the school. Before long, after being framed as the perpetual antagonist in the story of their own education, they began to see themselves as the Decepticons. Not belonging for long enough made them not want to belong. Not wanting to belong turned into finding something else to belong to. These students, after being hated and feared at school, went home to watch the *Transformers* cartoon and quickly realized that no matter what they did, they would not be seen as the heroes. The school, like the world beyond it, was built around and for Autobots who would always be the good guys. This meant that the students of color needed to embrace that they were always going to be seen as the bad guys. A group of good kids who took tests that said they were too smart to attend their neighborhood high schools got tired of being loathed and decided instead to be feared. After realizing that the loathing they invoked could be a strength if they banded together, they named themselves after the bad guys in the cartoon. They became the most feared gang in New York City. They became the Decepticons or Decepts.

If you grew up in New York City in the mid/late 1980s and early 1990s, phrases like, "The Decepts is outside" would stop the bravest souls in their tracks. The Decepticons were a street gang that was known for committing robberies and assaults. On March 1, 1989, the *New York Times* printed an article titled "A Gang Gives a Name to Students' Fear: Decepticons." The article captures the fascination around a violent gang of youth who committed robberies and random acts of violence. When rumors emerged that they were "about to invade schools . . . frightened parents . . . kept their children home on the days of the supposed invasion."

Although the journalist mentioned that not all the crimes attributed to these youth were committed by them, the article stoked the mystique around these young folks, who were later described by people like Hillary Clinton as "superpredators." Clinton, while giving a speech in the overwhelmingly White state of New Hampshire after the 1992 Los Angeles riots, which were a response to police officers mercilessly assaulting Rodney King, was following suit with an increasingly popular narrative about Black youth and their inherent criminality.

Many stories concocted about the violence that was committed by these young people were untrue exaggerations. The "superpredator" myth was fabricated by criminologist John DiIulio based on his grossly inaccurate projections of increasing criminality by youth. I remember coming of age in the 1990s and hearing stories about random shootings in broad daylight and robberies of police officers that were more tall tales than truth. This is not to say that there weren't some crimes committed, but what was most criminal was the mechanism in the American imagination that magnified the wrong these students did through the lens of a pervasive and grossly inaccurate myth about their superpredator and inherently criminal nature. It is also important to note that this narrative about having a criminal nature was also attached to not being intellectual or academic. My conversations with members of the Decepticons revealed a number of experiences they had in school in which they were regarded as unintelligent or not interested in school simply by being present and not being White. One of my interviewees remembered going up to the board to solve a problem in a math class, struggling a bit as he was working, and facing ridicule from a teacher who asked,

"How did you get into this school in the first place?" He remembered being comforted by another boy in the class who introduced him to the Decepticons. The reality is that the supposedly violent gang that terrorized the city was actually a group of young people trying to find their way. Their purportedly violent nature was rooted in fantasy and shaped by slim aspects of truth that got implanted in the public's imagination and magnified by the racism in society. Somehow, nerdy smart kids who gathered for solidarity in a world that saw them as being less than became the violent thugs the world imagined them to be.

The way that flawed grand narratives about young folks of color get constructed out of some slight truths plays out in a number of ways. Consider that the young people from the specialized high school happened to be attending one of the few schools in the city that had classes in which students could develop technical skills by creating tools. Students had assignments that included working in a foundry, doing technical drawings with T squares, and making a hammer. Making a hammer required everything from making a rendering of the tool to using a lathe to create it. This was a powerful intellectual exercise that allowed students to develop both technical and academic skills. The students learned to make the hammer and also how and why the hammer works. Students were proud of their work and would carry their hammers home after they made them. As they carried their hammers in the streets, narratives about why they had them started to form. Black and Brown kids carrying hammers who could possibly be part of the scariest gang in New York City were immediately seen as criminals wielding weapons. Soon, word spread around the city that Decepticons carried hammers that they hit people in the head with just for entertainment and/or before robbing them. At this point, the fear of the gang had grown so much that stories about them had spread across New York City schools. In the *New York Times* article described above, a young person was reported as saying, "Everybody's heard of the Decepticons. . . . They're everywhere." Young people across the city from different schools who believed they had no voice and just wanted to be acknowledged also started naming themselves Decepticons or forming their own gangs.

In the search for validation and safety that is a part of adolescence for all young people, whatever phenomenon can affirm them becomes what they gravitate toward the most. If schools validate you and make you feel safe, you develop a love for school and strive for perfection in education. If the football field or basketball court is where you feel validated and safe, you become an athlete and love sports. For the Black youth who became Decepticons, their crew/peers gave them validation, safety, and love. Sometimes, the only affirmation people receive is for being a version of themselves that is not who they truly are or who they want to be. This is as true for the Black folks who serve as cookies holding up White norms as it is for Black youth being shaped into gang members by schools that don't provide them with love and affirmation. This is not to say that these students never receive love and affirmation in schools. It is to say that they are only loved and affirmed when they perform as the thug in the imagination of those around them, which is distinctly different from their ratchet self (raw, authentic, and unapologetic in the expression of self), which can also be academic and intellectual.

The Decepticons I have engaged in conversations with over the past few decades have always described their "gang" not as a criminal enterprise but as a family. Common quotes include the following: "I just started by hanging out with my friends and just being together to feel strong and protected" and "I felt alone in school. They didn't want me there, so I went where I was wanted. I went with the brotherhood." Decepticons tell stories about navigating schools and searching for acceptance, voice, and validation within them. They loved education and went through a process of heartbreak within a system that didn't love them back. Schooling for Black youth has always been about unrequited love. The pursuance of an anti-school identity is trying to get the attention of the system you love by being what it sees you as or what it wants you to be. Any attention after the heartbreak then becomes good attention. A feature in a newspaper for being violent (like the Decepticons article in the *New York Times*) becomes a form of validation. Having people fear you when you are in a large group with your friends attracts attention. Chanting phrases in unison builds camaraderie, even if it is in a gang, and becomes a form of love. In search of love, the kids from the smart school turned themselves into gangstas. This then expanded to other kids from other schools who were also in search of love and attention. As a result, more Decepts were born.

The Decepts then grew in number to include the kids from the smart school who started the gang and other groups of kids who wanted the attention and validation the smart kids were receiving. They started what they called *legions* across the city and became a force. In an interesting way, the visibility that the Decepts received from the media for being violent created a battle among other groups of marginalized young people to see who could be the most violent. The Decepts' original members were high school students who connected to each other for safety, and its new members expected the incumbent members to be true to the violent stories the world told about them. The smart kids from the specialized school watched the new, more street-savvy members and wanted to impress them. The new members saw the original members as the embodiment of the stories around town and in the news. They were out to impress each other by being more and more violent. They were all auditioning for a role in the imagination of the public who saw them as ruthless thugs who were anything but academic.

When the new kids who recruited themselves into the gang (who were not necessarily attendees of the gifted technical school) saw that the more veteran members of their gang had hammers, they started carrying hammers as well. The new members had no idea that the hammers the veterans carried were class assignments. They carried them and figured that they had to be a weapon. Eventually, things became more sinister, and the hammer became the signature weapon for Decepts. Stories about assaults with hammers were everywhere. It instilled so much fear that at some point, the hammer was as feared as the gun. There was a powerful process happening in which it didn't matter if you had a gun or a hammer. The hammer sat through belt loops like a gun in a holster. The gun became renamed the hammer. They were both tools for building self-confidence and instilling fear.

If the hammer was called the hammer and the gun also was referred to as a hammer, these tools needed different names to be distinguished from each other. The recognition that the damage from the gun was much more than the damage from the hammer meant that it was a more powerful tool. The gun, being a more complex tool, started being named the ratchet. Just as the ratchet helped me put the bed together, the gun helped to get folks who offended or disrespected you "together" or to act in the way you wanted. You were dangerous if you had the ratchet. "Y'all better stop trippin' cuz I got the ratchet on me" was and still is a powerful threat that is used to blanket oneself in safety in spaces where one is vulnerable. The fear of revealing or releasing the ratchet kept folks respectful. At some point, in certain neighborhoods in New York City, it seemed like everybody had a ratchet or knew someone who did.

The ratchet is not welcome in the hands of everyone. The National Rifle Association and the Second Amendment of the United States Constitution declare that technically we all have the right to have one. In reality, that right is limited only to certain people. When the ratchet is being wielded by those who have historically been marginalized and feared, even in locales where having one is part of the cultural fabric, the right to bear arms gets revoked. As young Black folks across New York City were driven to go out (and simultaneously feared for going out) and get the ratchet, the punishment for having one became much more stringent. In the 1990s, random sweeps of groups of teenagers were the norm. In the 2000s, it became official practice of the NYPD to stop and frisk youth on the slightest suspicion that they were gang members. Laws were enacted to punish any Black folks who had the ratchet.

When rapper Jay-Z described the 1990s in New York as "back when ratchet was a ratchet," on the song "Marcy Me," he alluded to an evolution of ratchetness from the 1990s New York version to something different. New York in the 1990s was when people kept the physical ratchet for safety, protection, respect, and admiration. As a teenager in that era, I felt like I needed one. In the pursuit of a ratchet, I saved money and eventually connected to a person who could sell me one. I took the train to the other side of the Bronx, found the building I was told to go to, and walked into a dark basement. I shook the hand of a man who emerged from the shadows, and he handed me a cold piece of metal that easily fit in my palm but was heavier than I expected. My hand shook. He looked me in the eye and asked for the money. I handed it over and thought about what I had in my hand and what it meant. As I walked out, I was so afraid of being stopped and arrested that I was almost paralyzed. I had power in what I held, but it made me feel like it overshadowed the power I already had within. It was an external power source that didn't feel right. This led me to desire a different type of ratchet that could not be taken away from me. I ended up tossing the ratchet I had just purchased on the train tracks. I didn't want to have that type of power; I wanted to be the power. I didn't want the ratchet; I wanted to be the ratchet.

Rapper and social theorist Lil Boosie was ahead of his time in describing this phenomenon of being the ratchet and holding power. He was the first to describe the ratchet as an identity and not a physical weapon. He saw the ratchet more as a sensibility and way of knowing than a thing to display or use when one needed to exert power. He brought a very distinct Southern brilliance to the concept of ratchet that showed that it was a way of being in response to your surroundings. While New Yorkers and other Northern folks were all trying to get a ratchet in order to gain some power, folks in the South were *being* ratchet for the same reasons.

In both places, young people were undergoing a contemporary slavery in that their experiences in schools were, and in many ways remain, about producing work, staying in line, and being seen as less than. In the 1990s in New York City, the response involved getting the ratchet as a physical weapon. In the South, where racism was less hidden than under Northern respectability and appropriateness, the process of responding became more complex and layered. As the Decepts were rising in New York in response to not being welcome in schools, communities in New Orleans were rising in response to the fact that there were schools named after slave masters and Confederate figures that had predominantly Black student populations. In both New York and New Orleans, there were zero-tolerance policies that resulted in the suspension or arrest of Black youth at rates that were higher than those for White youth.

Boosie and his contemporaries in Louisiana were not only saying they were the ratchet but were declaring that we (all people) "all got some ratchet in us."[1] In other words, everyone has a piece of who they are that reflects a raw element of their authentic self they are forced to hide for the sake of acceptance. The issue is that some folks have to hide just about all of who they are while others can express themselves more freely because their ratchet is normalized. Boosie, in his interpretation of a song first recorded in the late 1990s by fellow Shreveport rapper and self-professed Ratchet King Anthony Mandigo, was not just introducing himself as ratchet; he was making a declaration that there was power in ratchetness. He was telling the world that ratchet is an internal weapon and a philosophy that pushes for a reimagining of what it means to be young, Black, vulnerable, seen as older than you are (robbed of childhood), dismissible, unintelligent, and feared. Dealing with all of these projections onto the bodies and souls of Black children creates angst that can be expressed either as wanting to grab a weapon or wanting to become a weapon. The point here is that when one becomes a weapon, one unearths a tool that lies within that helps the person to shape their own identity and define themselves for themselves.

Boosie proposed a theory for ratchet that brought visibility to those who exist at the margins. Building on this work, Nadia Brown and Lisa Young deconstructed the politics of ratchet while exploring the particular ways that it has been used to attack and devalue Black women.[2] In a powerful essay, they highlight the "oppositional practices" of ratchet folks and how ways of knowing and being that have been developed as a function of existing at the margins of society have become a tool for reclaiming worth in a world that devalues Black women. In a similar vein, T. A. Pickens describes how ratchetness is a performative strategy for liberating Black women despite or even because of the term being used in a derogatory manner.[3] These insights into what happens when Black women create life preservers for *all* who need it in a world that drowns them and other marginalized folks in self-doubt and second-class citizenship are powerful. Furthermore, these perspectives on the oppositional and performative aspects of ratchetness are important for educators to understand in order to make sense of how and why young people perform disinterest in schools in response to the ways that schools silence them and limit their expression of a full range of their identity. It is essential to recognize that weapons for defending against being typecast and tools for securing agency and claiming power will always find ways to manifest themselves. They may not always emerge in ways that make systems comfortable or in ways that seem immediately beneficial to those who find them, but they will show up. As long as schools continue to deny students opportunities to be and be valued for their true selves, students will find new ways to reject school and what it represents and unless those tools are fashioned to support them in their academic and intellectual development, they will be developed in opposition to school.

We cannot talk about academic underperformance or disengagement in classrooms without first recognizing that all marginalized groups develop mechanisms for dealing with being devalued. Decepticons did not appear out of thin air. They did not have an innate desire to instill fear. They were constructed as a defense mechanism from feeling fear. Over time, coping mechanisms become daily practices and then begin to form pieces of our identity. We turn to these practices to keep us whole and, in many instances, to keep us sane. We become ratchet to keep us from grabbing the physical ratchet and inflicting physical harm on someone. For Black women, who undergo a distinct form of oppression and violence, describing their ratchet forms of resistance as vulgar and violent is an attempt to disarm them from the beautifully complex weapons and tools they have created from the shards of a shattered societal image. This disarming happens at the hands of White dominant society but also from Black men who have been trained to devalue forms of ratchet other than their own in order to raise the value of their own forms of expression. This is how and why being ratchet has been transformed from a shared ratchetness as Boosie articulated it into a gendered expression that pigeonholes and frames Black girl ratchet as lowbrow when it is actually deeply complex and rich. We see these problematic iterations of ratchet on "Ratchet Girl Anthem" videos on YouTube in which Black men perform Black women ratchetness in ways that make fun of or devalue it. It is why the phrase "she ratchet" rolls off Black men's tongues with disgust or disdain and why it is spoken with such pride when an artist like Boosie describes himself as ratchet. It is also why we must collectively own and claim that we are a part of what we demonize and that it has formed us all. To devalue Black girl/woman ratchetness is to devalue ourselves. We have to accept Black girl/woman ratchetness as our own because it is our own. The viewing of a reflection of yourself as subordinate to you is the chief way that people can be convinced to support a distorted view of themselves. Unfortunately, too many have been trained to hate themselves and identify versions of themselves that they see in sisters as problematic. This process is the ultimate expression of self-hate and the chief way that we lose our ability to exist in the world with shared self-worth.

The argument here is that all people have some ratchet in 'em, and the absence of a space to accept and express that ratchetness will always have a negative impact on the learning of those who have it. We all have pieces of our identity that make certain folks uncomfortable. For young folks of color, these are aspects of who they are that many perceive to be negative or even dangerous, even when they are not. We exist in a world where we have learned to either willingly or unwillingly conceal these aspects of who we are for the comfort and/ or acceptance of others. For Black youth, the curbing of their ratchet selves for the acceptance of others comes at the expense of the construction of their academic identity. For others, all of who they are is accepted, and even their flaws are skewed toward being an asset of some sort. A loud White child has a voice. A questioning White child is inquisitive. A "smart-mouthed" White child is precocious. A Black child who expresses any of these attributes is bad. The reality is that the White child in these scenarios is expressing some ratchetness and value is seen in it.

Some folks don't need their ratchet for survival because they aren't being emotionally, psychologically, and physically assaulted. Their ratchet exists—as it exists for all of us—but is not essential to express because it has never been truly needed for survival. The contexts in which their ratchet may emerge have no significant consequence to their social or emotional well-being. For them, it can be neatly tucked away as a novelty that emerges when they have a few drinks or if they're really upset. For others, the ratchet identity is drawn upon to exert power when it is being taken away or to showcase strength when one is made to feel weak and vulnerable. For Black youth in schools, the experience of vulnerability and loss of power is an everyday experience. For Black youth, the conditions of their everyday lives make their ratchet fully developed and needed. Every experience in which they are silenced—every "Shut up and stay in line," "Be quiet, you're too loud," and "This is too hard for you"— forms the ratchet identity. Once formed, it is not something that can be tucked away, because it is weaponry for survival. A child whose sense of self has been assaulted will refuse to ever stay in line and will express discontent through both voice and body. The responses are visceral because they are necessary for navigating a world in which the very system, marketed as a way for Black youth to achieve power and status, is designed to make them feel powerless. For these youth, their ratchetness is on constant display because it has to be. This is why we cannot have a culture of selective acceptance of raw expression of self or ratchetness—where it can be expressed freely, celebrated, and used to exert power when expressed by White folks but then feared and demonized when expressed by others. The emergence of trending "Karen videos" on social media that were recorded by people on the receiving end of demands for voice, acknowledgment, and power by White women highlights an often unmentioned ratchetness being expressed by folks who demonize others for being ratchet. This reveals that the issue is not the demand to be seen per se, but rather that those who are in power (who have institutionally sanctioned power) resent both the expression of ratchetness and any claiming of power or sense of self by those historically positioned as powerless. Folks with power will name the expression of power by the marginalized as regressive and will frame a policing of that expression as advancement. In other words, there is always an unwritten belief (particularly in education) that Black folks are advancing if they are not being ratchet. This does not account for the fact that this version of advancement is about maintaining brokenness/powerlessness and teaching folks to endure it in silence.

Decepticons were the creation of a system that demanded that Black children suffer in silence. These young folks created an identity out of necessity and grabbed the ratchet to reclaim a sense of power in a school system that made them feel powerless. Once this fact has become accepted, it becomes the responsibility of the teacher/elder/community member to transform the existing system and allow the ratchet to be a tool for strength, power, and agency. There must be new structures/rules/norms that make ratchetness welcome and are applied to the free pursuit of academic knowledge and a demand for power and voice. In contemporary education, there is no space for these types of schools. In urban schools in particular, education follows a teaching and learning model that is rooted in only allowing the demand for (more) power to come from folks with power while keeping the folks who have been robbed of it silent and accepting of the existing norms. What we have today is contemporary forms of White teaching in the slave quarter.

Any teaching and learning experience that stifles the free expression of a population by making the experience about the production
of work/labor and the extraction of joy engages in a slave quarter
pedagogy. The only way to combat such a pedagogy is to be deliberate
about creating spaces where the expression of what is perceived to
be ratchet is allowed in the pursuit of academic excellence. In the
book *Deep Like the Rivers*, Thomas L. Webber explores education in
the slave quarter from 1831 to 1865.[4] In the text, a number of examples of White slaveholder teaching and the Black response to it are
described. In particular, the quest for opportunities for ratchet expressions among slaves in the midst of oppressive teaching contexts
caught my attention. Webber writes of the slaves' belief in their "stylistic superiority" to Whites—the slaves' better storytelling, creative
singing, and energetic dancing. He wrote of the slaves' sharper wit
and the ways that Whites "blocked their learning" because of a fear
that slaves were smarter. In particular, the fact that slaves found the
church services or the Sabbath schools of their White masters boring
and lacking in energy was fascinating. They rejected the pedagogy
in those places because they were "required to maintain the strictest order and were prohibited from shouting, moaning or dancing,"
which was antithetical to the freedom to shout and dance needed to
emotionally engage and truly learn. This is no different from today's
schools, where parents, school leaders, teachers, and students have to
be convinced that the strictest order and irrelevance of school to students' lived experiences must be accepted as a norm. I argue that we
must push back against this notion by embracing our ratchet selves
and teaching our young people to do the same while developing their
academic selves. The goal is to be ratchetdemic.

CHAPTER 4

RATCHET AS BEING AND FREEING

That the content of white teaching directly contradicted understand-
ings, attitudes, values, and feelings which slaves had learned from
birth in an educational process created and controlled by slaves them-
selves, was a notion too incredible and too dangerous to entertain.
To suggest that slaves were capable of molding their own culture,
of fashioning and maintaining their own educational instruments,
would be to undermine the most fundamental arguments with which
whites rationalized their enslavement of other human beings.

—THOMAS L. WEBBER, *Deep Like the Rivers*[1]

The legacy of slavery in the United States permeates every aspect of
our lives. Scholars like Kevin Bales and Ron Soodalter have written
about the links between contemporary human trafficking and slavery.[2] Others write about the slavery-like experiences of Black folks in
corporate America.[3] William C. Rhoden's book *Forty Million Dollar
Slaves* compares professional athletes to slaves on plantations who
were introduced to sports as a way to entertain their masters and
distract from the toils of everyday life.[4] Each of these comparisons is
powerful and provides insight into how the legacy of slavery persists in
the field of education, which takes each of the examples from slavery
described above and operationalizes it within an education-industrial
complex. This complex functions to coerce and entangle folks with

strong and free cultural expression into a system that profits from their presence and underperformance in schools. The education-industrial complex relishes removing minoritized youth from positions of power and purpose, and celebrates their vilification in society.

The reality is that contemporary schooling (particularly urban schooling) is often about the White slaveholders' teaching of Black children that stands in sharp distinction from the more informal (yet academically rigorous) and non-institution-focused Black teaching that has existed since slavery. This distinction is highlighted in the quote that opens up this chapter and its mention of a Black education "created and controlled by slaves themselves" that White folks just couldn't fathom or found too dangerous. This phenomenon—of fearing models for education created by Black folks and not believing a system created by those who have been positioned as less than could be a viable model for teaching and learning—is at the core of how slavery models of education persist. I want to be clear that White teaching is not about White people. It is about plantation pedagogies that were enacted by White people during slavery that are still being carried out today by the majority-White teaching force and held up by the brown cookies. White teaching or a plantation pedagogy is about disregarding and demonizing the "understandings, attitudes, values, and feelings which slaves had learned from birth" and the implanting of different ones that do not necessarily align to the souls of Black folks. I suggest that the teaching and learning that the slaves enacted had its own culture and educational instruments. It was ratchet in that it was expressive and stood in contrast to a system that functioned like trafficking in the ways it coerced genius from communities into institutions that demonized where they came from and used them as labor in an education-industrial complex akin to professional sports. To be more clear, I am suggesting here that both the education-industrial complex we have today and the system of professional sports, which renders Black bodies disposable unless they entertain and/or provide income for a wealthy class, are contemporary iterations of a model for "dealing with" Black bodies that has roots in slavery.

Today, many college and professional sports leagues maintain a power structure that, despite whatever compensation athletes receive, positions athletes as pawns to be controlled by the White wealthy class who owns/operates universities and/or professional teams and determines their worth or lack thereof based on a certain type of performance. The wholeness of athletes is not of any particular significance to institutions, as long as their performance in the one small slice of life (the field or the court) that the institution profits from reaps the expected benefits. The education-industrial complex is a system that creates an economy that involves jobs, real estate, and funding streams that line the pockets of individuals and organizations primarily concerned with performance on tests that do not capture the wholeness, genius, or potential of children. It is similar to professional sports and its legacy of mimicking slavery in the way it reduces complex people to performers of labor for the entertainment of the masses and the profit of the few. K–12 classrooms that carry traditions about teaching are eerily similar to plantation pedagogies in both their form and enforcement. This is a system where Black bodies are performing obedience and showcasing worth through test performance. Obedience is maintained by loud voices that bark orders and threats of punishment like suspension for expressing oneself and being free in thought, word, and action. This is a complex that invokes ratchet as a form of protest. I argue that the responses of slaves to the teaching structures forced upon them on plantations would be described as ratchet if expressed in contemporary classrooms. In much the same way, Black youth responses to plantation pedagogies in today's classrooms are natural expressions of a search for freedom in oppressive (learning) environments. They are simply trying to get free like their ancestors were.

Sociologist Jonathan Turner argues that human beings have core, social, group, and role identities.[5] These multiple identities are listed in the order of their emotional significance to an individual, with the role identity being furthest away from the authentic self and the core identity being the anchor of who a person is. These identities are essential for making sense of how "academic" identities that do not capture all of the individual get enacted and strengthened at the expense of other, more significant parts of the self that are part of the core identity.

Role identities are those we perform in different settings. We take them on because they are essential for survival. For many, being a teacher or even a student means taking on a role that one perceives is emblematic of how to be a teacher or student. For example, a teacher who has a prominent ratchet identity outside the school building learns to erase that part of the self to take on the role of teacher by remembering past teachers, watching other teachers, and receiving scripts for how to be a teacher from trainings and professional development. This person learns to walk, talk, and act in a socially accepted way that is defined by the understandings, attitudes, values, and feelings of the institution. It is not to say that all that is performed is inauthentic. However, it is essential to recognize that most of what a teacher becomes is developed from the script that teacher follows year after year. The more the script is followed, the less space there is for improvisation because of the risk attached to leaving the script—which then becomes a crutch.

A group identity is one that is shared within a particular group. For example, a group identity is shared by folks from the same hometown or folks who went to the same high school. It is a piece of the self that is shared with others who have a similar allegiance. Folks may enact roles based on their group identity. If educators see themselves as workers for the state and an extension of the institution, or if they see themselves as part of a collective whose goal is to police Black children's behavior, these teachers hold a group identity that reinforces the following of a social script that is shared by the entire group. Such teachers then take on particular roles and develop a role identity. This phenomenon explains why police officers protect each other or remain silent when other officers they share a group identity with enact violence on citizens. It is also why teachers maintain approaches to teaching that they believe align with a teacher group identity, even when their instincts and their students are telling them young people are being harmed by their practices.

Social identities are related to what Turner calls our "categoric units." This is the identity we hold that is related to gender, race, class, ethnicity, or sexuality.[6] When we operate with our categoric units, we are being guided both by nature and by societal perceptions of what it looks like to be in a particular categoric unit. For me, it is being a Black man and knowing that to be in my skin is to follow a legacy of teachers, thinkers, and preachers from generations before me who have positively impacted the world. However, it is also recognizing that when many see me, all that they see is my categoric units and all that their imaginations have created about me based on those units. My Blackness, to me, means I have something within me to be shared. For others, my Blackness means I am someone to be feared.

Of all the forms of identity, the core identity is the most important. It is the piece of who we are that Turner describes as "the accumulated cognitions and emotions that we have about ourselves as persons. This is the most powerful identity, and we work very hard to make sure that people honor and verify this identity because it embodies our core feelings and cognition about who we are as persons, carrying a sense of how we are treated and how we should be treated."[7] For most teachers, their core identity is what brings them to teach. A person chooses to teach because they care about young people and want to make a difference in the world. Their motivation to teach is deeply personal and tied to how they see themselves and how they want to be seen. Turner suggests that the core identity is the truest self, and I add to that concept by arguing that it is the part of us that we protect the most. When it is threatened or not validated by others, we respond viscerally and lose the capacity to give measured responses or feel controlled emotions. We go into protection mode and perform what biologists describe as *deimatic behavior*. Deimatic behavior in animals is a response to a threat that is designed to intimidate predators and dissuade or distract them from attacking. It can involve displaying the colors of feathers or accentuating other features that may give pause to an attacker so that they stop attacking or so that the animal being attacked can get away. In many ways, the deimatic behavior is a role performance. It is a role that the animal takes on for the sake of temporarily stopping an attack.[8] For Black youth, in a system of education where they are under constant attack or threat of assault, they take on deimatic behaviors in the form of role identities in response to threats to their authentic selves. In many cases, they never have the luxury to return to the self they were trying to protect because of the persistence of the attack. Schools don't stop assaulting a student's sense of self, so the young person becomes less and less of the self they are protecting and more of the aggressive self that is the protector. Over time they take on the protector self for so long, they cannot find what they were protecting to begin with.

When a person sees him or herself as intelligent/artistic/creative/brilliant and then goes to a school where there is no space to express any of these pieces of this core self, or when expressions of that core self are threatened, that experience invokes an authentic emotional and visceral response. That response is ratchetness—the chief mechanism for expression in moments of threat for the marginalized. It is the attitudes, values, beliefs, and emotions that come with being who they are in the world, all on display in their rawest form. It is the unfiltered expression of self of a particular person or group that runs counter to the traditional modes of expression or communication established and normalized by an institution. It takes on different forms each time it is expressed, but it is raw and unapologetic whenever it emerges. There is ratchet clothing that folks wear when their clothes are being policed, loudness when there is an assault on voice and volume, a type of art that is created when the only art that is valued in the world excludes them, and a certain type of teaching when the craft they love becomes so scripted that it loses its art. Ratchetdemic teaching is when one leads with the ratchet self in response to what has become of teaching. It is recognizing that students cannot learn any academic content if they experience the teaching as an assault on their core identity. A person cannot truly teach when all they are in the classroom is a shell of their true self and their craft has been reduced to a performance that does not reflect their passion for the art and craft of teaching. To meet the needs of students, teachers have to catch up to where youth are. Teachers have to reconcile their allegiance to a structure that harms their core selves and causes them to harm youth and their core selves. Ratchet youth need ratchet teachers who create classrooms where core selves are expressed freely and with joy. Otherwise, schools foster the performance of role identities that counter the core identity and cause youth to trade in their joyful passion for learning with an anger that hides this passion. Having to create and perform anti-learning role identities is deeply toxic. It permanently shifts the way that the core identity is expressed. What educators then get from young people is an isotope of the core identity. An isotope of a chemical element is a variant of it. Isotopes of an element have the same number of protons but different numbers of neutrons. The core identity is a love for learning expressed as joy. Its isotope is still a love for learning, but it will get expressed with/as anger, disrespect, dissatisfaction, and academic performance.

For example, a young person who has a desire to learn but who is not welcome or accepted in school doesn't change their passion for learning, but the young person may perform disinterest in school and develop an anger toward the school because it is the only role that young person is affirmed or recognized for. Consider hip-hop culture and the fact that it has always been a mechanism for the expression of the lived experiences of Black and Brown folks in the most vulnerable communities. Hip-hop artists tell stories that are reflections of an assault on their core identities. Whether the music an artist creates is a retelling of an experience, a fantasy narrative, a critique of society, or a grotesque exaggeration of wealth or sexual prowess, it often comes from a place of having some part of the core threatened. This is why the music is so emotive. It resonates with others who are going through the same experience. Hip-hop is a ratchet response to society. This is why educators who focus on hip-hop culture are so important. The hip-hop educator is the embodiment of merging worlds that society has deemed as separate who showcases that they are actually deeply connected to each other. Simply by walking into a classroom with one's hip-hop identity on full display (by how one dresses or speaks or the music one plays in the classroom) is a political act that tells the world that the teacher refuses to be defined by conventions that define intelligence and/or appropriateness narrowly. This kind of teacher, while self-healing by expressing the core self, is also modeling for students that it is okay to do the same. Hip-hop educators connect to young people because they are redefining norms around what is allowed in the classroom and creating space for core identities (particularly those around being smart or loving learning) to be expressed with joy. This is what is required to move toward creating and molding a radically different classroom culture. This is the beginning of ratchetdemic teaching and learning.

In the quote that opens this chapter, Webber writes that "suggest[ing] that slaves were capable of molding their own culture, of fashioning and maintaining their own educational instruments, would be to undermine the most fundamental arguments with which whites rationalized their enslavement of other human beings."[9] I contend that contemporary plantation pedagogies operate in much the same way. Suggesting that the culture of Black folks (particularly in forms that do not reinforce White standards) should be at the center of how children are taught is framed as trivial and/or lacking academic rigor. However, incorporating ratchet forms of self-expression like hip-hop culture (in the form of art, dance, poetry, and performance in the classroom) is necessary to undermine the plantation pedagogies that are currently in place and highlights that Black folks can learn on their own without existing curricular approaches and pedagogies that have been designed to harm them. To welcome Black cultural forms as legitimate educational instruments and ratchet cultural expressions as powerful for delivering information is a threat to the status quo. This is why a denial of culture and an erasure of all that culture produces, including educational instruments and pedagogical approaches that benefit those whose culture has been denied, is part of the playbook for those who maintain systems of power in education. What folks who deny culture have not counted on is the visceral response to the silencing—the expression of the core identity in ways that are intended to bring discomfort to those who oppose its expression. Black folks during slavery existed in a state of persistent denial of their humanity and culture. In response, the enslaved developed ratchet responses to White teaching. Their responses to White teaching then became the justification for why they were treated poorly. One of the basic principles of the teaching of slaves was to demonize where they came from (their land of origin) and blame them for the conditions they were placed under. The backwardness of Africa and the squalor of the slave quarters were important narratives implanted into the minds of the enslaved while educating them. They were blamed for the inhumanity of the slave master, and African songs and dances that helped them emotionally escape that inhumanity were barred. The very things that they used to heal from the assaults to their core identities were stripped from them.

Contemporary forms of this same process exist today. Examples such as narratives of the darkness of housing projects or certain neighborhoods and the association of song and dance as trivial or nonessential to learning are realities that Black youth have to endure in schools today. In many schools attended by Black youth, there are rules on appropriate ways of dressing, talking, or even wearing one's hair in school, which are extensions of plantation pedagogy. These are phenomena that I experienced in high school decades ago that are still present in today's schools. In the slave quarter, the response to this hyper-control over the body and mind was loud singing and dancing, pranks on massa and the overseer, and an outright rejection of the slave owner's vision of them. R. A. Bauer and A. H. Bauer describe the "day to day resistance" of the enslaved as involving slowing down work, feigning illness, or destroying tools.[10] Accounts from a book titled *The Unchained: Powerful Life Stories of Former Slaves* includes narratives of the enslaved mocking the slave master as a way of rejecting the master's idea of superiority and recognizing the moral superiority of the enslaved over their masters.

I suggest that students who reject doing work assigned by a person they feel morally superior to (that they feel they are better, kinder, more honest, and more trustworthy than) are enacting their own day-to-day resistance. Their rejection of what the teacher presents is an act of power and protest. In response, I am suggesting a reframing of the entire process of teaching and learning for youth that requires educators to rediscover/reclaim their ratchetdemic selves and then work with young people to leverage their ratchet protest to schooling into a mechanism for developing/strengthening their academic selves.

MY RATCHET, THEIR RATCHET, SAME RATCHET

As soon as I hit six feet tall, I found myself drawn into (attracted to) a persona that I ended up being drawn (created and constructed) into. I was Black, tall, and from a tough neighborhood. I quickly received the message from folks around me, media, and school that this meant that I had to be tougher, stronger, and more intimidating than I really was or wanted to be. I dressed in oversized hoodies, and my pants hung low. Somehow, those variables allowed people around me to create a vision of who I was that suited them. In the imaginations of teachers, media, and the police, I was a person who should be feared. I have written in a previous work on the hip-hop generation about how I could see the fear in the eyes of folks I encountered on the subway and in school. The way they clutched their bags or avoided eye contact spoke volumes about how they saw me. This fear gave me power in a world that made me powerless. It's a fascinating thing to only feel empowered when you are framed in a way that disempowers you. Somehow, I came to believe that being feared felt good. It was better than being invisible and was definitely better than being scared. Decades later, I often wonder how this happened. How did I slip from being Chris into "Devious" (my nickname throughout high school)? This wondering happens most when I work in schools in urban spaces and see new versions of me: same persona, same need to be feared, same masked vulnerability, and same rejection of a sanitized academic identity—just in skinnier jeans. What conditions transfigure preteen Black children into monsters in the imaginations of everyone around them? What makes so many of these children drawn to the images that others have drawn of them? What makes these drawn images flourish in places like schools? What is the mechanism that turns the role identity into something that affects the way the core is expressed? I have since conceded that these answers can be found somewhere in the historical metanarratives about Blackness that have existed since Blackness was first witnessed by White folks who only understood what/who they saw as the opposite of the good folks they weren't but wanted to be. What I can state with certainty is that disrupting these perceptions of Whiteness and Blackness can begin in classrooms and will begin with a more ratchetdemic approach to teaching and learning.

A few years ago, during a visit to a high school in the Bronx, I walked into a group of six or seven students who were being escorted to the principal's office by a school safety officer. They had been rounded up by the officer in what the school described as a "hallway sweep." Seeing them being herded down the hallway in single file with hands crossed in front of them triggered me, and I immediately walked over to the group and started asking questions. I asked the officer why the students were being walked down the hallway like criminals. He responded that he was "taking them down" (I assume to the principal's office) because they weren't in class. He responded assuredly that they had either been kicked out of class or had cut class and weren't in school to learn. He seemed proud of himself for "catching" these students. Though this seemed to be a justifiable response to a teacher who walked past us and nodded at the officer in approval, the officer's response yielded eye rolls and scowls from the group of students. I was surprised that none of them verbally responded, and my look of disapproval or concern seemed to signal to the officer that more of a justification was needed. He followed up by saying that he was "just following instructions. Something that these kids obviously haven't learned yet." In that moment, I was struck by his positioning of complicity (just following instructions) as something he had learned to do and was proud of. I then directed my questions to a young man who wore a bright purple and green Nike sweat suit that matched his sneakers. I asked, "Why were y'all in the hallway?" He responded that he had left his previous class late because he was talking to someone but was on the way to his next class. This is a phenomenon I have witnessed and written about thousands of times before: Black children being punished and not given the grace to explain misunderstandings of circumstances or misinterpretations of their behavior. I nodded as he spoke, and almost as soon as he finished speaking, another young man, with a freshly inked tattoo as indicated by the Vaseline glistening over it on his arm, said, "The teachers don't like us cuz we ratchet." He gave me a toothy grin that showcased his bottom row of gold fronts. I nodded as his peers laughed approvingly. There was something in what he said that resonated with everyone who was there. They were ratchet.

As I think back to that moment, I remember that it struck me deeply. These were students who were in the hallways for a number of reasons but mostly because they were unwilling to play the game of school as it had been presented to them. They were ratchet: acting and appearing unpolished, operating at their own time and pace, and unwilling to compromise themselves for the school or the officer who in that moment was the school's representative. Further conversation with these students revealed that there were battles within them that guided their decision to bend or break the school's rules. On one side was who they authentically were (a core identity and true self operating with joy and positive emotions), and on the other was who the school saw them as (a role identity operating with indignation). Another battle was between who they wanted to be (smart, loved, appreciated like all children, and free), and who the teachers wanted them to be (obedient, silent and attentive, and complicit with a system that only allowed them to be valued if they were not themselves). The unifying battle—the one that both students and teachers were going through—was one between freedom and complicity. This was the trickiest one, because freedom meant being themselves but that meant being seen as academically unfit or unprepared and perhaps seeing themselves that way as well. Complicity was doing what everyone in the school wanted, being seen as having the potential to be an academic success all while damaging their sense of self and worth.

Too many children are being told that if they act as themselves—if they are talkative, ask questions, laugh or talk too loudly, or express too much joy—they are disruptive to the classroom and unprepared for learning. These are the characteristics associated with being ratchet. When these same children are told that they have to be quiet and obedient to be seen as smart and prepared for learning, they believe that they have to choose between being themselves and being academic. Given the ridiculous binaries that school and society have created, which cause young people to believe they have to choose between being themselves and being "smart," educators must begin teaching from a drastically different place from how they were trained. The issue here is that the same phenomenon exists for teachers who have to choose between bringing life and joy to students and teaching for obedience, silence, and complicity.

If young folks are being told that being themselves in a pure expressive and joyous form that reflects their core identity is not welcome in the classroom, and if they see that those who are being celebrated for being smart and academically focused are the ones who are silent, quiet, and obedient, they quickly begin to associate who they authentically are with not being academic. They then begin to construct personas that are ratchet, in that they are expressive, joyous, loud (and powerful), and intentionally not academic. Students respond to schools that don't acknowledge their forms of genius either by changing their practices so that they align to what schools expect or by rejecting what schools want and choosing to remain as they are. My work with Black youth reveals that those who align with school norms about who they should be (particularly when those norms are starkly different from students' natural modes of expression) experience severe stress around learning. Those who reject school structures that do not make them feel welcome end up rejecting school and may attach the pursuit of knowledge to schooling. I suggest that the only way to truly allow the genius of all young people to be expressed and then attached to learning, gaining knowledge, and becoming academic is for teachers to allow all forms of genius to be expressed in the classroom. This process requires teachers to find and then model their ratchet selves, demonstrating how the authentic self can be used in pursuit of knowledge, even as they center it in their teaching. This newly revealed teacher ratchet self may not look like or be expressed in the same way as the version the students present. It may look and sound different. However, it will resonate with young people if it is an authentic expression of self that holds more allegiance to the students than to systems. What I am saying here is that all good teaching begins from a ratchet place. A raw, unadulterated, pure, and expressive energy is necessary to teach authentically and engage young folks academically. Ratchetdemic educators embrace young folks' ratchet selves and coalesce with other educators who are discovering and teaching from their authentic ratchet identity. Teachers who lead with their ratchet selves and who create contexts in which ratchetness is a means for engagement in the classroom create a space that allows young people to reimagine academic excellence.

GOLF RATCHET

A few months ago, as I was delivering a lecture on the need for teaching and being ratchetdemic to an auditorium of teachers and school administrators, a high school principal stood up in the middle of my talk and yelled to the room full of people, "I just don't get this ratchet thing. I accept people regardless of their culture. My school just doesn't accept abnormal behavior, and we shouldn't. None of us should." The scenario was bursting with irony given the fact that he just stood up and burst out saying what he felt right in the middle of my talk. His interrupting loudly because he felt something inside that he was passionate about was the most ratchet thing that had happened that day. In the moment, I suspended my desire to tell him how ratchet he was being. I stopped speaking and let him continue his rant. After a few minutes, he closed his rant with an emphatic and loud, "Now, excuse me," and he began to slide past people in the row he was in and into the aisle. He seemed to be walking out of the auditorium. It was rude and disrespectful, and I tried not take it personally. I clenched the microphone just a bit tighter to subdue my emotions, took a deep breath, and calmly asked him not to walk out of the auditorium. He stopped for a moment to glare at me with such rage and privilege that he seemed to glow. He couldn't fathom that he was exhibiting the very ratchetness he claimed not to understand. I let his ratchet be released and calmly said, "Sir, you made a statement. There may be some other people here who feel the same way you do. Perhaps, I can provide you with some clarity. To do that, I will need you not to walk out of the auditorium." He looked back toward the stage and didn't walk out. He stood in the aisle and faced me. The audience did not respond. They all seemed frozen in their seats. No one reprimanded him. They looked back and forth between us in complete silence as an awkward tension filled the room. After a few seconds that seemed to last forever, I continued speaking. He temporarily tucked his ratchet away and stood as I laid out examples of what he claimed not to understand without shrinking who I was and how I present.

I talked on, allowing unbridled expressions triggered by authentic emotion to have space. I mentioned that it was important to ensure that we do not allow people to be permanently judged by moments of frustration. I described a time when I witnessed a tenth-grade Black boy being called out of class and reprimanded by a school principal for having his head down on his desk. The principal had looked through a window to observe the class after hearing comments from the teacher about the boy not being engaged for weeks. He called him into the hallway, and I watched the boy attempt to explain himself as the principal reprimanded him. He was quickly scolded. I then played a video I had of the class when the boy was sitting in the back of the chemistry classroom excited that he had the right answer to a question the teacher had just posed. In his excitement, he put his hand up and started explaining how he got the answer. The teacher didn't acknowledge him. So he composed himself and put his hand up again and started explaining the answer more loudly. Again, he was ignored. This happened about five or six more times until he finally gave up and put his head on his desk in frustration. That then became his permanent position. Sixty seconds of not being seen turned into six weeks of disengagement. It turned into who he became: the kid who sleeps in chemistry. I argued that he became who he was because his initial enthusiasm was not validated by the teacher and he was not allowed to answer the question. I then talked about how some people have to hold on to certain personas that don't reflect who they are because their lives are almost entirely composed of moments of tension and frustration, especially within schools. I looked up at the gentleman in the audience as I explained this, and he seemed unmoved. A few minutes later, as I was explaining another concept, I noticed he had taken a seat.

I moved along with my lecture, explaining how essential it is for school leaders to reimagine professional development based on what we know about how and why youth take on/accept/present certain identities. Out of nowhere, from across the auditorium and in his new seat, I heard him yell again, "Oh, now I get it. I see what you're saying." In that moment, I followed my teacher instincts and invited him to share what suddenly brought him to such clarity. I created space for his ratchet. He walked up, grabbed the microphone, and said that he had a friend who was "golf ratchet." I was puzzled but allowed him to speak, reminding him that I was going to give him just a minute to explain. He then told a story about his golf buddy whom he described as having "really bad form and an awful swing. . . . He also doesn't have the best etiquette on the course." He continued and explained that he often went to the driving range with this friend.

However, he never brought this "friend" to more formal golf outings. "It would be embarrassing," he said. I asked if his friend was a good player, and he responded by saying, "As far as getting the ball in the hole, yes, he's pretty great—but technically, definitely not." As he explained further, it became clear that the issue was not the ratchet golfer's ability. It was his unwillingness to play by the rules, look the part, or seek validation from the other golfers. This led to him not being welcome among the people who saw the man who interrupted me described as "my actual golfer friends." He mentioned that if you saw this friend play, you would automatically assume he couldn't. However, when you got him out there on the golf course, he was amazing. Again, he declared proudly, "He's golf ratchet."

As I reflected on the entire exchange and processed the hilarious concept of golf ratchet, I found that there were some fundamental truths about his story that are worth noting. The first is that ratchet obviously exists in suburban White men. When offended, confused, or attacked, they will unapologetically express their ratchet without question or, in the case of my experience, any pushback from those who witness it. But unlike White men, folks of color are often demonized when they express themselves. The second is that the "golf ratchet" person did not lose opportunities to play when he expressed his ratchetness. Somehow, despite his unorthodox game, he had the resources to play the course. For young folks of color, what is perceived to be unorthodox in their approach to the classroom is almost immediately demonized by everyone from school safety officers to teachers. This often begins a downward spiral away from formal education that changes their life trajectory. Most importantly, after noting that the man who interrupted my lecture and the friend he described were both ratchet, I realized that there was a currency around doing one's own thing that both the man at my speech and his golf-ratchet friend expressed but that not everyone is afforded. These men made space for their ratchet while refusing to make such space for others. The man interrupted my lecture twice to have his questions considered without any consequence. His ratchetness was accepted and respected, and I had to ensure that he was taken care of. I then gave him a platform that required giving up my own. This luxury is not afforded to our young people, but going forward, it must be. In education, we make space for just about everyone except students, even though we profess that education is solely about them. A teacher with an unsatisfactory lesson is given another opportunity to show that they can improve. The schools that fail students are allowed a school improvement plan. A person who operates a charter school that kicks out students with special needs and verbally assaults teachers is given an opportunity to start a chain of schools. Yet students are rarely given chances to reimagine schools. We must ask ourselves why certain forms of ratchet from certain people are seen as resilient, brave, and determined, while others are seen as inherently negative. How have certain skills, dispositions, traits, and attributes become described as negative despite their complexity and the high acuity required to engage in them?

We move toward answers to these questions when we begin to accept that we live in a world where complex cultural expressions that require high levels of cultural/social astuteness, rhythm, wordplay, and understanding of powerful metaphors and analogies are viewed negatively by people who cannot engage with the culture on the level of those who are part of it. Having the ability to engage fully with a phenomenon but dealing with the perpetual frustration of not being able to access it leads to a tendency to reject that culture. Furthermore, it kicks up a sort of fox and grapes narrative where folks outside of a particular culture who cannot seem to engage with it, describe it as worthless or useless simply because it is out of their reach. The fox and grapes parable, attributed to Greek slave Aesop, best captures this phenomenon.

The fox who longed for grapes, beholds with pain
The tempting clusters were too high to gain;
Grieved in his heart he forced a careless smile,
And cried, "They're sharp and hardly worth my while." [11]

Because school culture is made inaccessible, young folks of color take on the view that school is not worth their while. They attempt to engage with academic content that is well within their intellectual reach, but that is held out of their cultural and emotional reach, so they respond by framing school negatively. The fox and grapes phenomenon is also present in many teachers who have not developed the ability to make sense of or connect with the rich and complex Black cultural norms and youth culture. They cannot reach the high cultural benchmarks of youth and end up describing the youth as disinterested in learning or even unteachable—"sharp and hardly worth my while."

Because those who do not understand Black youth culture and its ratchet expressions have the power to dismiss what they cannot understand, their misinterpretations of the richness of ratchetness are accepted as fact and used to describe the entirety of Blackness—that which they are unfamiliar with and cannot reach. Once again, consider hip-hop and the way that the whole of the culture has been branded by the misogyny, braggadocio, and hyper-capitalism found within parts of it, while ignoring the beauty of the whole of it. Then consider how other cultural expressions receive the benefit of a focus on what is good or redeemable about them or the people who represent them. Consider the reputation of brilliance bestowed upon Shakespeare and Greek mythology despite the violence and misogyny riddled throughout their works. Consider the fact that the forty-fifth president of the United States consistently insulted entire segments of the population, mocked people with disabilities, used misspelled words and poor grammar on public platforms, and still had the gall to proclaim himself a genius and be accepted by a wide swath of the population as such. This is an individual who consistently exhibited behaviors for which Black youth in urban schools have been suspended, expelled, or even diagnosed with mental health issues. When we begin to make sense of these hypocrisies and deep flaws in our society, our collective biases against the cultural freedom/expression of folks of minoritized populations emerge. It is at the point that we own our biases that we start moving from just recognizing ratchet to being ratchetdemic. It is at this point that we start developing the revolutionary spirit required to do right by the most vulnerable young people.

So far, we have established the importance of understanding the ratchet, knowing where it comes from, knowing why it is demonized, and working to include it as a tool in the construction of an academic identity. Our work now is to understand what teachers must do to begin the process of using this tool to unlock what has been sealed away and free young people as we redefine academic excellence. I suggest this begins with the teacher looking inward and asking what they need to do to allow young folks to be free. Teachers must ask: How can I model a more authentic version of myself so that my students can see/experience/feel what it looks and feels like to be free, ratchet, and educated? How do I move beyond the mold I have been forced into that maintains the status quo? My answer is, you just do it. Like James Baldwin describes in his powerful talk to teachers, the teacher has to go for broke:

> Any citizen of this country who figures himself as responsible—and particularly those of you who deal with the minds and hearts of young people—must be prepared to go for broke. Or put another way, you must understand that in the attempt to correct so many generations of bad faith and cruelty, operating not only in the classroom but in society, you will meet the most fantastic, the most brutal, and the most determined resistance. There is no point in pretending that this won't happen. . . . The obligation of anyone who thinks of [one]self as responsible is to examine society and try to change it and fight it—at no matter what risk. That is the only hope society has. That is the only way society changes.[12]

The first step in going for broke and unleashing the ratchet is for teachers to look at the educational system as it currently exists and name the structures that harm teachers and students. The next step is to identify the practices WE (teachers, principals, district personnel) enact that endorse these structures. We must understand that if we do not interrupt certain structures by interrupting them in our practice, we endorse and maintain them. Ask yourself: What ways has the school pushed me to teach in a way that does not resonate with what is in my heart and soul? What practices/rituals that harm young people have I inherited from my parents/elders/past teachers/administrators? How am I continuing a legacy of bad faith and cruelty in the classroom by continuing to follow along with the curriculum I was given? The process of naming the structures of schools that continue to harm, while identifying the ways they manifest themselves in our personal/everyday practice, is essential to going for broke, but the process begins by interrupting the status quo as it manifests within you. Interruption is first about revealing to yourself what needs to be overhauled and then going for broke in attacking that thing.

This work quickly unearths a number of issues within the school. It makes clear that buildings will have to be shaped differently, certain rules will have to be eliminated, the order of the school day will have to change, hiring practices will have to shift, teacher recruitment will have to be done differently, the subjects that are taught will have to be overhauled, and assessments will have to be revised. The process will reveal the need to face history/tradition, the effects of it, and, in some cases, the effects of those effects—some of which will remain unknown until they reveal themselves through this process. Furthermore, this process of naming, if done properly, will reveal that the individual educator or school leader after revealing what must change, must recruit a critical mass of folks to break tradition and shift a school's climate and culture. The reality that there is always something to be done will emerge, but that reality will grind against the simultaneous realization that many of these structures are impossible to shift without shared responsibility and collective transformation. Shared responsibility and collective transformation cannot happen with people who have not seen the value of being ratchetdemic, and the only way to recruit others to this philosophy is to be it. The individual teacher must see that the way to recruit peers to do the work is by unearthing the revolutionary within themselves. Teaching students to break out of the mold that supports the structures that break their spirit requires a certain temperament, disposition, and individual responsibility. To teach and go for broke requires educators to find and lead with their ratchet.

I argue, like James Baldwin does, that to fight against structures that perpetrate violence on young people, the teacher must refuse to be a tool for the enactment of that violence. Going for broke is both breaking the mold of who you should be (as defined by the school system) and working toward what the school could/should be (a space that welcomes, fosters, and grows the students' ratchet, even as they thrive in traditional pursuits). Going for broke is shattering expectations of normalcy by taking cues from the youth who are most ratchet on how to find and express your own ratchet self, even as you model how to be freer in the classroom. In this process, it is important to note that the goal is not to be like your students. It is to be as unapologetic, raw, and honest as you can be about who you are, while creating space for your students to express their authenticity and vulnerability in ways that have never been allowed before and that support their freedom to learn and become academically successful.

CHAPTER 5

ELEVATORS, HATERS, AND SUCKAS

A seven-by-ten-foot painting of Black people with dark, indistinguishable features and bright lips, happily entertaining White picnickers and begging for change, hung on the south wall of the first-floor stairway landing at the St. Petersburg City Hall in Florida for decades. The painting, titled *Picnicking at Pass-a-Grille*, went up in 1945 at the same time as another, titled *Fishing on the Pier*, which featured a White couple leisurely fishing. The second painting hung on the north wall. Both paintings were commissioned by and paid for with federal funds from Franklin Delano Roosevelt's New Deal, which supported an artist named George Snow Hill to do a number of public works projects. These two pieces of art were supposed to depict everyday life in St. Petersburg and went through both federal and state approval before they were finally hung. The painting on the north wall was pretty innocuous. No one made any comments about it. The one on the south wall drew offense almost immediately. Placing both paintings across from each other as depictions of life in the city spoke volumes about how Black folks were seen in comparison to Whites and revealed the deep racism in the city.

The images were sending a message about how Black folks were viewed by society, and they immediately requested that the painting be removed. Some argued that the painting was harmless and that the painter had no ill intentions. However, it was apparent that the racist painting was emblematic of a certain penchant Hill had for racist imagery. In a previous painting, Hill featured Black workers in a cotton mill being supervised by a White man in a suit. Another featured five Black men in tattered shorts, like escaped convicts pulling a cart through a swamp. The normalizing of caricatured Black servitude in Hill's paintings was part of a pattern that was similar to the way that folks normalize false perceptions of Blackness and its association with an anti-academic, anti-intellectual, and ratchet identity. Society hangs false perceptions of Blackness prominently for the world to see and, in so doing, creates a narrative.

Hill's paintings of Black characters entertaining White picnickers provided much to be interpreted about society and, in so doing, provides deep insight into schooling. Like Hill's paintings, schooling today often engages in a fetishizing and subsequent devaluing of ratchet Black performance and expression. Black children are often trotted out to perform Blackness for school visitors or tell stories about how the school saved them from their troubled lives outside of the classroom. I have attended a number of school events with educators and school leaders during which young Black kids step, rap, and sing to hand claps from adults who appear entertained by the performances but not struck by the genius in the forms of expression. The students' loudness/expressiveness/ratchetness is performed for entertainment but is then framed as problematic and/or distracting in the classroom. My argument for ratchet expression is not an argument for performing ratchet for White folks. It is about expressing all of who you are for your benefit and refusing to be painted a certain way based on an artificial, contrived image of you that is always less than.

The fact that the painting was displayed in city hall, the heart of the city, says much. St. Petersburg City Hall was constructed in 1939, at a time when Black folks who lived in the city were feeling the effects of gentrification. They were being shuffled to the outskirts of the city because of the perception that their presence in the downtown area would negatively affect the newly developing tourism industry.

City hall was technically open to all, meaning Black folks could enter to conduct business, but the painting not only made it clear how they were perceived by the White folks of St. Petersburg; it reinforced the notion that the city and the hall were for White people. The city hall was the site of the founding of the St. Petersburg White Citizens' Council in 1954, which was a response to Black citizens using state facilities like swimming pools, which were technically open to all residents but in reality unavailable for Black folks. City hall was the place where White folks gathered to affirm their perceived superiority. Because of this fact, having an image of Blackness in a narrow and grotesque form hung prominently made sense. A respected Black journalist for the *St. Petersburg Times*, Peggy Peterman, once said, "There wasn't a Black person I ever met that didn't despise that mural."[1] Yet it remained.

When false perceptions of you have been allowed to take up space like that painting, no one has to tell you that you are not welcome. Rejection is in the air, and you can't help but breathe it in. Your interactions are shaped by it, and your sense of self is infected by it. When you formally or "appropriately" push back against the image of you that lingers over you, the hope is that something shifts in the imagination of those who see you as less than. When Black folks asked nicely for the painting to be removed, they hoped for the humanity of White folks to be activated. When students are quiet, raise their hands, modulate their tone, memorize all the information, write between the lines, and pull their pants up, they expect to have the image of them as nonacademic removed. When they are still seen as less than, despite their efforts to make White folks and their institutions comfortable, it is crushing, and eventually the facade of decorum breaks. Someone reacts. In the case of the painting at city hall, folks did all the right things the right way to have it taken down. They wrote a number of letters and made formal public statements, but the powers that be were unresponsive. Enoch Davis, a Black reverend from that era, writes in his memoir about going to a city council meeting and asking for the painting to be removed: "The members of the [city] council listened and laughed but did nothing about our request."[2] The message was clear. Doing things the prescribed way or bending yourself to meet their demands only leads to exhaustion while remaining under the same conditions that led to your initial frustration.

In 1966, in the midst of heightened racial tensions, a young man named Joseph Waller made several written requests to the city to have the painting removed. Following the pattern of all requests before him, none of his letters received a response. Finally, after he wrote to the mayor of St. Petersburg, describing the painting as "despicable" and "derogatory," the mayor responded, revealing his ignorance. Writer Peyton Jones documented the mayor's response as, "I find nothing offensive. . . . I must admit that I have looked at this mural for the past ten years with nothing but admiration."[3]

After this, Waller took to protest. He gathered with other members of the community in front of city hall to demand that the painting be removed. In the midst of the protest, White onlookers gathered at the spectacle. At one point, Waller heard some of the White observers making fun of a Black woman who was speaking. He had grown tired of doing things the "right" way. He had enough of the city's disregard for Black folks. He walked into city hall with some friends, ripped the painting from its frame, and made a run for it. With the painting dragging behind him, Waller ran through downtown St. Petersburg with the police chasing after him. It was an act of righteous indignation that was rooted in a desire to be seen as more than the caricatures in blackface he removed from public display. As the painting was dragged, the images were ruined; it must have felt gratifying. Waller left an empty spot on the wall in city hall, and the entire debacle earned him close to three years in jail. The event turned Joseph Waller into a self-described Africanist and a civil rights advocate (he later changed his name to Omali Yeshitela). The punishment for Waller was unjust. He faced consequences for choosing to disrupt, but he emerged with even more resolve and a career as an author and founder of a social movement that advocates for justice.

Yeshitela has spent his life working toward a recognition of shared connections among people of African descent and challenging their exploitation across the globe. To be ratchetdemic is to draw from this tradition of shared connections among Black folks. It is to recognize that issues around race and injustice require the spirit and dedication of Joseph Waller/Omali Yeshitela. Joseph Waller's work of ripping a painting off the wall of city hall is the work of a ratchetdemic educator. Representations of young people that hang in the imaginations of the public must be pulled down through teaching that empowers, uplifts, and creates classroom contexts that allow for students' full authentic and academic selves to emerge. This work includes naming those who operate as oppressors of African people within schools as neocolonizers. The work is recognizing that schools are designed to be the exemplar of "Americanism," a very particular image of America that is about sameness and uniformity at the expense of humanity. Yeshitela champions African internationalism and, in doing so, recognizes that "the ideas of African Internationalism are opposite and contradictory to the ideals of Americanism. The ideals of African Internationalism promote freedom from oppression and injustice."[4] I contend that the type of freedom Yeshitela argues for plays out in classrooms when teachers are free to be themselves in the pursuit of modeling freedom for young people and creating just classrooms where their students feel free to be themselves. His critique of "Americanism" is not just about how brown cookies hold up white filling; it is a questioning of how it is even possible for the Oreo's white filling to be the benchmark of excellence.

Yeshitela sees people who have power and allow injustice to happen as operators in the tradition of colonizers. Just as the English, Belgian, and French colonizers established political control over African nations, those who teach young folks of color to accept that they are subordinate and substandard become neocolonizers. Teaching, when an educator does not disrupt the devaluing of ratchet expression, becomes a form of cultural imperialism. It creates unequal relationships to the content being taught and damages the students' relationship to that content and their belief that it is for them. If I teach in a way that forces young people to erase their authentic selves in a chemistry classroom and that practice results in them hating chemistry and choosing not to pursue science, I have colonized their learning and enacted a pedagogical imperialism that limits their academic potential. I understand that terms like *neocolonizer* and *cultural imperialism*, like *neoindigenous* and *neoindigeneity* (which I have used in previous work), seem unnecessarily complex to some people. I have heard arguments that it is offensive to call someone a *neocolonizer* if they have chosen to help the less advantaged in an urban classroom. I have also heard that folks take offense to naming urban youth as *neoindigenous* if we cannot trace their biological Indigenous roots. I argue that offering to help young people, however honorable, does not erase what is felt and experienced by those young people as a result of your work. I also argue that this naming/framing/theorizing is about drawing connections among marginalized people in the African internationalism tradition, not about erasure. The marginalized experience different forms of shared expression. I name myself as an extension of you not to erase you but to recognize you, connect with you, and strengthen us. A ratchetdemic educator from a racial or ethnic background that is different from the students is not the same as a ratchetdemic student. However, they are both limited in their self-expression and freedom to be by a school system that silences them both. They are not the same, but they are both victims of the power structure and can be strengthened together. Neoindigeneity, for example, is about recognizing similarities in forms of oppression (for example, through schools and schooling) with a particular emphasis on recognizing the violence imposed on the Indigenous, whose experiences have been erased by power wielders and left generally unknown to those undergoing new iterations of the same oppression. This naming is not about claiming a position or essentializing but focusing on the effects of Americanness and White supremacist practices on us all.

My thinking here, driven by Yeshitela's work around the concept of African internationalism, is to connect folks to their Indigenous roots and push for solidarity that transcends geographic divides, activating a mission and vision of work that is ancestral. Transforming education cannot happen without a recognition that it is a system that has taken on colonial structures that oppress Indigenous folks and does the same with urban youth, who I call *neoindigenous*, to forge solidarity with those who once occupied the same land and still experience the same marginalization. The educational system cannot be fixed unless there is a snatching of the picture from the wall and a run from city hall. We must snatch the image of anti-intellectualism of youth of color from the metaphorical city hall—the district office, the school, the classroom—even while recognizing there will be challenges and obstacles as we engage in this process. Joseph Waller did not leave the experience of running from city hall with the painting unscathed. One does not depart from the teacher training one received in the university or school district and not expect some resistance. However, if the goal is freedom, a departure is essential. The untwisting of the brown cookie from the white filling is essential. In the process of becoming more ratchetdemic versions of ourselves and enacting more ratchetdemic pedagogy, we must recognize that resistance will come. Much of it will come from places and people you expect to resist your work, but it will also come from brown cookies—melanated folks who are tethered to White supremacist ideologies and who are committed to ensuring that White norms and institutions are protected. Some of the tension/resistance that will come will manifest itself as an internal strife that comes from your heart telling you to find your authentic self again and from your head reminding you that you have much to lose by giving up the position, title, and social capital you have earned by continuing to deny your true self.

As you work toward ratchetdemic identities and pedagogies, you will encounter three types of people: elevators, haters, and suckas. You meet elevators on your journey who shake you up and take you higher. Haters are on your path to discredit you and your work because they believe they deserve your platform and/or the love you receive for doing your work. Suckas are people fundamentally opposed to Black joy and wholeness and don't see any value in your work to empower young people. They each come from both the same and different racial and ethnic backgrounds as you. Some use the same "woke" language you do. You must have particular strategies for dealing with each one. This requires developing the ability to identify who you are interacting with. This is especially the case for educators, who have to answer to so many people positioned as their superiors in the school system. These "superiors," or "bosses," are not necessarily in the business of healing Black children and may be either elevators, haters, or suckas. Because the education system is built on hierarchies designed to place people in positions just above the others as tools for leveraging power for those highest within the system, we have to be more wary of those with institutional power than those who have been robbed of it. Consider a school that has general staff of various kinds: assistant teachers, teachers, lead teachers, deans, coaches, assistant principals, and principals. Then consider that the system is structured in a way that dangles the carrot of promotion in front of the person who occupies an essential position and distracts them from mastering the role they are in pursuit of, a role that is framed as "more important" or next in the hierarchy. Good teachers work with their eyes on being principals instead of mastering the art of teaching. Good school leaders/principals have their eyes and heart on the district office before mastering the art of leadership. Stakeholders in education who prioritize position and power over impact are easily convinced by the system that the only way to reach "the next step" is by stepping on the person or people in the position below you. The entire system becomes a recipe for disaster that forces people to take on roles that make them into haters or suckas. When educators get on the track of chasing position instead of being the best for the young people in the role they currently occupy, the first thing they lose is their intuition.

Intuition can be described as the use of natural knowledge that draws from instinct or feeling rather than what is considered to be traditional sensemaking or reason. It is a powerful force that we all have experienced in some way. You may be walking down a street and are struck by a feeling that you should make a left instead of going straight toward your destination. As you make the turn, you realize that there is a car accident that very well could have involved you if you had continued straight. Somehow, your intuition told you to turn even though the path to your destination was straight. When situations like these happen, we are affirmed in our belief in and thoughts about ourselves. Oftentimes, when you retell the experience to another person, they doubt that it happened or ask how you knew to change direction. The typical response to these types of situations is, "I just had a feeling."

While many question whether intuition is real, a number of psychologists believe that it is. They believe that intuition is a phenomenon that is formed from a culmination of previous experiences and previously acquired knowledge.[5] I agree but also want to consider that intuition may be drawn from previous knowledge beyond a person's own experiences; knowledge that may be ancestral or generational can inform intuition. Your people's and your people's people's experiences also shape and guide your intuition. This is especially the case for folks who have been historically oppressed and marginalized. For these folks, intuition is not just a suspension of institutional logic but a move toward a new logic and sensibility that can be described only as a spiritual connection. When you learn to tap into your intuitional knowledge, you enact intuitional teaching that operates in stark opposition to institutional teaching. To operate from and with intuitional knowledge is a mode of existence that lays bare the connections between schools and other institutions that stifle the agency of folks of color. A ratchetdemic educator operates with intuitional knowledge and recognizes the ratchet responses that youth have to schools may be based not only on their present experience but on their historical trauma. A teacher barking orders at a student may trigger an unsettling in the spirit of a student whose ancestors underwent a similar experience at the hands of a slave master on a plantation. The mechanics of this process—a post-traumatic slavery disorder described by researcher and author Joy DeGruy—are experienced as physiological responses to stimuli resembling or replicating past experiences. The student's intuition may trigger a fear and distrust that then sparks a righteous indignation with the structure of the place, an anger with the school because of its similarity in structure and norms to the plantation. Without being able to articulate it, their intuition awakens the reality that they are in a place that is supposed to be educating them but tells them they are worthless. It has them in rows like cotton fields and forces them into labor that benefits everyone but them. Everyone gets a paycheck—teachers, administrators, testing companies, publishing companies, and police officers/security—everyone but young people and their families. It evokes an intuitional anger, a righteous indignation—a ratchet expression.

This righteous indignation is anger with the structure of schools; frustration with the norms/rules deliberately designed to disengage young people; and distaste for the blandness of curricula, especially while witnessing the complacency of all who hold up empty creme filling in its varied forms. Eventually, all these emotions also become anger with oneself for being a brown cookie holding it all up. One has to be mad at the system and one's role within it before fighting it. As philosopher and activist Maxine Greene once wrote, "Without the ability to think about yourself, to reflect on your life, there's really no awareness, no consciousness."[6] She went on to say that "consciousness doesn't come automatically; it comes through being alive, awake, curious, and often furious." That furiousness is what moves teachers to do good work. This is what gets teachers to begin teaching ratchetdemically.

One of the most pervasive and problematic issues for educators— particularly educators who come from similar backgrounds as their students but who have lost their connection to their backgrounds— is that they feel no indignation. They operate comfortably within institutions that awaken indignation in students. These students' intuition tells them that this type of place/structure has broken their ancestors before them and will inevitably break them as well and will respond accordingly. Righteous indignation is a fire that burns away institutional and societal respectability and allows ratchetness to lay bare. Folks operating only with institutional knowledge and who live a life based solely on meeting others' standards have been trained to turn a blind eye to the injustice perpetuated by schools. They have grown to accept that young people are being silenced in multiple ways. When you have grown to accept injustice, there is no indignation. This means there is no fire to burn away the junk (doubt, worthlessness, despair) deposited in the psyche by schools. Without righteous indignation, you sit in and with these negative emotions and then project them onto students.

Folks who only have institutional knowledge are bound by norms, rituals, and rules that cover, stifle, and suffocate their intuition. The institution buries the intuition and inhibits the ratchet within young people from being able to breathe. Suffocating the ratchet stops it from being a tool that unlocks the natural genius of Black youth. Unless the ratchet is allowed to breathe and indignation is allowed to be expressed, schooling becomes nothing more than a game of hide-and-seek between who you are and who the institution wants you to be. You lack awareness that you are in a game that has been designed for you to lose—the house always wins. The work then is about recognizing the different types of players in the game of school who use institutional norms as the rules of engagement. One must understand what their role is and what the roles of other players in the game are. The ratchetdemic educator gauges the purpose/intention of those who operate in the space. One must be aware of the elevators, haters, and suckas mentioned earlier in the chapter and learn to engage with each according to who they are. It is essential to remember that elevators are designed not just to bring you up but to bring you closer to your mission of being a revolutionary ratchetdemic educator; haters are designed to break you down emotionally, psychologically, and spiritually and distract you from your purpose;

and suckas are designed to take you away from your mission by growing apathy and implanting flawed perceptions of those you serve. Knowing who is working with you and who is working against you is essential for surviving a system designed to break young people and use teachers to execute this goal.

ELEVATORS

Consider a situation in which you get on an elevator in a high-rise building. Your goal is to get to the top floor of the building where there are beautiful and expansive views. On a bright day, when you get to that top floor, you develop a new vision/perspective. You can see for miles behind and in front of you. I call this top floor a place of light—a place where an understanding of the past, present, and future is revealed. This is the ideal place from which every teacher must teach to do good work, because it is where they receive a vision of the teaching landscape that they could never perceive just by graduating from a teacher education program and walking into the school building. The past is seeing history and historical trauma, the present is understanding the ways that the past impacts the now (along with new forms of oppression), and the future is being able to imagine a ratchetdemic world in which the pedagogy transforms how young people experience school and the world moving forward. While there is no space to delve too deeply into a next frontier beyond the place of light, I argue that on that top floor is a helipad. On that penthouse level, you can get on a helicopter and fly high above the entire building. You can see the entire world through a lens that you would never have on the ground.

Once educators recognize that just walking into a building or just walking into a profession or position will not give them the vision/perspective they need to be effective in that position, they learn to find the elevator to take them higher. The elevator is an individual or group of people whose goal is to challenge you to see from a different vantage point than you have been trained to. Their challenge to you may come in the form of statements that question your credibility to teach or lead, challenge your patience, or disrupt your comfort. Buttons will be pushed. The most important thing about elevators is that the challenges they give you, however grating to your ego, are wrapped in love and a desire for you to be better. For example, while coaching a teacher who repeatedly complained about "the most rude and disrespectful student" she had ever had, I decided to walk into the class to observe the student. I showed up early, sat in the back of the class in an open seat a bit separated from the rest of the class, and watched students file in. One student showed up earlier than her peers, said good morning to us both, and sat down. Others quickly filed in after her until the bell rang and the teacher started her lesson. All was going well until I realized that the student who came in early interrupted the teacher a lot. It started with an abrupt, "Nah Miss, you not explaining it right," as the teacher tried to explain how to solve a mathematics equation. The teacher rolled her eyes and kept going. A few minutes later, as the teacher attempted to get every-one focused by flicking the class lights on and off, this student said, "How you don't realize yet that that don't work?" Over the course of the lesson, a few more of these instances occurred. I quickly realized why she described the student the way she did. She did interrupt the lesson a lot and could be described as rude because of how she inter-rupted. However, I noticed that when she spoke, she was providing the teacher legitimate critiques of her teaching. The student was an elevator. If the teacher heeded her words, she would have taken her pedagogy higher. She needed to get on the elevator and deal with the frustration and deal with the pushing of buttons.

Educators can stand in the elevator and be proud of themselves for just getting in, or they can allow the elevator to take them to the top floor where they can witness and be in a place of light. It may have been a challenge to get to the elevator, but that challenge is fruitless unless you decide to "push buttons," get your buttons pushed, and withstand some discomfort. This is part of the process of an elevator taking you higher. On elevators, there can be a moment of discomfort once you press the button and begin to move. Pushing buttons in this context is challenging the elevator in your life to offer substance after the critique and then accepting that your body will shake with that initial discomfort that inevitably comes before going higher. For many people, that initial jolt once on the elevator with the doors closed is scary. For example, asking the student what she meant when she critiqued the teacher may have been uncomfortable, but it could have led to a recognition that there are things the teacher could do to better explain the lesson or understand why flicking the lights on and off doesn't work for getting students to be quiet. The major point here is that some people are designed to take you higher but will put you in a place of discomfort on your path to getting there. They will say things to you that will hurt your feelings or give you advice that will be hard to take. They may shake you up or make you believe that you would be better off stepping out of the elevator. Despite this, it is essential that you heed what they say even if your institutional logic may be telling you to do something different. Elevators can be anyone. They may be colleagues, professors, or parents; however, the greatest elevators in an educator's life are students. They will tell you what they need from you if you provide the space for them to speak freely and elaborately as they critique the structures that you put in place to affect their learning. Once you understand the intention of the elevator and withstand the temporary discomfort of their critique, you will end up higher. Listen to your elevators.

HATERS

Another group of people that ratchetdemic educators will come in contact with are haters. Haters are people who have a singular goal of disrupting the work of those who are operating successfully in their mission to transform a classroom, school, or any other institution. Their approach to this goal is to use any means necessary to discredit, devalue, or disassemble the work that someone else has done. There is no place where haters are more prevalent than in education because the field has become so saturated with folks who focus only on institutional knowledge, goals, and attainment. So, the few who operate with an intuitional approach and actually connect with young people become targets of those who cannot do what they do. Haters will attempt to showcase why you do not deserve the love and attention that you are receiving from those who really matter because, in their mind, they deserve that love and attention. When you operate in the world from a place of radical truth—in which there is an honesty about the flaws of the institution, a revelation of the history of oppression that schools replicate and your role in this process—you tap into a light that emanates from you and connects to young people. This is especially the case when you learn to spot the elevators in your life, listen to them, overcome the discomfort when they take you higher, and allow them to guide you toward light and a more expansive vision. When you operate from a place of light, folks are always going to "throw shade." Shade is the main currency of a hater. Hating is projecting darkness toward a person with light because the hater cannot understand why that person has the impact they do. Folks will lie, distort, manipulate, and maneuver to undermine folks with light and what they stand for. The biggest and most vocal haters are those who technically have the same credentials or position as the person they are hating on. They compare themselves to the person with light through an institutional lens and using an institutional audit—they compare degrees and other credentials like years in the classroom and/or schools attended and feel like they match up. However, even though the hater may technically, institutionally, or academically fit the bill, they may lack the intuitional ratchetness necessary for authentic connection. Their thought process is always, "What makes X so special? I teach just like this person does in the same type of neighborhood this person does. Why do they have the type of impact they have? Why don't I get the recognition that they're getting from students, parents, and communities?" The reason the hater doesn't have the same type of impact is because they are endorsed by institutions and not people. They lack a certain ratchet intuition that cannot be gained unless one takes the time to truly know oneself and how that self can connect to those one is teaching.

Many may misconstrue hating as simple professional jealousy or see a hater as a random competitor. It is far from that. Competition from coworkers is different from assaults on a person's work and character because they are fulfilling a mission that is larger than a professional role or task. Consider two teachers in the same school with the same credentials who have classrooms right next to each other. Each takes on a different assignment. One comes to work with the goal of keeping their job by making the administrators happy. The other comes to work to be the best teacher for their students. Inevitably, their approach to teaching will vary and the way they are perceived by the students will vary. The responses from students will reflect a certain love for the teacher who strives to be the best teacher they can be and for the content being delivered that will be unmatched. When this happens, the other teacher's inadequacies in connecting will become revealed and the hate ensues. The teacher who connects and teaches with an intuition that reflects the students' true ratchet selves will get reported to the administration for a number of things that have no relation to the effectiveness of the pedagogy but everything to do with not aligning with institutional norms. Phrases like "the class is too loud" or "the teacher is unprofessional" start floating around the school building. Before long, the rigor of the instruction will get called into question.

The next level of hate gets more personal. The hater's way of dealing with their inadequacy is to level personal assaults and question the other teacher's integrity and truth. The intuitive teacher will hear that they are not a good teacher, that they do not belong in a classroom, and that they are too loud and lack decorum. This type of personal insult is hard to hear and too often bruises the ego. Thoughts like "How dare they talk about or spread rumors about me?" will arise. This is when those who operate from light fall into the trap that takes them off course. The ego begins to operate and the person who is light begins to engage in a back and forth with some person or group of people whose intention is to snuff that light out. When there is no preparation for or awareness of the purpose of shade, light will expend energy on preservation of self without a recognition that light shines brighter when there is shade. There is no need for the teacher to be distracted from their course by battling an agent of the institution when their mission is to change lives by leading with intuition. The best way to handle a hater is to do your work and ignore them.

SUCKAS

The third type of individual a person with light will encounter is the sucka. These are people who are opposed to the fundamental ideas behind this book: that all young people have the potential for academic excellence and that all young people (particularly those from historically marginalized and oppressed populations) possess a genius that educators must recognize and cultivate. Suckas require a particular response because their intentions are more dangerous than those of haters. Suckas hold beliefs about young people or certain groups of people that are at their core racist, sexist, or homophobic or that center on a denial of the full humanity of a person or group of people. While the hater may be a good person conditioned to believe in the power of the institution and thus averse to the intuitional, the sucka has a fundamental belief that is simply against freedom. They are hell-bent on denying the ratchet. In education, a field that has historically been about providing equal opportunity in theory while maintaining historical inequity in practice, suckas will often follow the institutional hypocrisy and not share their perspectives in a direct, open, and outright way. What they will do is test the air by depositing their ideologies into the space in subtle words and expressions. They then wait to see how their biases are either challenged or accepted in an attempt to shape institutional norms and pedagogies. Pedagogies that reinforce biases about Black youth begin with suckas shaping norms by subtly sharing their harmful perspectives without critique. How young people are treated in schools begins with statements that question these students' abilities or with comments about a particular kid's neighborhood or potential. These words are doused in racism that is covered up with language of concern and justified with manipulated statistics and partial truths.

A couple of years ago, prior to the recent global health crisis, I was invited to a school district that had recently received a large federal grant to address "achievement gaps for youth of color." After the award was announced, the district convened a meeting and invited a number of experts to a conference to discuss the education of urban youth. At the event, I was part of a panel of experts who were charged with discussing how their funds should be spent. On the panel, I suggested a focus on teachers and teaching that would revolve around identifying community gifts/assets and using them as the anchors of teaching. I shared strategies for valuing context and ways that it would help young people reimagine their relationships to school and academic content. As I shared my suggestion, a hush fell over the room. A question was raised about how much this would cost and who would provide the training. I replied that, if done properly, this would not be as expensive as other initiatives the district had previously put in place. Then, another person on the panel made some verbose statement that closed with "but the big focus that we should have is on the digital divide. Young people need to have access to technology and that will close the gaps." In response, eyebrows raised and members of the district asked about cost. The answer was that "it would be expensive to equip all the young people and their families with technology, but it is a necessary thing to do." Heads of people from the district nodded in unison.

I quickly came to understand that the questions about the budget that were coming from the people in charge of the meeting were not concerned about doing the most important work. They were interested in the most expensive work. The meeting was for ideas that would help them spend their money in the quickest way and not on what would impact Black youth most positively. They had a budget to spend, not solutions to find. Before I knew it, the entire room was talking about the digital divide and buying computers and iPads for thousands of families to close technology gaps. My suggestion for understanding community and leveraging that knowledge into pedagogy was dismissed. There weren't even questions about access to broadband or using the technology. I left the meeting in disgust and feeling that this entire enterprise was a waste of time. I traveled back across the country and carried on with my work emphasizing culture and community.

About two years later, I received an email inviting me back to the district for an event aimed at evaluating their grant and hearing them share the outcomes of their research. I went to the event and sat attentively as their team dazzled the attendees with colorful charts and graphs wrapped in language around equity, social justice, and the amount of money they had spent on devices and preloaded software intended to address a number of gaps. Finally, at the end of the day, one of the speakers closed the entire event with a litany of statistics related to the Black youth in the district that ranged from test scores to suspension rates and then said, "It's unfortunate that despite all our efforts and the enormous investment we made into this community, there was no significant shift in outcomes. We will keep trying to get them there though." This statement, said with incredible conviction, was responded to by a rousing round of applause and a person or two on their feet. I sat there frozen to my seat because I couldn't believe what I was hearing. Somehow, giving to the students you have psychologically and intellectually broken down devices they neither wanted nor needed had become reconfigured as another way to blame them for the dysfunction you created.

This was racism masked as care, and it exemplifies exactly how suckas move. They sprinkle their racism in the air. They don't say it outright. They allow it to take up space so we can breathe it in. We rarely confront and counter them in efforts to be civil or "keep the peace." The truth is we cannot keep the peace with suckas. Every time they say something that is opposed to the freedom of young people, and every time they reinforce tropes about the dysfunction of Black and Brown children, we *must* counteract their words with responses that say the opposite. I should have stood up and said, "No! That's not what happened. You spent money to make yourselves feel better and never addressed any real issues." I didn't, and I regret it. "You know how those kids are" has to be combated with "Yes, I know how they are. They are brilliant, magical human beings who need us to be better versions of ourselves in order to help them express their genius." "The kids from that neighborhood are so loud and obnoxious" has to be matched with "They are so energetic and prepared to learn." When suckas speak and attempt to deposit their negativity into the space, ratchetdemic educators snatch their words from the space and hand them back to them. When we allow suckas to fill the space with harmful words without combating them, we allow them to fester and to contribute to the acceptance of dishonest articulations of Blackness and ratchetness. Before long, the environment we share with them becomes toxic, and we start to accept and then project the words that we allowed to take up space onto young people. All too often, young people breathe it in themselves and develop a view of themselves that is flawed.

In describing the effects of suckas and the best way to deal with them, I am always reminded of my many attempts to garden, despite a hectic schedule that includes teaching, coaching, writing, and being present with my children. I always begin my plan to garden with the best intentions. I place my flowers and plants in the ground with care and tend to them as best I can. However, when I can't get to them in about a week, weeds eventually creep up into the flower bed. As soon as I see them, I pick them and ensure that the conditions for my plants to grow are sound. Unfortunately, I will often get a bit too busy to fully tend to my garden. When this happens, weeds slowly start growing again, and although I know they are no good for my flower bed, I leave them because I "have no time." My thought is always that one small weed or two won't hurt because I can get to it later. After a short time, I look up, and the entire flower bed is covered in weeds.

When this happens, I am always alarmed and motivated to finally do something.

I go to the garden and start pulling all the weeds I can find. Inevitably, however, I always end up with a major dilemma because I find a weed growing close to a flower that looks just like my flower. The width of each stem is similar, the shoots look almost identical, and even the leaves are similar in structure. At this point, I can no longer tell the difference between my flowering plant and the weed. It is almost as though the weed has intentionally taken on the look of my plant and grown directly next to or under it. Most importantly, the flower I delicately planted and planned to watch grow stops growing and blooming. By ignoring the weeds, I have stifled the growth of my plant. At this point, if I were to clear my garden of the weeds, I would also clear it of some of my flowers. All of this could have been avoided if I'd just taken the time to diligently pick the weeds every time they grew next to my flowers. The combating of suckas is daily work. In every instance in which it becomes clear that an educator's presence with young people does little to edify and much to vilify, we must respond by picking those weeds away from our children right away. We must understand that suckas are there to steal faith and hope. They are there to stop our flowers from growing. Address the weeds right away. Don't let suckas and their words against young people fester.

When the words of suckas are left unchecked to grow like weeds and occupy our space, they impact not only the students who are presently in the classroom but those who come to it in the future. What I mean here is that words that go unchecked float in the air and coagulate with like forces to form the spirit or framing of a place. They occupy the space, form its structure, and then impact it for generations to come. I often lecture on the difference between space and place and the need to recognize that while we do not see space, it impacts everything that happens in a geographic place. Space is an untouchable phenomenon that carries all the emotions that those who previously and presently occupy the place put into it. All the things that are felt and never said or said with ulterior meanings to deliver a message are in the space. Those who fail to see or feel it (the present and the past) end up shaped by it without their consent. Educators who recognize space transform their place. By pumping positive affirmation into a space, we erase what has been deposited and implant what should be.

Educators tend to attribute issues that emerge in classrooms to contemporary events or recent history. They do not recognize the power of space. As a result, they try to address people they think they know and fix what they see with tools that are not equipped to touch space. Unbeknownst to them, what they are fighting is not anything that they can physically see but is something that is in the space. This is the history of the United States and the reality of its slowness to impact any significant change in the education of Black folks. There is a preoccupation with what we see and not with what exists but cannot be seen—the dimension that is consistently being shaped by history, words, and ideas that inform what we do.

The field of education has inherited a historical failure to address suckas and what they have done to shape space. Their words have gone unchecked and formed the structure of how we do school. Today, we still breathe in the toxic effects of the words our founders imbued the space with. The only way to change how we operate in the everyday is to counter each statement that has been put into the space by speaking directly to acknowledge it, speaking directly to counter it, and then tackling its effects. What we currently do is attempt to tackle space with a denial of it and then become concerned when issues we think we have tackled continue to reemerge. The bottom line is that we have inherited a long history of naming folks of color as nonacademic and unintelligent. We come from eras in which it was politically correct to suggest that certain populations should only live in certain areas and attend certain schools. It was incredible to believe that all children could perform at the same academic level as their nonminoritized counterparts. Schools have not yet cleared the space from these eras. We have not spent enough time refuting each statement and belief that we inherited with counterstatements that affirm and celebrate those who have been historically marginalized and seen as less than. The fact is that institutional logic dictates that we move forward and celebrate progress that sounds and looks more diverse but ignores what exists in the space. On the other hand, intuitional logic dictates that we recognize the past and the space. An intuitional approach focuses on affirmations, mantras, and even prayers with a specific goal of clearing the space. It requires affirmations that call youth into their brilliance with as much fervor as their ancestors were called stupid or less than. It requires acknowledgments of those who occupied the land the school sits upon and moments of silence in honor of past generations and ancestors who have been harmed by schools. Educators need to develop mantras that remember the past, acknowledge its role in the present, and introduce a more just and powerful future for young people. All of this must be done through speaking, singing, dancing, rapping, drumming, and affirming the value of our youth in the most raw, unapologetic, and ratchet ways possible. The only way to get young people to express academic genius in a way that we have never seen is to recognize that it is already there. It was there before they walked into the institution; the institution that grants the credential to teach is the same one that robs teachers of the intuition to do so.

CHAPTER 6

CAGES AND CONDITIONING

If the people in your circle don't inspire you, you don't have a circle, you have a cage.

—NIPSEY HUSSLE

Shortly after the release of my last book, *For White Folks Who Teach in the Hood . . . and the Rest of Y'all Too*, I visited schools across New York City, trying to work with teachers whom I knew required a different approach to teaching and learning. I would hear from students and parents about their belief that things weren't quite working in particular schools, and I would volunteer to help. I listed off my credentials and experience in hopes that these would convince administrators and teachers that I could help. Overwhelmingly, their response was no. They didn't want my help and seemed offended that I offered. A few mentioned that they "don't have time to work on the teaching because they have state exams at the end of the year to prepare for" or that they were "doing just fine" despite a school's statistics and reports that indicated the opposite. Their statements seemed ridiculous to me. How could a person in charge of a school not have time to address what seemed to be the obvious inadequacies of teachers and unmet needs of students? At the same time, I was receiving a number of messages from educators around the country who wanted me to train them on reality pedagogy. As these requests filed in, I didn't focus much on them. I was consumed with trying to make inroads in the city where I had attended school and had worked as a teacher. I wanted the work to focus on the hood—my hood. There were people I loved in my hood. What I saw to be the effects of poor pedagogy were manifesting themselves on the streets where I walked every day in ways that I couldn't help but notice. Every time I saw youth violence and aggression in my neighborhood and others nearby, I knew that something was going poorly pedagogically. Yet the invitation to help these schools never came.

When I did get the rare invitation from the places where I wanted to work, it was from teachers who would come to me like they were going rogue. Some would whisper, even though no one else was around, as they described the constraining structures of their schools, their unwillingness to keep doing the same thing, and that they felt unsupported. These teachers would tell me that they used my book to justify powerful work they were doing in isolation and under the radar. I would be handed hardcover copies of the book with the dust jacket removed so that no one could see the title. In some cases, teachers told me that they would place the book in their administrator's mailbox or subtly drop it on the desk of colleagues who needed it. I also received anonymous requests from parents and community folks asking me to reach out to their school administrators and convince them that their staff needed the book. One time a parent approached me and asked if I could just show up at a school and give a professional development workshop to teachers. This is why it came as a surprise when I received a letter in the mail followed by an email and a number of phone calls by the board of trustees of a school requesting that I visit. The headmaster and teachers signed the letter, which was not an invitation to speak or train anyone but instead to observe a wing of the school that was implementing aspects of my work to see if it aligned with my vision. A quick online search of the school revealed that its students were almost all White and very affluent. This was the kind of place I would've never dreamt of attending when I was in school. The annual tuition for the school cost more than my college tuition for four years. The place seemed doused in excess and it was a bit off-putting. However, knowing that they were deliberately implementing my work at a time when so many were afraid to engage with it or did so in secrecy moved me to seriously consider their invitation.

Considering this invitation meant reminding myself that the teaching strategies I laid out in *For White Folks* were not only for those *Who Teach in the Hood* but truly *the Rest of Y'all Too*. While my deepest allegiances lie with young folks in the hood who were being broken by schools, my vision was and still is to transform all schools for all young people. I still went back and forth about accepting the invitation until I received the fifth invitation from folks at the school, which referenced my work in a detailed fashion and was hand signed not only by the school leader and teachers but by a number of students. At this point, I could not help but accept. The letter mentioned that "a segment of our school community has devoted themselves to deeply studying and exploring your work around reality pedagogy. Its tenets have fully transformed our high school math and science classes." This final letter indicated a commitment to a transgressive pedagogy that I often have to struggle to convince school leaders and district personnel to implement. I became convinced that this affluent private school was worth visiting.

After I accepted the invitation, the dates for the trip and my transportation were quickly set in place. In less than a week, I found myself preparing for a flight across the country. I got to the airport, looked at my ticket, and realized that the school had put me in first class. This was an unusual but welcome luxury, and as I boarded the plane and settled into the comfortable seat, I felt extremely valued by the school. I had never been offered a first-class seat to deliver a lecture, let alone to just show up and observe folks in a school implementing my work. About a half hour into the flight, after being pampered with pillows, snacks, and beverages, I felt so honored by the invitation and the way I was being treated that I felt compelled to begin working on a presentation to deliver at the school. This was not a request they had made or even something they had hinted at. I just felt inclined to do it because I felt so valued. My thought was that if they valued me enough to get me a first-class ticket, I could value them enough to give them a phenomenal presentation. The way I was treated moved me to want to do more.

Later, as I reflected on this experience, I realized that this vignette could serve as a valuable lesson about teaching and being ratchetdemic. Valuing and respecting youth, and sending them messages about their worth, even before you begin teaching them is the beginning of this approach. Furthermore, taking the risk not to draw conclusions about what they present but rather looking beyond the surface to connect with what lies beneath is a necessary exercise. The folks at the school could have very well said that this book was for White folks in the hood, and that we are more than just White folks and are not from the hood, so this book isn't for us. I am sure that some folks in the school may have experienced some discomfort with the title of the book. That did not stop them from engaging with and then implementing strategies from the work. Creating ratchetdemic classrooms is about ensuring youth are seen, not judging them for what they initially present, treating them like they have value, and making them comfortable. Teachers often ask me how I reconcile the tension between making young people feel valued/comfortable and meeting high academic standards. I am always baffled by this question because that tension doesn't exist for me. Reaching high standards/academic rigor and creating contexts for freedom/comfort are one and the same for me. The comfort of the youth (culturally as well as physically) is a precondition to engaging in rigorous work. When a tension exists in the mind of a teacher or school leader around this fact, it reminds me that the current system of education has led otherwise intelligent people to draw senseless conclusions because they have been conditioned to see things a certain way. The reality is that any young person will adjust their investment in academic tasks to the connection they have to the teacher and to the amount of love the teacher expresses for them and their culture in the classroom. Youth will meet or surpass academic expectations that educators hold for them when these expectations are held concurrently with a value for what makes them feel most culturally, physically, and emotionally comfortable.

Another question I am typically asked is whether young people will be prepared for the "real world" or if they will be "college and career ready" with the type of pedagogy I propose—a pedagogy that advocates for freedom of expression and thought and that focuses first on the emotional and psychological comfort of young people. I respond by describing the trip I presented earlier in this chapter. I did not have a terrible time adjusting to the first-class seat. It may have been a bit awkward to get offered a drink within minutes of sitting down and having an airline employee help with placing my bag in the overhead compartment but once I realized that this was the norm, I reveled in the experience. I enjoyed it and was excited to work on a presentation because of it. I felt that my hosts valued me. In much the same way, in the classroom, a value for the student in their most ratchet form that ensures their comfort positively impacts their willingness to engage academically.

Every young person has an easier time adjusting to being valued than existing in a world where they are devalued. They may test to see if the love they are receiving is genuine (by testing boundaries or questioning the person giving the love), but once it has been tested and proven, they adjust to it quickly. Furthermore, I argue that there is no academic rigor without love. If you don't value the young person you are teaching, they will perceive academic rigor and high expectations as punishment. Challenging students academically without loving them is an application of force that only results in resistance. Without love, there is no growth, no movement. The net force is zero. Teaching with love eliminates the resistance. I use the word *love* here to mean valuing the students as they are and seeing them as deserving of the best without desiring that they change for your comfort and acceptance. This valuing of young people is the most essential ingredient for their academic success because it triggers their desire to commit to something larger than themselves. In the case of my travel, it was because I was valued that I decided to work on a presentation even though one wasn't expected of me. It was the care for my comfort that moved me to work on my presentation while on the flight. The love/valuing that one receives activates the desire to work harder and ignites the academic talents that already exist. This simple construct is hard to grasp for many people whose work in education is so deeply rooted in a deficit view of young people that they cannot see anything to be valued in the student and cannot express the type of love necessary to activate the students' inner desire and ability to do more. The reality is that one does not work harder at tasks that one has no emotional connection to. Showing love or expressing the value one has for another person activates their passion to work harder at any task. This is why the argument for more authentic/ratchet educators is so important. Young people connect deeply with real people and are more willing to be vulnerable, forge relationships with, and learn from them.

Once off the plane with a newly created presentation, I walked to the baggage claim area where I was greeted by three school employees. They were dressed in navy blue suits, and the man in the middle held up an iPad with my name on the screen. They seemed to spot me right away and greeted me as I approached them. After the pleasantries, one of them said, "Dr. Emdin, do you mind if I grab your bags?" Another one of them quickly asked if he could carry my coat. I shook my head to both requests and kindly said, "No, thank you." They looked at me and then at each other in a perplexed way. The exchange continued for almost a minute with them asking endless variations of the same offers. After they realized that there weren't enough "We'd really love to help you" and "We really don't mind" statements to keep me from holding on tightly to my bags and coat, they relented and asked if I would come with them to the waiting car. The reason I did not hand them my things wasn't that they seemed untrustworthy. In fact, they seemed very nice. It was that my experiences in urban America have given me a high level of skepticism whenever I find myself interacting with folks I do not know or trust.

Nothing about their seemingly good intentions would have convinced me to accept their offer. Even though the offers to carry my bags were accompanied by smiles and an acknowledgment of my long trip, I still held tightly to my bags. They were mine to carry, and I was okay with that. Even if it meant that I was going to be more physically uncomfortable carrying the bags, I was more comfortable with my own baggage. Giving them up in that moment would not have made me feel safe. I would have been more preoccupied with where my stuff was going than the effort that was made to ensure I was treated well. I understand that for some, this comes off as paranoia. However, I want to be clear that every interaction in the world for those who have been historically devalued and denied is a test of the authenticity of those who suddenly profess to love you. There is no new adoption of anti-racism and culturally relevant discourse alone that will automatically cause me to let my guard down and trust you until you prove yourself beyond words with deeds.

The whole scenario with carrying my bags at the airport serves as a powerful lesson for educators who may be so caught up in offering what they think students need to be comfortable that they overlook their responsibility to find ways to understand what their students actually need. In other words, comfortable is relative to the realities of the individual. The educator must provide the resources to make the student comfortable and also accept when the student chooses to hold on to the emotions that belong to them and are a part of them. Our work is to understand and respect a student's decision to not give their bags/burdens away even when the educator is willing to help carry them. Without a test of whether or not you truly value me, I choose to carry my own baggage. Once I see the real you and can trust you, I will have no issues handing over my baggage, but you cannot judge me because previous experience says that I should trust myself with my baggage over anyone else.

With bags in tow, I followed the school's employees out of the airport to an awaiting vehicle. Once in the car, I sat and thought about my unwillingness to hand over my bags to people who had gone out of their way not only to pick me up from the airport but to ensure my flight was comfortable. I had to sit with the experiences that made it so challenging for me to trust others or have them prove their trustworthiness. It was in that moment that one of the larger issues at play in the education of youth of color that is often overlooked came to the fore. This phenomenon has been described in academic research as *hypervigilance*, where individuals develop a sensitivity to particular behaviors in others that are often rooted in previous experiences that may have been traumatizing. Many consider it a psychological issue that isn't healthy for the person who expresses it. When it is possessed by the oppressed in particular contexts, it can be a gift. Youth from certain communities will always move with caution and scrutiny when dealing with educators because of both their own experiences and those of their ancestors. Somehow a predisposition to vigilance is coded into the genes of folks of color and gets activated in scenarios in which they are being told to cast their burdens aside by folks who don't have the same experiences they do and who have a history of taking advantage of them when their guards have been let down. Not understanding this phenomenon often results in viewing expressions of vigilance and caution as rudeness or personal offense. Hypervigilance gets expressed as ratchetness in certain scenarios. The role of the educator is to do as my hosts did on that trip. They accepted the fact that I chose to carry my own baggage but did not stop showing me the love and respect that they had since the initial invitation.

Finally, we arrived at the school. I was shown a number of beautiful buildings and told where they came from. The football field was a gift from alumni, and the state-of-the-art science center was built from donations that came from the grandchildren of the school's founders. The campus looked and smelled like affluence. As I walked around with my escorts and observed the students, I witnessed a lot of uniformity in their cultural expressions. Students all engaged with adults with an overall air of curiosity and confidence, but no one seemed to be pushing any boundaries. All the students appeared to be content with what they were being told to do. In my mind, these were excellent lambs on the way to becoming sheep.

As I walked through the hallways of the school, I felt a bit uneasy. It sank in that I was being asked to offer my expertise to a group of people that I knew were more privileged than those for whom the ideas were developed. I had spent my entire teaching career in urban schools that served youth of color and spent just as much time studying the ways that teaching and learning naturally happens in communities that were rich in culture and ingenuity but lacking socioeconomically. Yet here I stood in a place dripping in wealth and being asked to give to those who already have. I tried to suspend these feelings as I walked in and out of a number of classrooms, strolled around, and listened to students exchange with their peers. As I listened to them, what struck me most was how similar they were to the students I traditionally worked with in terms of style of dress and overall persona but also how different they were when they engaged with adults. When they talked to their teachers, they seemed more self-assured and confident. There was an overall air of belonging that was fascinating. Somehow, I didn't want my work to be happening successfully here. Not because it wasn't good to see how folks were interpreting my work, but because this was not the population I had designed it for.

As I walked the hallway with my hosts, I overheard a teacher engaged in a powerful dialogue with students about climate change. As we turned the corner, a young White student came running down the hallway with hair swinging and a reckless abandon that was usually reserved for the playground. He bumped into me, looked up curiously for about a half a second, and continued scurrying along the hallway without saying a word. My response to a happy child who happened to run into me in any other circumstance would've been to share his joy. In this instance, because I was coming from a place of critique and scrutiny first and because I knew that this type of joy is not the norm in urban schools with youth of color, I interpreted the joy he was expressing (especially because he bumped me) as rudeness. Bias has a way of shifting beauty and innocence into something bad, rude, or problematic that needs to be fixed. It turned a happy boy running down the hallway and colliding with a visitor into a rude kid who was barreling down the hallway and unapologetically bumping into me. I took a mental note of this rude kid. I would mention this when we debriefed later.

After this exchange, I stepped out of the hallway and into a set of classrooms that was described to me as the school's model for reality pedagogy—the approach to teaching and learning that I champion and that centers all learning on the realities of youth in the classroom. In these classrooms, the students asked more questions, moved about a bit more, and were a bit noisier than their peers in other classrooms. As I walked through this section of the school, my cynicism about their enactments of reality pedagogy surged. I almost didn't want them to get reality pedagogy right. However, with each visit to a new classroom, my skepticism was challenged by good practice. I observed youth giving teachers feedback on instruction in cogenerative dialogues, students delivering instruction with coteaching, a group of students enacting cosmopolitanism by walking with the cafeteria staff carrying what appeared to be materials for cooking, and students generally free to question and be questioned. At one point, I walked into a chemistry classroom to observe a woman who was identified by the school as the "reality pedagogy teacher." In her class, groups of students engaged in a number of activities using different modalities. One group listened to what seemed to be hip-hop through headphones plugged into a single device as they bobbed their heads (albeit with much challenge to find a common rhythm). A few sat in a small circle working through problems with pencils in hand and worksheets askew on the floor in front of them. One seemed to be lying down at the back of the class on a huge bean bag chair with a textbook open, its cover facing the ceiling. Another small group was engaged in an informal conversation with the teacher. As I walked from group to group, I noticed that even though the students were engaged in different activities, they were all covering the same chemistry content. From those who were attempting to rap to those who were doing more traditional problem-solving drills, the level of engagement and academic heft of the exchanges were at a high level. Still trying to find a problem with the school and their use of my work, I spoke with the teacher and asked if and how the content was covered before the students broke out in their diverse groups. She explained that her classes were pretty traditional until she asked students to give her feedback on her instruction in cogenerative dialogues. The students suggested that they could lead their own discussions and then selected peers as co-teachers who could lead a number of activities. I nodded, as this all sounded familiar to the steps in my approach to instruction. I then walked around the room to look at the walls of the classroom. I discovered pictures of the young people on vacations in places around the world and of their "service" work in a neighboring community where they volunteered at a community center tutoring "less fortunate" kids and doing toy drives for them. The teacher mentioned how this builds cosmopolitanism and focuses on various youth contexts. The students had created a community within this classroom that was stronger than the bonds they had to other classes. Exasperated with no immediate holes to punch in their adoption of reality pedagogy, I asked about the boy who ran recklessly in the hallway and bumped into me. I was told that he was running to his animal physiology teacher from the chemistry class because he was curious about whether the gram molecular weight, which is called a mole in chemistry, had a connection to the small mammal that bears the same name. In awe of what I was witnessing, I asked, "You mean to tell me that boy was running all crazy and bumped into me because he was excited to learn?" "Yes," replied the teacher as she chuckled. "As you mention in your work, I encourage the students to always seek out answers to the questions they have and give them the freedom to explore their own ideas."

Despite whatever preconceptions I had of this school or this classroom, they had created a space where the students were learning on their own terms. At this point, all I could do was chastise myself for not wanting to see that these people were actually doing good work for their students. I quickly realized that I wasn't upset at the school or the teacher—I was upset that they had the courage to do what is right for the young people they serve when I knew that so many schools that are attended by mostly Black youth are not courageous enough to do the same. They took ideas from a book titled *For White Folks Who Teach in the Hood*—without being upset that they were being called White folks and without being intimidated by the fact that they were not in "the hood"—and took the risk to implement new ideas because they knew their students deserved more. This is not to ignore the immense material resources present in this school. On the surface alone, they had an animal physiology teacher and an amazing laboratory that other schools just didn't have, but the pedagogy didn't rely on those things. It relied on and gave credence to the students and their genius.

Before leaving the school, I asked to give the presentation I had planned on the plane. Because they had not expected a formal presentation, they couldn't get their faculty together. Instead, they suggested I give a presentation to or at least have a conversation with a group of students. I took this as an opportunity to gain further insight into who the students were and how they were experiencing reality pedagogy. As I sat in an auditorium with a group of about fifty students, many of them expressed their excitement with the new approaches to teaching and learning being implemented in their school. They enjoyed the new process, but they never mentioned feeling like the pedagogy that was already in place was particularly problematic. They were enjoying the instruction now that they were free to explore their personal interests and believed that their teachers were putting more effort into listening to their concerns, so they enjoyed school more (even though they were pretty much enjoying it already). They mentioned feeling valued as individuals and as a group of students. During these conversations, I was struck by the ease with which they spoke with me. There was a refreshing honesty about how they spoke that struck me because of how similar this was

to the responses I get when connecting with youth in urban neighborhoods. However, there was also a certain irreverence that I usually
do not experience with other young people at that age. They looked
me straight in the eye and responded to questions without hesitation. They asked me about my job as a professor and my research
and nodded in agreement with points I made, like we were peers.
One middle school student mentioned that he had read my book and
was considering writing a response article or review of it. Another
mentioned that she was working on her own book about education.
What I came to realize is that the combination of their privilege and
schooling experiences gave them extreme confidence. There was a
sense of being equal to anyone who came to speak with them. With
the implementation of reality pedagogy, their self-assuredness came
with a new sense of freedom that affirmed them even more. They
walked right into their greatness like it was a birthright. It was almost
like they were genetically predisposed to a sense of worth. The new
approach to pedagogy simply endorsed what was already there.

As I witnessed this freedom to learn on full display, my thoughts
immediately went to the young people for whom this experience is
reversed. Students who experience teaching that affirms that they
are not intelligent. Children who interact with adults who pull them
back in line if they seem too confident and who interpret student
curiosity as sassiness. When certain children speak too confidently or
present themselves as more than they have been portrayed to be, they
are seen as a problem. In far too many urban schools, the challenges
of poverty, coupled with school environments that favor pedagogies
that police free expression, are at the root of young people's brokenness—a combination of financial and emotional insecurity mixed
with a denial of agency. Black youth have been robbed of emotional
wholeness and self-assuredness and denied a chance to demonstrate
their brilliance. They just want a shot at showing their genius, but
they are denied it at every turn. Most importantly, they are conditioned to accept being less than who they are. In fact, if I were to
identify the most significant difference between the affluent school

I visited and the schools with Black and Brown youth I most often work in, it would be related to the absence or presence of freedom. In the affluent school, teachers and students had been conditioned to believe that young people can and will be academically successful; in urban schools, the exact opposite is the case. There is an expectation in urban schools (even within the students themselves) that the students are problems to be solved and don't deserve to be free. The largest difference between schools that create whole human beings and those that do damage to young people is freedom. In some schools, there is a belief that teachers can and should move beyond established curricula for the sake of the students' learning. In other places, the scripts teachers are given in the form of curricula and lesson plans are gospel to be followed without interpretation. Students and teachers have both been conditioned into believing in the rhetoric of institutions (like schools) and their tools (like curricula) whose primary function is to keep students from being free and keep teachers from being who they need to be to help students be free.

Conditioning is a physiological phenomenon wherein an organism's responses to a stimulus become more predictable and frequent based on the rewards received for responding in a desired fashion. Over time, the connection between the physiological response and the reward becomes so strong that the response becomes completely involuntary and gets associated with anything that is associated with the reward. In layman's terms, if something you want and enjoy is associated with a certain behavior, you are more likely to behave accordingly. This notion goes back to Russian scientist Ivan Pavlov's famous 1890 experiments with dogs. Noticing that dogs would salivate when presented with food, he began ringing a bell whenever he fed the dogs to associate the two stimuli. Before long, the dogs became conditioned to salivate at the sound of the bell alone, even when no food was present.

In much the same way, teachers have been trained in teacher education programs and professional development sessions (even those focused on cultural responsiveness and equity) to align themselves with perceptions of students and pedagogical practices that institutions endorse, reward, and prize. This is especially the case for those I call excellent sheep, who enter the teaching profession having always been good, nice, and complicit students whose sense of worth is tied to validation by the institutions that name them as excellent. The culture of the institution often dictates the nature of the instruction and what is considered excellent (in teachers and students). For example, the affluent school that I described earlier in this chapter created an environment in which the teacher who incorporated reality pedagogy was affirmed for doing something that improved the student experience. She was further validated when the school invited me to come and observe her work. The approach to instruction she employed allowed her to move young people both within and beyond her classroom. A context was established that supported other teachers taking risks to employ new types of teaching practices that positively affect students. In the school, there was a normalizing of teacher agency and student freedom. Excellence was attached to risk-taking and being ratchetdemic. The opposite of this can also very easily happen. In any situation in which there is no recognition or compensation for innovation, there will always be stagnation. This is the case even if you talk about equity, culture, and social justice. Teachers will not be innovative and young people will not be able to grow until it is shown that the culture of the school rewards ratchetdemic expression and sees it as part of being academically successful.

The environment created in schools—what is celebrated and what isn't—can create the conditions for the type of pedagogy that takes root. I recognize that up to this point, the push has been for individual teachers to discover their own ratchet. That remains the message. We cannot rely on institutions to endorse practices that run counter to what they have been built upon. However, once individuals take up the charge pushed for here, it is essential to recognize that the ultimate goal is for institutions to transform so that this individual work can be supported by a transformed leadership. Conditioning for servitude within an institution requires an individual who is willing to tolerate being less than and a person designated as a leader committed to keeping that individual in that position. Institutions alone cannot condition individuals to be less than their whole selves. It requires people within the institutions to accept this "less than" position and enact this mission even at the expense of their own freedom.

What is most fascinating about the process of this conditioning is that it doesn't begin with students and schools in the present. It is a historical process that is inherited and continues unless deliberately interrupted. The reason the school I visited had the structures it did was because it had been in existence for about a century and had always believed that those who attended it were going to be the leaders of the world. Its students and graduates have always been part of a higher socioeconomic class, and the association of that social class with intelligence had been deposited into the bones of the institution. Even when there had been no true indication that they had an intellectual or academic advantage over their counterparts, the idea of the superiority of the White affluent population the school primarily served had been ossified into the collective consciousness of everyone on that campus. I use the word *ossify* here to bring clarity to the process by which false ideologies about the intellectual or even behavioral superiority of White middle-class students take root. Ossification is the biological process that transforms flexible connective tissue into hardened bone. This process is important because, among its other functions, bones support and protect the organs and provide structure and support for the body. However, the skeleton, the structure of human bodies, begins as a jelly-like cartilage that is neither hard nor fixed. Bone becomes the strong, fixed, and arguably most powerful part of the body when a cell within the jelly-like structure slowly and naturally begins pushing out organic material to the exterior layer of the cartilage. Over time, this material hardens and then becomes bone. What is jelly-like and almost flimsy in its original form becomes the strongest part of the body when messages from its interior/core get sent out to the entire structure. Even after a person dies, bone remains after decomposition.

In education, many cartilage-like, unstructured, and unsubstantiated philosophies and belief systems about people of color get released from the center, or core, of the institution to form rigid structures that we come to accept. *These students are hard to teach. This school is hard to staff. This neighborhood is violent. These kids are bad.* Once they have been formed, they become such a piece of who we are as a system that we cannot operate without them. Much of biological ossification occurs during infancy, just as the ossification of false and flawed narratives occurred during slavery—the infancy of this nation. These narratives are now a piece of who we are today and because of that, we must fight feverishly against them. I do want to be clear that the idea of the superiority of one group does not get ossified without the positioning of another group as inferior. It is in the narrative of the other as inferior that power maintains itself and excellent sheep continue to thrive at the expense of others. This is why we must teach young people to see themselves as the geniuses they are: to see and accept themselves as being able to learn, deserving of love, having a right to be in the classroom, and being comfortable in expressing themselves freely as they learn.

We must create a ratchetdemic new normal that reimagines what classroom norms are while pushing back against the narratives that have been ossified into the structure of the school. Young people have to be reconditioned to see themselves as worthy of love and grace and as growing into their genius. The failure to grasp this basic premise—that love, grace, and a sense of self are at the core of improving education—is at the root of much of what is wrong with contemporary education. Affluent, "well-educated" White folks create conditions that allow their children to be free and worthy of all that is good in the world, while educators in urban neighborhoods teach youth to condition themselves to not being loved, not getting second chances, and only having value if they score well on arbitrary assessments, which those who hold power and position themselves in an upper-class have never been beholden to or valued to begin with. The current approach to pedagogy is framed around getting Black and Brown youth to be equal to their White counterparts, but in reality, the focus is on centering Whiteness and comparing everything else to it. This results in certain students feeling superior, smarter, more academic, or intellectual than everyone else and others feeling the opposite.

Over the last decade, epigenetics has transformed the field of biology by challenging assumptions that scientists had previously made about what gets passed down from generation to generation. More specifically, they have been studying genetic markers and how they consistently emerge across generations. As new as the field of epigenetics is, the concept it relies upon was developed in the 1850s by scientist, philosopher, and artist Conrad Waddington, who suggested that if we understood environmental stimuli and considered developmental plasticity (changes in the connections of neurons resulting from learning and interactions with the environment), we could almost determine who we become. This is a powerful biological construct but should also be a powerful one to consider in education. Waddington was telling us that the mechanism that sends information throughout the body, and that is partly responsible for determining who we become, can be told/trained/conditioned by our environment. What we have been exposed to and how we have been treated historically shapes what our neurons tell our body. These factors can impact our physiological makeup. Joy DeGruy describes a post-traumatic slavery syndrome that African Americans experience as a result of hundreds of years of subjugation. In her book, she asks, "Isn't it likely that many slaves were severely traumatized? Furthermore, did the trauma and the effects of such horrific abuse end with the abolition of slavery? No, it did not end with slavery, and yes, slaves and their descendants were and are undergoing trauma."[1] I suggest that schooling, which places young folks in metaphorical cages and inhibits them from being free, is a contemporary form of historical phenomena like slavery. It creates similar feelings in students. They feel contemporary forms of the same stress, fear, and anger their ancestors felt, and schools serve as spaces that condition them to accept those feelings and normalize them. In addition, students whose ancestors were not enslaved but who share race or socioeconomic background as those who were also feel the terror of the contemporary pedagogy. Even experiencing that trauma for the first time will affect generations to come.

One of the most powerful experiments conducted by epigeneticists was a research study that revealed that newborn mice carry generations of information from their ancestors in their DNA.[2] In the experiment, male mice were first introduced to the scent of cherry blossoms. They were then electrically shocked while they were exposed to the scent. Later on, they were exposed to just the scent without the shock and began to react like they were being shocked. The mice had learned to associate the scent with the shock. They had been conditioned to fear the scent. These mice were then bred with female mice. Scientists observed that the adult offspring, when exposed to the scent of cherry blossoms, began responding as though they were being shocked. Not only did they physically respond to the scent, but their biological makeup was affected. These were mice that, though they had never been shocked, were born with altered brain structures. Even more remarkable, scientists discovered that many generations later, the descendants of the mice initially exposed to the stimuli responded to the scent like they were being shocked. This experiment in many ways confirms what folks of color have tried to articulate for centuries—that there are ancestral effects to traumatic experiences that are carried in the genetic code of current generations.

For our purposes, it is essential to address the traumatic experiences related to traditional/formal education for folks of color who, at some point in this country's history, were outright denied an education. Even when they were provided an education, it was substandard and they were made to believe that they were not even worthy of the poor education they were receiving. There is historical trauma associated with formal learning that we must consider when educating the descendants of slaves who, at some point in this country, could be killed for being literate. If we consider that formal education is equivalent to the cherry blossoms in the experiment described above, much can be revealed about young folks and their reaction to the education they receive within institutions that carry traditions that police Black bodies and deny the freedom to move, question, and express culture. Historically, the cherry blossoms of formal education have been introduced to folks of color with shock pedagogy—an approach to teaching that attaches terror in the form of punishment and policing of the body to learning. Teachers who hold biases about the students they are teaching and enact teaching practices that do not affirm students create generationally traumatic conditions. The youth are being shocked by poor pedagogy in much the same way that their ancestors were shocked by the varied forms of racism that denied them agency. When a young person sits in a classroom with a teacher who does not believe that they are smart enough to succeed, or if the educator has a persona or approach to dealing with young people that shames students or makes them feel less than, I argue that offenses against their ancestors may be triggered. Consider a number of audio and video recordings that have made the news of White teachers furiously yelling at Black students and the ways that the teacher's exertion of power and expression of uncontrollable and displaced anger are reminiscent of historical narratives about the ways that slaveholders interacted with slaves. Shock pedagogy is evident in the 2016 *New York Times* video of a White teacher from Success Academy in New York berating and ripping up the work of a Black child while her classmates sit frozen with hands clasped in fear. Another video that same year caught a White teacher in Baltimore furiously screaming at students, calling them the N-word, and telling them they would end up getting shot.

When youth begin responding to the rage of their teacher, they may be responding not just to their present conditions but also to historical biases against their ancestors who underwent similar experiences. I am suggesting that a teacher's angry yell, a police officer's violent words, and a slave master's demands are connected in the spirit of Black children. In much the same way that future generations of mice responded to the scent of cherry blossoms as if they themselves had been shocked in the presence of this scent, I argue that these young people have been genetically coded to identify the flaws in the curriculum, the inauthenticity of the pedagogy, and the superiority complexes their teachers hold. If one were to listen to the dialogues these students engage in with each other and others they love and respect or if educators set up cogenerative dialogues with students, they would hear warnings and predictions that indicate a hypersensitivity to a number of things that are commonplace in the classroom. One would also hear powerful and accurate predictions that could be described as premonitions. As soon as a teacher walks into a school, students can correctly tell you how long that teacher will last. In one instance, a student I was having a conversation with told me, "She ain't coming back after winter recess," regarding a teacher who didn't teach her and she hadn't directly interacted with. When the teacher didn't return after the break, I asked the student how she knew that would happen, and she said, "I just be knowing. Her energy was off."

In another instance, five different students who had the same teacher at different times of the day all called the teacher a racist and said so with such conviction and truth that there was something they knew and felt that the adults couldn't see. When an adult tells a young person that their intuition is wrong or doesn't honor it, that young person will reject what the adult teaches and will do everything in their power to fight against it. Pushing back becomes affirming and even healing. In other words, my decision to not accept a person who sees me as less than is an opportunity to claim some power over them. I am suggesting here that young people who are unaware of the racist histories of schools and schooling will reject pedagogy that is tinged with the scent of their ancestors' trauma because even when they cannot articulate what they are feeling, they still feel the shock from the oppressive practice. "I didn't like how she made me feel when she raised her voice" has to be seen as a legitimate complaint for a person whose ancestors endured being barked at. "All we do here is sit in the seat in rows . . . and do his worksheets" is a powerful response for a person whose ancestors picked cotton in rows and saw no benefit from the work they did. We have to honor student responses to these phenomena. Our work is to help these young people know that what they are experiencing is legitimate and that their responses may have some deeper meaning. It is up to the educator to let young people know that their aversion to pedagogical violence is a sign of their intuitive genius. Their ratchet responses are a weapon to protect themselves from a harmful pedagogy and represent a survival instinct activating itself. Our work is to tap into that instinct and drive it toward learning.

CLONES

Clone: Make an identical copy

Cloning: Imitating or replicating another thing
and then functioning as a separate entity

In one of the schools where I conduct research, I remember being awestruck while watching a new teacher who had a certain magic in the classroom. The sister had flow. Lessons began with images from the neighborhood and then transitioned into stories that grabbed the students' minds and hearts till they seamlessly landed on academic content. Her high expectations for students and high emotional intelligence created a classroom that was simply magical. This was teaching in its purest and most ancestral form. She spoke and I heard grandmothers' voices and griots telling stories. I remember one lesson in which the science class started with a discussion of Meek Mill and Drake's rap beef, moved on to a conversation on the need for scientific argumentation, and ended on a discussion of Newtonian physics. She had a gift. Her hand claps for emphasis of scientific formulas and comfort with talking about herself and her challenges with science made the class feel like light. She was ratchetdemic in the purest sense.

I also remember an assistant principal in the building having it in for her. There were pop-up class visits and random critiques of her instruction. One day, she mentioned to me that the assistant principal had walked into her class and reprimanded her in front of her students because a few students still had their hats and hoodies on in the classroom. She had had enough and responded to the administrator in the same tone as he spoke to her: "I realize they have hats on, but they are learning. Please leave my classroom because you are interrupting us." Students' eyes opened widely when she spoke up for herself, and they cheered her on. One kid said, "That's why nobody like him. He's mad petty." The administrator was livid. He grew increasingly unpleasant after that interaction. There were no morning greetings, and no flexibility was given for her to do the types of lessons she usually did. Notes would come in about the noise in her class even when the volume was not disruptive to other classes. At one point, she was so uncomfortable that she asked me to speak with the assistant principal, even though I was only at the school in my role as a university researcher.

A few days later, while reporting some observations of other classes I was working with in the school, I subtly mentioned this particular teacher's class and what I enjoyed about her lessons. His brows tightened, and he told me the same story she did but from a very different perspective. He mentioned that he visited her class like he usually does for all teachers and realized that there were several of the school's rules being violated. Young people were sitting in the wrong seats, they were talking, and they were not following the school's dress code. He mentioned that this has frequently been the case with her class. Finally, he said what I thought was the most important thing, "The students all go crazy over her and her class like she is some type of hero, and I don't understand why." As I attempted to respond on the teacher's behalf and mention the learning that was happening, he said, "It doesn't matter what is being taught or how it's being taught if the students aren't learning to follow the rules." I was taken aback and didn't respond as he continued talking about a few other random things until the meeting was over.

Weeks later, I noted subtle changes in her classroom. The most obvious was that students had their hats and hoodies off and seemed quieter than usual. This wasn't something that I had noticed before, but it was glaringly obvious now. Previously, the instruction was so high powered that I didn't notice whether the students were wearing hats and hoodies. Now I began to notice small things that hadn't been important before. Most importantly, I noted changes in the teacher. She wasn't as enthusiastic or passionate as she used to be. She was still a good teacher, but her magic seemed to be missing. One of the most heartbreaking things to witness is someone becoming something other than who they are simply because they have been convinced that not being themselves is more valuable. In this case, an enthusiastic educator with a natural talent for teaching and unbridled enthusiasm for this work started teaching within an institution where her gift was threatening to the administrator. He had lost (or maybe never had) the type of connection that she had with students and used the school's rules around clothing and noise to devalue her magic. His goal was to extract her ratchet and put her on a course toward chasing a vision of herself that looked like him. The reality is that this vision of who she was expected to be was not created by him but was enforced by him. He was a clone of some prototype of a teacher/leader and he couldn't see her for who she was. He was a hater.

No one can trace the reason why young people need to take hats off in school, and it is important to note that young folks in the most affluent schools are not seen as less intelligent if they choose to wear a hat. There is no connection between staying seated and learning. There is no research study that connects being quiet to intelligence or learning. In fact, there is research that indicates the opposite. The rules of engagement of schooling are imposed by folks who have lost the very things that make the people they are critiquing/assessing so special. There was nothing the assistant principal was doing every day to be a hero to students. There was something in the teacher that he wished he had. However, because he was the person in power and she had gotten worn down by his critiques, she decided to start becoming something she wasn't. She was getting cloned into being a version of him that was some version of teaching and leading that did nothing for students. In schools charged with educating Black youth, it has become normal for educators to have their natural talents eroded by the institution. We then watch these same educators rob students of their genius. It is a classic case of replication of oppression in which folks who have undergone or are undergoing trauma enact that same oppression on those over whom they have power until they all become clones of each other. In this case, a Black woman was being harmed by a Black school leader who was attempting to make her a clone of himself.

In biology, cloning is the process of producing an organism with the exact genetic makeup of another through either natural or artificial processes. The idea of human cloning has been the subject of many science fiction books and movies in which duplicating a human being results in irreparable damage to the world. Scientists have argued that creating clones will inevitably lead to a world in which people are born simply to become experiments. Others have argued that clones will lead to a societal sameness that would wipe out biodiversity. Furthermore, a number of polls identify that a majority of Americans oppose the idea of cloning. A 2000 Gallup poll showed that 90 percent of Americans opposed the idea of human cloning. Most people seem to recognize that creating exact replicas of other humans is deeply problematic. They also understand that there are a number of bioethical issues (such as creating "designer babies" and embryos for experimental purposes) that make cloning en masse a problem. However, even though most of us agree about creating clones, we rarely acknowledge that schooling in the United States and in many places across the globe is a system of what I call *educational cloning*. Educational cloning is not too far off from its biological counterpart. It is a process in which one tries to make certain students into replicas of other types of students. It operates through a process whereby teachers are made to be soulless and militaristic clones who teach subjects and content instead of students. Educational clones manage classrooms rather than facilitate learning and engagement within them. By *militaristic*, I mean that teachers are deployed like military officers to view young people as the enemy of the institution. These young people are then forced to become clones of some imaginary perfect student.

Contemporary education, particularly for Black youth, has become almost singularly focused on making them into clones of people they are not with the goal of distilling and removing the essence of who they are. This process is justified by focusing instruction on academic standards that do not consider standards and norms within communities, implementing curriculum that is static and not reflexive enough to meet the culture of young folks, and conducting assessments that do not capture the complexity of students' social lives and real-life experiences. Any young person who stands outside the mold created by particular standards, curriculum, and assessments is framed as being outside of what it takes to be academic. Our schooling system has become one in which we are not just making clones but dismissing young people we deem uncloneable or who refuse to be cloned. If you choose to not be docile and sheeplike enough to be cloned and if you are unwilling to bend to particular cultural expectations/norms, school is framed as not for you. Black and Brown youth in particular are expected to be sheeplike in order to be seen as brilliant. Schools don't want living, questioning, thoughtful, outspoken teachers or students. They want quiet, docile, cloneable sheep.

WHITE SHEEP, BLACK SHEEP

In the book *Excellent Sheep*, William Deresiewicz describes elite universities occupied by upper middle-class students as spaces where uniformity is fostered at the expense of individuality and emotional well-being.[1] He argues that affluent and so-called "excellent" elite universities like Columbia, Harvard, and Yale are classified as Ivy League and top tier because they provide their graduates with endless resources, social connections, and promises of prominence if the rules and traditions of the institution are followed. Deresiewicz does not mention that many of the rules and traditions of these institutions were created in an era when people of color were not considered good enough to attend these schools. There was (and is) an institutional and societal perception that folks of color were just not excellent enough to attend these institutions. White folks who had been similarly positioned as not smart enough or White enough (e.g., Italian Americans) were able to increase their social value and status (eventually leading to acceptance into Whiteness) by distinguishing themselves from Black folks and claiming a moral and/or intellectual superiority in both their literary work and social interactions.[2] Maintaining the narrative that Black folks are less than is one of the chief ways that White mediocrity maintains itself.

In Deresiewicz's work, like in society writ large, he suggests that we should feel sorry for the students at elite universities (the "excellent sheep") who are undergoing a number of stressors in pursuit of the excellence required of them. We are supposed to recognize the fear, anxiety, and stress they undergo. In a roundabout way, he argues that the world should be more understanding when excellent sheep make mistakes. This is because of the immense pressure on them to be excellent. What we do not see is that no matter what happens, these White sheep will always be seen as excellent. Meanwhile, their minoritized counterparts, who have little access to these institutions or have to give up much more of themselves to be seen as worthy of being on these campuses once they arrive, are rarely seen as excellent. They are seen as lucky, considered to be there only because of affirmative action, and undergo various forms of institutional racism.[3] The permanence of classist notions of excellence for certain people is predicated on the permanence of an ideology that there is an underclass doomed to exist beneath them that is incapable of excellence. We are being told to acknowledge the struggle of the elite class for whom "the prospect of not being successful terrifies them, disorients them, [and] defeats them," but no acknowledgment is given to the fact that their excellence is predicated on the framing of Black and Brown youth and those who are socioeconomically disadvantaged as inferior to them.[4] This ideology filters from universities into K–12 schools. In fact, the chief strategy for recruiting teachers for Black schools is to target excellent sheep from elite universities who have learned their entire lives (perhaps not explicitly but certainly implicitly by how Black folks are positioned in media and society) that Black folks need to be positioned beneath them in order for them to feel excellent.

For Black youth (also expected to be sheep and never seen as excellent), their perceived flaws, which are actually essential, unique parts of their lives, become magnified while they are compared to excellent White sheep whose flaws are hidden and whose accidental successes are magnified. This is why being ratchet takes on such a negative connotation in the imagination of most people. Just existing in Black skin in a public place is seen as disturbing the peace. Being expressive and being Black is seen as a crime. Sometimes it seems that the only way Black youth are accepted is if they are invisible or subservient. They are only accepted if they are sheep and they are never seen as excellent. They are always seen as black sheep. We have seen endless videos of White people calling police on Black folks just for doing everyday activities like barbecuing or walking into their dorm room or apartment building. On the other hand, White youth are given the grace to make mistakes. White college students are recruited to work with Black children, and nobody cares about their GPA; a 2.5 will do. Just say you care about kids and that you're organized, and use the words *equity* and *social justice* a few times, and you too can be hired to help the less fortunate by teaching them. Schools hire excellent sheep to reinforce to our children that, in the eyes of society, they are black sheep. Black folks, who see obvious flaws in the sheep who are charged with teaching and leading our children, are told/forced to accept them as excellent despite these flaws. They are told that these excellent sheep are there to help the black sheep with their flaws, which are often fabricated and then magnified by the excellent sheep. My use of the term *black sheep* is not just about phenotype. Yes, Black folks are framed as black sheep because they are Black. However, there is a bit more to explore here. The term *black sheep* is an idiom that refers to a member of a family or organization who is considered not just different but also disreputable. This does not necessarily mean that the black sheep is flawed or naturally deficient. It means that the black sheep has been identified as bad on some arbitrary assessment of goodness that allows other sheep to always be seen as excellent.

In an article for the *New York Times*, Margo Kaufman discusses the experiences of the "black sheep" of a family by saying that "the black sheep needs to be there for the holidays to remind the rest of the family of how wonderful they are. . . . Otherwise, one of the white sheep might look quizzically at someone else and say, 'Hey, you look a little gray.'"[5] This phenomenon is powerful for educators to consider as an analogy for what happens in schools. It helps us to consider that the reported academic underperformance of Black youth is intentional and designed to create an inferior group so as to maintain the perception that another group is excellent. Without black sheep in the school system, the grayness of White sheep's excellence would emerge. The reality is that certain students and schools have to underperform so that others can be seen as overperforming. This is part of the design of schooling. In order to disrupt this system, schools must redesign themselves to accept the expressions of Blackness previously deemed unacceptable. For that to happen, every person who works within a school has to redesign their thinking about who are excellent sheep, who are black sheep, and how those categorizations (even though we oftentimes don't realize we are classifying that way) can be disrupted. Can we consider that the black sheep—the ratchet ones who are positioned as less than—are actually closest to the ideals we profess to value in those who complete school: individuality, resilience, and creativity?

The point here is that formerly excellent sheep who have come to realize that they are far from excellent (because they lack individuality, resilience, and creativity) become teachers who use their positions to affirm themselves as excellent. The school system gives them no space to teach from a place of honesty about the charade that their own education has been. The only way to get away from a system of education in which Black and Brown young people are being forced to be exactly like "excellent sheep" who are deeply flawed and who themselves need saving is to introduce a ratchetdemic approach to teacher preparation, in addition to instruction and learning. In teacher education, excellent sheep must offload their privileges, reveal their imperfections, acknowledge their undeveloped ratchetness, recognize the more complex and layered ratchetness of young people, and, most importantly, create contexts to allow for the leveraging of both the teacher's and student's ratchetness to construct a ratchetdemic pedagogy.

Understanding the dynamic between excellent sheep and black sheep is essential for the future of schooling. We must recognize that academic excellence has become a synonym for proximity to excellent White sheep or White ideals and an antonym for raw, unapologetic expressions of Black brilliance. Since we have established that excellent sheep are all named excellent simply because they all look and act the same, we have to unveil the charade that operates by forgiving their flaws and acting like the privileges they are afforded exist because of merit. Consider the historical narratives of Ivy League students who were accepted into these institutions because of donations from family members; legacy preferences (in which admissions are skewed in favor of certain applicants because of family relationships to the school); or situations in which there was outright lying, cheating, and bribery. Then consider narratives in which folks critique affirmative action programs for being biased even though those programs benefit folks who have been disadvantaged and positioned as less than by excellent sheep. My point here is that we are expecting black sheep (those who engage in the world in nontraditional ways and are positioned as outsiders) to be like excellent sheep (advantaged folks who suffer from uniformity and a lack of purpose and creativity) so that they can be academically successful. However, if all black sheep became like excellent sheep, everyone would be manipulating the system to get advantages they did not earn while wallowing in normalcy and mediocrity. That will never get us to academic success.

In many ways, the story of David and Goliath provides a powerful example of how education has functioned for black sheep but also gives insight into how it can be reimagined to allow black sheep to operate in their full genius. In this story, there was an impending battle between the Philistines and Israelites and a challenge from Goliath (the Philistine giant) to fight anyone from the camp of the Israelites. The winner of the battle would gain domination over the people from the losing faction. Goliath was not only a giant, but he was adorned in heavy armor made of bronze. He also had a shield that was being carried by men who accompanied him and that made him extremely intimidating. He and his armor bearers sent the Israelites into pandemonium. Despite being a chosen people predicted to overcome any obstacles placed before them, the Israelites developed an intense self-doubt regarding their ability to defeat Goliath.

In the education system, young people from urban communities are like David, community members are like parents, and activists are the Israelites. They are all living under the threat of the Philistines and Goliath, who are the institutions whose sole interest is controlling the Israelites and their land to expand their kingdom. Saul, the king of the Israelites, represents teachers. Goliath, an ever looming and threatening force, is large in size and shouting threats that include everything from closing and privatizing schools to firing the principal and teachers and turning to state control. As expected, the Philistines' mission and Goliath's threats send the Israelites into a frenzy. Goliath's armor bearers come in the form of district personnel and employees of departments of education who storm schools with clipboards and useless rubrics, holding test scores as threats over teachers' heads and using fear as a weapon for getting complicity with superficial requests, often resulting in no effective change in pedagogy. Today, as the Philistines send Goliath and his armor bearers to threaten and intimidate the Israelites, David sits prepared to go to war. He knows within his soul that he can defeat the giant that has been sent to conquer the Israelites and make them parts of the Philistine empire.

Malcolm Gladwell, in his book *David and Goliath*, provides some details about this story that often get erased.[6] He shows that David, despite being seemingly outmatched, was not an underdog in the battle against Goliath. He was actually an expert with the slingshot. The slingshot, which on the surface appeared to be an unsophisticated weapon with no value in battle, was the key to victory against Goliath. When young folks in 1990s Brooklyn went to get the ratchet, they went to get their weapon. When David went for his ratchet in the battle against Goliath, he grabbed the slingshot. In academic spaces, the ratchet is looked down upon, just as Saul looked at the slingshot when David went to grab it in the battle. In fact, David declared he could best Goliath even before he went to get his slingshot. Saul insisted that he couldn't, but David somehow knew that he could. This is what young people do every day in classrooms. They tell us that they are equipped to defeat the giants sent to slay them. They can be successful at assessments, surpass standards, and achieve at academic tasks, but the Sauls in their lives won't listen. Eventually, if David is lucky enough, a Saul does listen to him, and David can get his ratchet.

Prior to allowing David to get his slingshot, Gladwell mentions that Saul attempted to prepare him to fight Goliath by getting him to put on the same type of gear as Goliath. Saul believed that if he made David a clone of Goliath in terms of equipping him with the same gear and weapons, he would improve his odds in battle. Even as he placed heavy armor on David, Saul never saw David as legitimate opposition to Goliath. The reality was that David did not need to be equipped the same way as Goliath; he needed to be equipped the way that was best for him. The armor Saul placed on David simply weighed him down. Test prep doesn't prepare our Davids to slay Goliath. Having them look, act, and talk respectably will not assist them in battle. Eventually, David, against the best advice of Saul, decided to take the armor off. He went with the weapon that made him most comfortable. He grabbed the ratchet. The rest of the story is part of legend. David, the underdog, won.

Gladwell discovered that David's slingshot had the same force as a gun—a significantly more sophisticated weapon. The slingshot appeared simple, but it was tailored to David's abilities. Therefore, it was what he needed. Just as young folks have mastered the use and expression of their ratchet in their everyday lives, David had used his ratchet successfully in arenas outside of the battlefield many times before. David was more equipped to win the battle than any of the Israelites who thought that the only way to survive was to join the Philistines. Unbeknownst to anyone, he had been preparing for the showdown his entire life. As a small shepherd boy, he had been practicing the use of the slingshot against animals that were trying to attack his sheep. His small stature made him quick, and his bravery made him special. Gladwell also notes that Goliath, because of his unnatural height, possibly suffered from a condition that impaired his vision. He walked in with armor bearers, who made him more intimidating, simply because he needed them to see. Everything that made him intimidating was simply masking a number of his deficiencies.

Our education system—armed with rubrics, benchmarks, and standards aimed to intimidate Black youth in schools who are positioned as black sheep—is there to scare Davids with intuitive knowledge, quickness, and weapons for survival that will lead to their victory. Davids with their ratchets will always conquer a blind giant if Saul gives them the space to take the armor off and use the weapons they have perfected. In education, young folks are always attempting to take off the armor. Every time they express their culture in classrooms that silence them and reject institutional classroom norms, they are attempting to take off the armor. Raised voices when the teacher wants silence, deep questions that go beyond what is on the lesson plan, and tapped beats on tables while the teacher is demanding silence are all attempts to take off the armor so students can take on Goliath. We never see the power of the slingshot if it is never allowed to be taken up. We cannot get young folks to take on the challenges of the world if we don't uncage them from the armor we have placed on them.

CHAPTER 8

SOUL WOUNDS
AND WHITE GAUZE

It was in the 1990s while living in New York City that I first came to understand the intimate and unhealthy relationship between race and education. It was also around this time that I got introduced to the power that came with carrying the ratchet. Among those who study history, art, and culture, that decade (1990–2000) has emerged as one of the most significant cultural and artistic renaissances of our time. In rapid-fire succession, young people who had either recently been in or were currently attending schools began creating and releasing music that gave deep insight into the urban experience. They referenced schools and education often, talked about what it looked and felt like to live in Black bodies in White spaces, and described their living and learning conditions more vividly and accurately than any media outlet or academic ever could. Dead Prez announced, "They schools can't teach us shit. My people need freedom, we trying to get all we can get."[1] Nas asked his listeners, "How can we exist through the [false] facts written in school textbooks?" and then declared, "F**k a school lecture. The lies get me vexed-er."[2] In other words, the lies told by teachers and written in textbooks only serve to stoke the anger of young people who are in search of the truth. In the reporting of their realities, they were describing what it was like to be caged with armor that kept them from fighting wars being waged against them. Over the boom bap of hip-hop beats created from samples of their parents' and grandparents' records, they were not only baring their souls but crying out for help.

Hip-hop was, and still is, raw ratchet and unapologetic expression, and those who understood what the young folks were trying to express (because the older generations had also experienced it when they were in school) could see that hip-hop lyrics were a response to what I call a poor teaching in schools disorder (PTSD), which, like post-traumatic stress disorder, requires a number of serious interventions. Hip-hop educators—those who have learned to value the culture of young people and use it to reimagine how teachers teach and systems operate—understand that rap is simply the traumatized individual's attempt to engage in cognitive/talk therapy and counter negative feelings about the self in real time. HiphopEd(ucators) often reference the song "Juicy," recently identified by the BBC as the greatest hip-hop song of all time, as a way to gain insight into the realities of young Black folks undergoing stress/trauma at the hands of schools. In the song, the opening track to a masterful album, nineteen-year-old rapper Biggie Smalls dedicates the album to "All the teachers that told me I'd never amount to nothin'."[3] He was signaling to the Black youth in schools who have been told over and over again by those charged to teach them that they were worthless. Like David prior to his battle with Goliath, Biggie was pushing back against the narrative of worthlessness being cast upon him by using hip-hop as his slingshot. Ironically, Biggie, in his era, was telling the same story that contemporary artists like DaBaby are telling today. Lyrics like "All the teachers they thought I was stupid" and "I just put diamonds on all of my teeth, now they probably think I ain't intelligent" speak to narratives about Black youth and judgments being made about them.[4] In the case of DaBaby, the diamonds in his teeth exemplify ratchetness. You see someone with diamonds in their mouth and it is supposed to automatically mean that they don't care about anything of substance. That is not the case. His declaration of his intelligence is wrapped in his highlighting of the stupidity in seeing him as not intelligent because of his teeth. DaBaby's words are what being ratchetdemic is all about: uncovering the stupidity of the presupposition that there is an absence of intelligence based on society's association of physical attributes or stylistic choices with intelligence. Being ratchetdemic means claiming intelligence/genius/brilliance that is rooted in a core identity that is more visceral than visible but when expressed visibly gets perceived superficially as ignorant or not intelligent. Biggie and DaBaby, like David who conquered Goliath, use poetry and music as the chief avenues for sharing unsaid truths and providing new perspectives for those whose realities have otherwise been erased.

Prior to his showdown with Goliath, David was most known for writing poetry. The Bible's Book of Psalms is a collection of poetry that contains musings, beliefs, and affirmations by David and his contemporaries. The most notable psalm by David (Psalm 23) is one in which he speaks of fearing no evil and defeating his enemies. The lines in this psalm read like an affirmation that prepares one for battle. The affirmations in the poetry of the oppressed are the fundamental components of their self-therapy and healing. The words that the marginalized create to heal are the skeleton that a ratchetdemic teaching philosophy is built upon. If you don't have any affirmations of self-worth or declarations of how you will overcome the struggles that have been placed before you, you are missing an essential part of healing and teaching and being ratchetdemic.

For hip-hop's psalmists, the poetry they create through hip-hop prepares them for battles in schools and beyond. Their music gives insight into their psyche. They are telling us what happens when we take their slingshots from them and then cover them in heavy armor. They are attempting to heal themselves through their music even as they are forced into classrooms that give little to no time to healing or that prescribe medicine that is not in the form or dose they need. The structures of schools have been more about caging, cloning, and conditioning young people into complicity than providing a space to listen to young people as they speak about the pain of being sent to battle without the tools they need to win.

When you are sent to battle and are handicapped by the removal of your slingshot (the banning of expressions of ratchetness) and forced to wear unfamiliar armor (standards that do not consider who you are or your need to be free), you are being set up to lose. Your natural willingness to go to battle will eventually erode as you keep being placed in a war you are destined to lose because you are ill prepared. In contemporary schools, too few people directly interrupt the process of setting our children up to lose and even fewer question themselves for making the students poorly equipped to deal with the trauma of schooling. Even when schools finally do own their role in stopping children from learning and healing, there will be those who argue for more armor—more restrictions on the students' ability to be free.

Recently, I visited an institution that had started identifying itself as a "progressive high school." The school's new administration rightfully recognized that the young people who attended the school had undergone some trauma with the previous administration and required a more humane school space. Too many students had gotten suspended for minor infractions like being loud in gatherings and using cell phones. Students had also been punished for arbitrary and subjective markers of disrespect or anger like talking back and being rude. The new administration believed something had to change. In response, they decided that they would follow an ever-growing trend to have the young people employ mindfulness and meditation to help them deal with their emotions. Within a week, the new administration had the entire school working through an article the principal shared about mindfulness. Within a month, the adults at the school were working with the youth to bring attention to what the students were doing in the moment and teaching them how to meditate. The principal argued that the skill the students needed most was how to be reflective when they behaved in ways that would warrant suspension. An adult would say a child committed an infraction, like being disrespectful, and the student would be called out. Instead of being suspended or sent to detention, the student would then sit and be led through a mediation exercise to think about how and why they offended the other person.

In many cases, even when they learned to be present and meditate in silence on the experience, the young people could not identify what they did wrong or how they offended the adult. The students felt that being given the time to process was beneficial, but they were not finding the wrong in their behavior. Before long, word of the meditation and socioemotional learning school reached the district. The school was lauded for being ahead of others in meeting the needs of young people. However, when I got to the school and engaged with the teachers, they could not see the benefit in the practice. Teachers said that "the kids were still being rude and disrespectful." One teacher mentioned that the students were being even more indignant than before because they were no longer being suspended.

After talking with the young people, I realized that they had a different perspective. They saw power in the meditation, but it simply highlighted to them that they were often not wrong in conflicts with teachers. Sitting in a calm room reflecting on what was called an "almost fight" by someone who doesn't understand "the dozens" is a tough thing to do. The dozens—a cultural phenomenon within Black communities that involves a game of insults that ratchet up with each round for the sake of expressing and developing wit, charm, assuredness, and confidence for both participants—looks like an "almost fight" to someone who is culturally unaware. A student who gets sent away to meditate on why they did something may understand why they did and have a different perspective on what they did than their teacher. One student brilliantly said, "They just trying to brainwash us to just sit there and do nothing. The teachers are the ones that need to meditate on why they're mad at everything." That statement—the most poignant analysis of the entire initiative—captures the problem with trying to fix a student or responding to a problem you see in the student without recognizing that the problem lies with the system and its agents. The question has to be, Why do we continue to use "progressive interventions" to enculturate young people into the established culture of schooling? When will we recognize that even mindfulness, socioemotional learning, and restorative practices, if nested in a perception that the youth are broken, will only serve to maintain the existing structure?

Schools will never blame themselves for not being designed for young people. What they will do is try to fix young people who respond to problems the schools created. The approach in the scenario above is routine and emblematic of the ways that schools respond to the issues they create. There were too many suspensions. It couldn't be our fault; let's get the kids to meditate and think about why they're wrong. That approach was not a solution because the problem was that teachers were identifying behaviors that were not significant enough to warrant students being taken away from class or being punished. Like in the story of David and Goliath from the previous chapter, Saul (the teacher) does not question the effectiveness of the armor because he believes it is part of what gives Goliath power. There is more faith in the armor than there is in David (the student). When the student in armor goes to battle and merely survives, it is seen as a victory. There is no consideration that they may have been battered and wounded in the process. Schools don't address this woundedness and its implications (impostor syndrome, self-doubt, and questioning of self). They choose not to see the very evident wounds and bandage students up unhealed.

Educators who focus on the needs of folks of color have always advanced the need for pedagogies that are centered in revolutionary thought/practice. For example, multiculturalism in education emerged in the mid-1990s as a necessary response to centuries of schooling that gave power to just a few at the expense of all others. James Banks suggests that "it grew out of a civil rights movement grounded in such democratic ideals of the West as freedom, justice, and equality."[5] He argues that "multicultural education seeks to extend to all people the ideals that were meant only for an elite few at the nation's birth."[6] Those goals are tough to argue. How could anyone not want all young people to have the power reserved only for the elite? In a similar vein, and in many ways evolving from multicultural education, is culturally relevant pedagogy (CRP) and its significant offshoots like culturally responsive and sustaining education. This work, championed by brilliant educators and thinkers like Gloria Ladson-Billings, Django Paris, and H. Samy Alim, advocates for education that is fundamentally rooted in academic achievement, cultural competence, and social consciousness. CRP, like multicultural education, requires a revolutionary spirit to be enacted. A teacher must be attuned to something bigger than just delivering information to take on approaches to teaching that have roots in and continue to carry a legacy of social justice and equity. A system of education that has committed itself to, or at least seriously considered, these approaches to teaching and learning for the last twenty years could not possibly fail Black children. Yet here we are, over twenty years since these terms became part of the discourse in teacher education programs, and nothing significant has shifted in the education of the most marginalized young people. In fact, they have been more wounded than ever before because there is a perception that their needs are being met because of the popularity of the rhetoric. The reality is that powerful phrases like *cultural relevance* and *multicultural education* have become absorbed into the lexicon of American education and lost their power. My conversations with scholars who coined these phrases and concepts always reveal their frustration with the way their ideas have been robbed of their meaning even as they have become popular in a number of influential places. For example, across the country, there are classes in schools of education and beyond that are developed around cultural relevance, responsiveness, and competence. However, teacher candidates who leave these institutions maintain the same types of teaching that have always been in place when they get in classrooms with young people from diverse cultural backgrounds. Within contemporary classrooms, there is a gross corruption of the work of culture in education and a gross distortion of its purpose and intention.

I have sat in multicultural education classes that don't discuss civil rights and culturally relevant lectures that don't mention race or class. What is happening in education is the adoption of the language of revolution and institutionalization of theories of/for emancipation for the sake of neutralizing the agency of those whose cultures have been historically marginalized. If I can welcome your words and nullify your intent, I can convince the public that my goal is to empower you, even if all I actually do is reinforce the status quo and maintain power. Furthermore, if I can put enough effort into telling the world you are welcome here, I don't have to put much effort into transforming the place to make you actually feel welcome. This narrative is most evident in a powerful story about a good friend who was a Black student at a predominantly White university. Years ago, his smiling face was Photoshopped into a picture of White students at a football game. That picture was then featured on the cover of the institution's admissions booklet as a means to showcase its diversity. This sleight of hand—in which institutions display an interest in radical ideas (like inclusiveness and cultural relevance) while reinforcing and supporting the status quo—happens in various forms and across various contexts in American society. We see it when a past president celebrates a Tuskegee Airman during a national address and then gives the Medal of Freedom to a person who is best known for pushing racist tropes and reinforcing negative stereotypes about Black people. The mention of a hundred-year-old Black military aviator who fought for the nation's freedom then becomes a distraction from the celebration of a person whose presence opposes the airman and what he represents.

A final example of the manipulation of powerful words, phrases, and concepts is evident in the historic election of Brian Kemp as Georgia's governor. Following his election by a narrow margin, an article ran in *Essence* magazine that revealed "a judge could demand that Georgia Gov. Brian Kemp reveal his methodology for purging 700,000 names from state rolls between 2016 and 2018."[7] The story revealed that Kemp worked as an election official overseeing the gubernatorial race in which he was a candidate. He ensured that a large number of votes were either called into question or not counted in an effort to ensure that he would win the race. What I find most fascinating about this case is the rhetoric around voting rights that Kemp used in public. He was the prototypical politician who urged that "everyone must ensure that they go out and vote." However, in privately recorded conversations that were leaked to the media, he was captured lamenting what would happen to his campaign if everyone who could vote actually did. This narrative is the perfect way to describe what happens in schools. Like Kemp's nice words about voting, institutions use nice words like *cultural relevance* and *multiculturalism* without shifting their work to meet the needs of marginalized youth. The use of the words is simply a tactic to cover up a festering wound that is caused by the damage institutions are inflicting on those within them who are having their ratchet suppressed. The words of the institutions become like gauze wrapped around untreated wounds, a nice white wrapping around the denial of voice and agency intended to suffocate the response to that denial—the ratchetness beneath.

In urban communities across the country, folks who profess to care about Black children argue that the absence of rigorous academic content is the core reason why they are unsuccessful in school. In response to, and in many cases solely because of their public narrative of care, these people have been given full license to work within or even open schools that solely target young people of color. In these schools, bastardized notions of care and academic rigor are used to justify problematic pedagogies. For example, a school in Louisiana that created a number of viral videos showing student acceptances to college operated with a public face of care for students. A *New York Times* exposé about T. M. Landry College Prep told a powerful tale of hypocrisy.[8] Before the exposé, a number of interviews featuring the school operators saying how much they loved their students and treated them like family were littered across the media. However, beneath this public facade, students reported intense emotional and physical abuse and a culture that was characterized by fear and intimidation. In the school, like in society, the word *rigor* was partnered with phrases like *college* and *career readiness* and framed as an extension of care. Somehow, rigor and care have been reframed to mean being like excellent sheep: getting kids into the "right" school and having them looked upon as valuable in the eyes of society even if that means harming them. Students who attended T. M. Landry, the Louisiana school that turned into a media darling for getting Black kids into Ivy League universities, now tell tales of being physically and verbally slammed by the school principal and threatened. They tell stories about how their documents were doctored and their confidence was shattered—all while their pain and trauma were hidden under the pristine white gauze of college acceptances. Inevitably, the bleeding ratchetness under the gauze of college acceptance came seeping through. That is exactly what happened in this story. Young folks got bold, loud, and honest. They alerted the media to the fraud in the school. They refused to be silent about their soul wounds and did not allow the gauze to stop their wounds from bleeding through.

The reality is that there are people who are being wounded by a bevy of inequities and who are also robbed of their voice when they attempt to articulate their pain. There are places where soul wounds are inflicted more intensely and more consistently than others. For the people who are at the epicenter of targeted oppression, not only are they fighting to heal, but they are constantly being retraumatized by those outside of their culture profiting from their wounds without giving voice to their realities. A school that opens in an urban neighborhood that professes to improve the conditions for Black children but whose pedagogy reinforces or doubles down on the same violence that the students' ancestors experienced cannot be allowed to operate without critique. Such a school is no different than a newly gentrified neighborhood where business investors see gold mines in the form of real estate and tax breaks and turn a blind eye to community displacement and loss of cultural resources. In much the same way, new charter schools led by profiteers with no love for the people and their culture simply serve to profit at the expense of traditions that are lost, cultures that are erased, histories that are rendered valueless, and souls that are wounded.

Soul wounds are created by assaults on culture that result from the policing of cultural expressions. The wounds are inflicted by teaching, teachers, and schools that claim to love culture but see it as superficial. Teaching that causes soul wounds does not recognize that "culture is part of the soul. As human beings, we are all part of a culture and not separate from it."[9] Therefore, an assault on culture in teaching—or a misrepresentation of culture or its expression as non-academic—amounts to a soul wound. The work of transformative educators is to not allow pedagogy to critique our ratchetness but to critique the education system that is comfortable with conditioning us into not being seen as brilliant. Our ratchetness is our resistance. I have established that we cannot have a pedagogy predicated on assaulting culture without a recognition of the conditions that initiate a raw and ratchet response. Here I want to make clear that those who have been wounded will always attempt to heal. Young people who stand face to face with police officers, look them in the eye, and say they are not moving are not being defiant because they want to be rude. They are claiming space. They are attempting to heal.

When soul wounds start healing, they slowly become scabs that inevitably heal over and become scars. The scars serve as reminders of the past wrongs but don't carry the same type of pain as the wound. Too often, youth never get to the scarring and full healing because their wounds are consistently being picked at. When Black students show up at a school that reprimands them for being too loud, they decide to just say nothing. When they get asked to adjust their attitude because they are silent, a scab is getting picked at. When they are told to lie on their college application to construct a story about poverty instead of joy in their neighborhood so they can get accepted into college, a scab is getting picked at. The ratchet young person is raw and bleeding, and when a path for healing cannot be developed, they find their own. They turn cold and disinterested, and if they're lucky, their wounds scab over. They leave their experiences in school like the scab—contained and hard—and end up putting on an unapproachable exterior. It is after they leave school that they can finally heal.

When the wounds that schools inflict get picked at as youth attempt to heal, this is educational excoriation. Excoriation is an obsessive-compulsive disorder that is marked by so much picking at the skin that it significantly impacts all other aspects of one's life. When one picks at a wound before it heals and goes through excoriation, the physical wounds impact how one is seen and how one sees oneself. But there are also deep emotional wounds. Phobias and traumas develop when one's wounds are constantly picked at. I have previously mentioned poor teaching in schools disorder (PTSD), which develops when students go through teaching and learning that does not focus on empowering, healing, and accepting what they bring and what assets they have but instead consistently corrects, reprimands, and belittles. The person who undergoes this is then permanently marked by the wound even if it heals.

In Yoruba culture in western Africa, tribal marks are inscribed on the face and body during childhood by burning or cutting the skin. I spoke with a Yoruba elder about this process, and he described how the marks are treated and allowed to heal by being allowed to touch the air and be touched by it. After healing, the painful marks from childhood are not erased. They remain in the form of what appears to be etchings in the skin that are not hidden but become symbols of connectedness with others from the same background or shared experience. There are different incisions or markings in the skin for different tribes, and some are quite complex. However, regardless of the markings, when they are all allowed to heal and not reopen, they can shift from painful reminders of a traumatic experience to badges of honor that become anchors for the community. Allowing them to heal is not wrapping them in white gauze the minute they start bleeding. It is allowing the wound to breathe and then helping it to heal.

When the soul wounds from everyday interactions with adults in school are deep and then constantly reopened before they can heal because of the excoriating nature of contemporary schooling, they cannot be covered up with a pretty curriculum. In the current approach to schooling, surface bruises and deep lacerations get covered and dressed the same way. Metal detectors in school buildings that suffered from crime in the 1980s when there was a drug epidemic remain in schools simply because the young people who attend them are Black and Brown. Bars on classroom windows, old textbooks, instruction that does not reflect who the students are, policing and criminalization of normal behavior like walking in groups, punishment for self-expression, and extraction of the art and culture of the community—each of these are wounds that are ignored and covered with words like *equity* and *social justice* that come from the mouths of teachers who have no idea what those terms really mean. When blood seeps through the dressing and turns the pristine white gauze of words and phrases red, we blame the wounded for making the dressing dirty and simply try to wrap it with more layers. A curriculum with no flexibility for reality, when wrapped around a wounded person, cannot stop the blood from seeping to the surface of the gauze. "Poor classroom behavior" and inattentiveness when a curriculum does not reflect reality is simply blood seeping through the white gauze of the curriculum, making it clear that there is an untreated wound that lies beneath the dressing. Commands like "Stand straight," "Don't talk too loudly," "Enunciate," "Don't ask too many questions," "Follow me with your eyes at all times," and "Why don't you know that?" serve as the scratching at the wound, and teaching becomes a never-ending cycle of excoriation and then wrapping gauze around the wound.

The Nigerian ritual of the tribal marking ceremony is one in which wounds aren't just covered up. It includes piercing the skin with a knife but also placing snail secretions on the cut, pressing charcoal dust into the wound, and then letting it naturally heal. Urban schools have their own rituals that result in young people being marked. It is a sad truth that millions of young people have become a part of a tradition that limits who or what they can become. If they attend certain schools, it is a given that they will be berated. They will be ignored. They will witness some sort of violence. However, just because this is a ritual in schools does not mean that educators cannot create the spaces for healing even within those schools. Ratchetdemic classrooms are the healing secretion, charcoal dust, and freeing space that allow wounds to heal. Those who have experienced this healing together will have tribal marks and become part of a tribe. This surpasses location and time and is apparent every time I engage in a conversation with young people who have healed together in a class or a school. There are cadres of young people who have gone through a learning experience with a teacher who changed the trajectory of their lives and who still bond over that healing experience. That ratchet teacher who sees the students' ratchet selves and uses it as a mechanism for learning and growing together creates a connection that, like tribal marks, lasts forever. The system cut us, but you gave our wounds air and charcoal. We ended up marked, but our healing and our marks bind us forever.

The tribal marking ceremony described above that mars the faces of children is not as popular in Nigeria or Africa writ large as it once was. In 2003, the nation passed a Child Rights Act that banned the practice. There is a collective recognition that there is some long-lasting emotional pain that comes with the marks. Consequently, the ritual has been practically wiped out. In the United States and other countries that claim to be more civilized, there has not been an abandonment of our inhumane rituals. Within schools, we still harm young people with zero-tolerance policies and other policies that criminalize them and damage their sense of self. Not only do we persist in inflicting these soul wounds, but we deny that we produce them in the first place. This denial of soul wounds is fascinating because even though we deny inflicting them, we consistently attempt to cover them up. We are always either reopening wounds before they heal through excoriation or dressing them up so they can never heal—all while claiming that the wounds never existed or were never inflicted.

AGNOSIA: A NEW DIAGNOSIS

This denial of a person's truth in the face of evidence that their pain is rooted in your practice is one of the most callous things a person can do. Yet in education, this is the norm. Far too often, I engage with teachers and principals who claim to believe in students and the transformative power of education and who follow norms that run counter to the words they say. For example, I remember a meeting with a school principal who wanted me to work with her staff to improve the outcomes for their students in math and science. After visiting the school and assessing their issues, I recognized that the math and science issues needed to be addressed by first working with the teachers to change their perception of young people. When I mentioned this to the principal, she quickly cited Paulo Freire's work about conscientization. This wasn't a traditional conversation I would have with a school leader, but I appreciated that she was making connections to theory, which is sometimes needed to make sense of what needs to be done to improve everyday teaching and learning practices. Conscientization is about developing critical consciousness about the world writ large and developing an understanding of the many tensions and inconsistencies that exist and one's role in them. I figured that she and I could use this concept as a grounding point for our conversation. After the meeting, we visited some classrooms together. As we walked down the hallway, students scattered and cleared a path for her. I thought nothing of this at the time.

We then walked into a history class where a teacher was delivering a masterful lesson on the transatlantic slave trade and its implications for the students' lives in schools today. We stood quietly at the back of the classroom as we watched the lesson. I was enjoying the interaction between the students and teacher and looked to the principal to give her a slight head nod of approval. But when I looked over, I saw that the principal was scowling as the teacher taught. The teacher was unconcerned by our presence and gave the students a writing assignment. As the students excitedly began writing, the principal walked over to the teacher and whispered to her. The teacher was obviously upset, but luckily the students were too caught up in their writing to notice. After the assignment wrapped up, the principal and I walked around the classroom together for a few minutes and then visited another classroom. Hours later, when we returned to the principal's office, I asked her about the conversation she'd had with the teacher. She pointed out that she hadn't interrupted the lesson even though she could have. I commended her on this. I then again asked what she had whispered to the teacher that got her so upset. She said that she'd told the teacher about being too political and possibly upsetting the students. These were students who were happily and excitedly engaging in the lesson and the writing task. It was the best lesson I had seen that week. I quickly challenged her critique of the teacher. I mentioned the student engagement and the quality of their writing. She pushed back. She insisted that the teacher was wrong. She could not see the hypocrisy in citing progressive work that welcomed both the historical and contemporary concepts that affect the lives of young people while disparaging this practice in real life. She was suffering from agnosia—a cultural agnosia.

Agnosia is a medical condition that affects the part of the brain that controls visual and perceptual understanding. People with agnosia are able to see but unable to process what they are seeing. For example, a person with agnosia may be looking at a beautiful landscape and rather than say, "I see trees and the sky," they would say, "I see green things attached to brown ones with blue things floating on top." They can witness the phenomenon, but they cannot understand what it is; consequently, they cannot fathom what it means. When a person suffers from agnosia, they often have to go through severe therapy and, in some cases, surgical processes to rectify their inability to process information.

I suggest that we start identifying people who suffer from cultural agnosia. When people suffer from this condition, they can witness the cultural expression or practices of a person or a particular population but cannot process the beauty and gift that they represent. Cultural agnosia may play out with a principal who intellectually or theoretically knows what conscientization means but lacks the ability to make sense/meaning of what it looks like in real life (as in the example above). It most often plays out with educators who visually see youth of color and their naturally ratchet forms of self-expression but lack the ability to see these expressions for the genius and brilliance they possess. These are people whose entire worldview is shaped by a condition that robs them of the ability to see beauty. They cannot see the linguistic genius in street slang or the pedagogical magic in hip-hop cyphers. They misidentify inquisitive and intellectually curious young people as rude and disruptive, and engaged classrooms as loud or distracting. Just as those with agnosia have brains that cannot process what they see, too many educators have a heart that simply cannot feel the pedagogical value of ways of knowing and being that are outside of the canon or other predefined markers of academic value. In education, we have allowed those with cultural agnosia to define the way we look at young folks of color. Those who can see the youth for who they are become silenced or the teacher version of excellent sheep. A ratchetdemic pedagogy does not allow for those with cultural agnosia to lead schools and classrooms. We speak loudly and boldly with our words but mostly with a ratchetdemic pedagogy that heals as it teaches in whatever way makes the most powerful connections to the young people we are charged with guiding to self-actualization through education.

CHAPTER 9

FRENEMIES AND ENERGY

In his short story titled "Of the Meaning of Progress," W. E. B. Du Bois describes a period of time when he was a teacher in rural Tennessee.[1] He describes the challenges of attending a teachers' college, finding a job as a teacher, overcoming racism, and convincing Black families to see the value of a formal education in a world that demanded only their labor. I've always loved reading about that period of his life because it is an essential part of who he became that is often erased from his story. People remember him as the first African American to earn a PhD from Harvard and as a writer, thinker, and cofounder of the National Association for the Advancement of Colored People (NAACP), but most do not recognize that he, like many great Black scholars and intellectuals, formed many of their thoughts about freedom, equity, and social justice when they were teachers. I believe that the erasure of this piece of his story leads to a general lack of attention to the activism inherent in teaching. It also masks the role of teaching in shaping the lives of those who effect major change in the world.

Teaching, which is one of the most revered professions in the Black community, is the boot camp to be an enlisted officer in the army for social justice. Derrick Aldridge writes of the long history of Black teachers and traces it back to Africans who taught each other during slavery, during and after Reconstruction, and beyond. The strongest folks always choose to teach. Of those who have worked as teachers, the best of us remain in the profession in some way for a lifetime, the luckiest among us still work with schools and have the gift to witness the genius of young people every day, and the rest of us are perpetually shaped by the time we had in the classroom. I use the term *boot camp* not to describe teaching as a struggle or to attach the work to military training but to make clear that it is where the basic skills to change the world come from. It is by teaching that we begin to truly see the flaws of society. It is when you are in the classroom with the most marginalized youth that the urgency and drive to change the world becomes realized. Teaching in the neighborhoods where the people have been described as "too fast" and "too loud" is where you find your ratchet and develop the energy to do your best work. Those who have taught or worked closely with young people who are fighting vigorously for agency develop a certain way of looking at the world that differs from those who have not worked with them. You learn to fight by being in classrooms with those who have something to fight for. This does not mean that there aren't people who have been enlisted, called, or signed up to change the world who have not taught. It is to say that those people have not learned all that they are supposed to if they have never worked in a classroom. Being an educator is as much about learning as it is about teaching. Those who teach, especially those who teach with a full understanding of the privilege of teaching—and what it means for who they will become in the world—end up transforming our society and empowering the next generation.

Today many of the activists who put their careers on the line for the sake of the betterment of Black folks are former teachers. Consider actor Jesse Williams, who starred in *Grey's Anatomy*, one of the most popular dramas on television. He has repeatedly used his fame to advocate for civil rights. He has been a significant part of the Black Lives Matter movement and has created a number of organizations/platforms that not only highlight systemic inequity but work to address the issue. Also consider Congresswoman Maxine Waters, who faces the most heinous personal attacks for advocating for the well-being of folks of color in the face of a tyrannous government. She has publicly spoken out against the rise of White nationalist organizations; authored numerous pieces of legislation that address giving voice to the marginalized, including laws that support more equitable federal contracts to minorities and women; increased tenants' rights; and increased funding to education programs that serve communities of color. I suggest that these two people do the work they do because each spent integral parts of their lives as teachers. Williams taught high school in the Philadelphia public schools for six years. Waters entered politics after working as a teacher for close to a decade and witnessing inequity in education firsthand. These two models for what teaching can ignite in the soul of a person serve as exemplars of why teaching is so important, even if one's journey leads them outside the classroom. For both the aspiring teacher and those who are already on this journey, it is in the classroom that their vision of the world becomes clear. In particular, the work of Black teachers has always been as much about the world outside the classroom as in it. It has been about delivering academic content but also addressing inequity and transforming society. Michele Foster's brilliant work on Black teachers highlights this feature of Black teaching that got lost in the mass displacement of teachers after the desegregation of schools. In her interviews with twenty Black teachers born between 1905 and 1973, Foster describes how these Black teachers "did not try to imbue their students with traits like tractability that so often characterized the teaching of white Northern school teachers."[2] In other words, complicity was not always the goal of good education for Black folks. Tractability—being easily shaped/handled or malleable—is the opposite of being strong, vocal, and expressive, which are traits at the core of a ratchetdemic identity.

With a ratchetdemic educator, young people are given permission to reveal their true academic selves and discard the appropriateness and respectability that gets in the way of their free expression. Whether you are in the classroom temporarily or for the rest of your life, know that if you approach teaching with a recognition that your job is to remove what inhibits your students' genius, you will be offered the gift of having their powerful perspective of the world revealed to you. Once this perspective has become revealed, a person cannot see the world in the same way. The roadmap to freedom has been drawn by our ancestors and hidden in the hearts and minds of our youth. The educator must possess a certain ratchet and youthful energy for that truth to be revealed. This is not to say that teaching well or revealing our purpose requires one to be childish. It does require that we be childlike. To be childlike means to be filled with a youthful curiosity, a willingness to use the imagination, a pursuance of play, and a sense of pure joy. It also means not being consumed by rules and order. This childlikeness is the key that unlocks one's ratchetness. Freedom and the energy to pursue one's true self is unlocked in both the teacher and the student when both are operating with a certain *expression and recognition of each other's true selves*. It is for this reason that the erasure of teaching from the Black intellectual tradition is so problematic. When there are no Black teachers and/or allies who have developed an understanding of ratchet/authentic/childlike ways of knowing and being, there are no opportunities to depart from systems that reject more innovative and culturally attuned ways of teaching, and these systems are then allowed to continue to inflict violence on Black children.

This erasure of Black teachers and Black teaching has roots in the 1954 landmark Supreme Court ruling in *Brown v. Board of Education* in which the justices unanimously ruled that racial segregation of children in public schools was unconstitutional. This powerful decision was intended to allocate equal resources to Black and White children because of the inequity that was present in Black schools under the previous "separate but equal" policy. The *Brown v. Board of Education* case led to Black students being sent to White schools en masse and eventually led to the closing of many Black schools and the displacement of those schools' Black teachers—who were not being hired by White schools, even if these schools had a new population of Black students. The school superintendent of To-peka, Kansas, which was ground zero for school integration, explic-itly stated to Black teachers that because "the majority of people in Topeka will not want to employ negro teachers next year for white children, it is necessary for me to notify you now that your services will not be needed."[3] There was a butterfly effect—a scientific con-cept that can be simplified down to the notion that small things can have nonlinear impacts on a complex system—that Black folks and other folks of color have never recovered from. We have not been the same since. Black teachers pursued other careers, and over time, a collective amnesia arose about the role that Black teachers played (and play) in the lives of young people. When Black kids attending White schools became one of the chief indicators of racial progress, the Black schools and their now unemployed Black teachers were rendered useless. This broke a major tradition in Black communi-ties that previously revered the teacher as much as the preacher. In fact, it is known within communities of color that good teachers are always preaching, and good preachers are always teaching, because their work requires being both educative and soul affirming.

This is why the mass displacement of Black teachers who worked in all-Black schools prior to desegregation had not only a horrific effect on Black children, who no longer saw themselves in the adults in their schools, but on the Black community writ large. Not only did we lose our teachers; we lost a critical mass of revolutionaries who did not get the training to fight for justice that comes from being a teacher.

When Black folks don't teach, we lose the ability to see the world through the eyes of the youth, and we can only see what we have been trained to see by institutions that don't have the wholeness of Black folks in their vision. Communities that have been historically marginalized cannot get to freedom unless they are sharp (stead-fast, hopeful, attentive, responsible, and powerful) in their pursuit of strong relationships with young folks. For educators, our primary work is not just to teach them but to learn from them. This is why my work has always been anchored in reality pedagogy and its tools for gaining insight on how to teach from those one teaches. Reality pedagogy teaches teachers to understand that their effectiveness requires a knowledge that only the students have. To do this work well, we must lay ourselves bare before the students. It is only then that we can bear witness to the inequities young people are dealing with from their unique vantage point. I argue that insight into the reality/ lived experience of a group of broken people is what drives folks to commit themselves to social justice and activism. The transgressive spirit of many potential leaders has been lost because the preparation for harnessing that spirit or energy, which comes from having been in the classroom and learning from and with young people, has been lost. Too many potential leaders have either willingly or unwillingly been removed from their natural inclination to be a freedom fighter because they have been convinced that they couldn't or shouldn't teach. Many of them have a calling and a desire to teach but have chosen not to because they couldn't see a path to being their full ratchet selves in the classroom. They remembered their teachers and realized that they didn't want to be like them. When we create a new way of teaching, we benefit the young people we teach, but we also teach them to teach. We open up truths about where we need to go as a society and recruit others into the classroom.

My teaching story goes back to my experiences as a student. After a challenging time in high school, I stumbled into my undergraduate studies, found science, and discovered I was good at it. I ended up graduating from college with degrees in physical anthropology, biology, and chemistry and then completing a master's degree in natural sciences. After causing my mother a ton of heartache as I attempted to navigate high school, it seemed she was finally proud of me. Her thoughts were that I would pursue a career in science or medicine, as those careers were aligned with what I studied in college. After I graduated with my master's, she would tell anyone who would listen that her son was a scientist. As I was deciding what I wanted to do with my career, she consistently suggested medical school or a lucrative offer I had received from a pharmaceutical company. Neither of those paths really spoke to me, and I eventually took my father's advice to "try teaching until you find what works for you." Teaching was supposed to be something I did for a year or two until I figured out what I really wanted to do with my science degrees.

I walked into an after-school program in a middle school in the Bronx expecting not to enjoy this work at all. Then I started interacting with the young people. I remember the first time I explained a math concept that they were having trouble with in their math class and heard the entire room of twenty or so young people all sing, "Ohhhhhhhhhhhhhh, now I get it," as they jumped excitedly around the room because they learned how to solve for a variable in a simple algebraic equation. There was something about their response to learning that set my soul on fire. After my first week, I remember calling my mom excitedly and telling her I wanted to come home to tell her some incredible news that was too big to share over the phone. She seemed excited. I rushed over, knocked on the door, and she gave me a big hug. She then asked, "What's her name?" I was puzzled for a second, and then it hit me. She thought my excitement was about meeting a woman. It wasn't. This was bigger. I had found what I wanted to do with my life. I laughed and told her it wasn't that. I grabbed her hand, walked with her to the couch in the dimly lit living room, and said, "I want to be a teacher." In that moment, even in the room without much light, I saw her excitement turn into disappointment. It was a look I hadn't seen since I got suspended from high school for spray-painting graffiti on a wall. The interesting thing is that my father was a teacher. At one point, my mother had been one too. I learned later that her mother was a teacher, and my grandfather was a news announcer called "The Teacher." The craft I had chosen to pursue was in my genes. However, my mother was not fully convinced that teaching was the right profession for me. She was worried that it didn't pay well enough and didn't see it as valuable, compared to other professions. So my decision to teach came with her disappointment. But I knew that something got activated when I heard the joy of learning from those kids. I also felt that something was wrong when a year-long class could not teach these students something they had the ability to understand in five minutes of learning with ratchetdemic energy. Those early moments are what brought me to do the work I do today. They are the inspiration for this book.

For Du Bois, his time preparing for and then teaching in the hills of Tennessee sharpened his insight on the ways that race and racism impact education. In "Of the Meaning of Progress," Du Bois describes graduating from the segregated teachers' college and looking for a teaching job. During his rather unsuccessful search, he realized that he was not viewed as an equal to the White graduates of the institute and that finding a place to teach was incredibly difficult. As he continued on his journey, he encountered a twenty-year-old woman named Josie who excitedly mentioned to him that her community needed a teacher. Du Bois accepted the job and spent the next year teaching Josie and others in her small community. This was Josie's first opportunity to attend school, and she was excited. What is most compelling about how Du Bois describes Josie is that she "longed to learn, and thus ran on talking fast and loud, with much earnestness and energy." His description of her fastness and loudness as attributes attached to a longing to learn is striking because contemporary classrooms attended by youth of color often connect fastness and loudness to being anti-intellectual or nonacademic. I have heard endless variations of the phrase, "If he could just calm down, he could learn something." My response is always, "He probably ain't calm because he's excited to learn something." Excitement to learn is expressed in ratchet ways that are demonized in contemporary schools but that are closest to Josie's and other Black students' truest selves. When Du Bois describes Josie as speaking with an energy—which is not something that can necessarily be measured but can definitely be felt or experienced—it reminded me of the energy of urban neighborhoods evident in church sermons, children playing double Dutch, and adults greeting each other with handshakes that start with connections of the eye and end with finger snaps and hugs. This type of energy, when harnessed, can spark genius. It is also the type of energy that good teaching fosters and that folks who don't have it are intent on either silencing or devaluing it.

Du Bois's story of Josie ends with him moving on from his teaching job after a number of challenges with keeping the school open but returning to the town years later to discover that Josie had her energy drained from her until she died. She left school and went on to support her family financially. She carried the labor of providing for and protecting her siblings, and her fast-talking, loud, and earnest passion for learning was taken from her. She ended up being a shell of her former self and her energy was gone. As he reflected on his life as a teacher, Du Bois wrote, "My journey was done, and behind me lay hill and dale, and Life and Death. How shall man measure Progress there where the dark-faced Josie lies?"[4] He could not make sense of progress when Josie was denied an education and forced to live a life as a shell of who she could have been.

In schools populated by youth of color, like Josie, young folks are taught to suppress their natural energy and make decisions that are more about survival (and making other people in their lives more comfortable) than about identifying and pursuing their educational interests. They are forced to bend to the needs of teachers who would rather they be compliant than express their earnestness and loudness. They are forced to choose memorization and obedience over the pursuit of their interests and passions. They are robbed of their ratchet energy. We must recognize that there are enemies who oppose the progress and growth of young people and their teachers and that these enemies are often the individuals working closest to students. Even family and friends may be opposed to the progress and growth that students and teachers pursue. When Du Bois writes about Josie, he mentions her loving family whom he enjoyed spending time with but who would not allow Josie to pursue her dream of going to school. To meet the needs of her family, "Josie shivered and worked on, with the vision of schooldays all fled, with a face wan and tired."[5]

Sometimes, the enemies and energy stealers of your progress are people who are close to you, who prioritize a version of you that is different from who you want to be. Most times, they are people who do not have your earnestness and energy, and their jealousy gets awakened because they recognize they can never match what you bring to the world. Du Bois suggests that this may have been a piece of what did Josie in—a family who failed to see her as anything more than a worker to sustain their livelihood despite her obvious passion to pursue a formal education. Enemies to progress not only work to police youth self-expression but also to drain young people of their energy. Energy is an intangible attribute/force that cannot be quantified but that drives everything. It is the internal motivation to do and be what the heart desires. It is depleted when you get consumed by individuals and institutions that want you to support their goals instead of fulfilling your heart's desires. In Josie's case, her energy was stolen by those who did not see the value of the education she so earnestly desired. Her family could only envision her as who they needed her to be. They became frenemies. The word *frenemy* is a portmanteau of friends and enemies that I use to describe situations in which folks present themselves as friends or profess narratives that seem to be intended for the benefit of a person or group but who function in opposition to the full actualization of that person or group. When young folks have their energy stolen by educators who love (or profess to love) them but do not allow their energy in the classroom, these teachers become frenemies.

Over the course of my career, I have attended a number of conferences in which stakeholders in education gathered to discuss the landscape of urban education. At these conferences, I discovered that *urban education* stakeholders are actually the culturally misinformed (who appear not to recognize their own cultural competence gaps) who struggle to reach and teach these children they view as problems to be solved. The whole idea of using coded language to name/describe Black children signals a discomfort the education system has with facing itself and who these students are. An educator who is fearful of being outed as biased, or fearful of not being accepted by folks who themselves may be biased, showcases that they are not ready to truly teach because they have not achieved a comfort with themselves. This indicates an inability or "achievement gap" in the person. In other words, if you have not achieved a place of earnestness and comfort that enables you to name what you see and discuss it at a conference or in any place, then you have not achieved an elevated state of awareness and unapologetic comfort with who you are; you may have a ratchetness achievement gap.

At conferences on social justice, equity, and closing the achievement gap, attendees are mostly White, and their discourse captures the most powerful and progressive words and phrases I have ever heard. White folks and their Oreo endorsers (Black folks who serve as brown cookies who hold up White supremacist ideologies) sit with legs crossed and pointer fingers pressed against lips and brows and incessantly talk about equity, diversity, and socioemotional learning without being able to say Black children are suffering under the structure of schools that we are holding up. These people describe each other with words like *caring*, *committed*, and *anti-racist*. Who is the woman with the pink shawl who says she doesn't see color? Oh, she runs the equity program for the district. She is part of the group who meets to discuss BIPOC youth. These are youth who happen to never be in the room when they are being discussed. The general narrative seems to be that students don't need to be in the room because folks who claim to be their friends are there to speak for them. These friends say all the right words, ask each other all the right questions, cite the right people, and feel they have the answers. Quotes from Michelle Alexander and Ta-Nehisi Coates roll off their tongues. Yet the schools they talk about and the young people they claim to represent and support remain lifeless under their leadership and their "work." We are never to critique these folks or call them to task because they are "friends of the community." I argue that many who are framed as "friends" are not the ones who can solve our problems. In fact, our extension of friendship to them is a trap to drain us of our vital energy. This is the issue of White saviors and friends of the community whose chief goal is not about young people but positioning themselves as the ones to help young people be better. They need to be the ones who provide those young people with resources and give them what they need because they need those young people to remain in subservient positions in order to be affirmed. Keeping those kids as a perpetual problem allows them to see and sell themselves as the students' heroes.

From 1883 to 1916, an annual conference that was organized by a group of wealthy philanthropists gathered at Lake Mohonk in New York to discuss Indigenous Americans. They were described as "reformers interested in Indian Affairs," and their goal was "to discuss Indian matters and make recommendations."[6] These were people considered at the time to be so invested in the needs of Indigenous populations that they called themselves "Friends of the Indian." Members of this community presented themselves as caring and concerned citizens, and they gathered to decide what was best for Native American people. They described their meeting as "a work of love."[7] However, notes from these conferences revealed that these *friends* described Native Americans and Blacks as "savages" who were "uncivilized." In fact, any reading through the proceedings from these meetings reveals a shared self-righteousness and overall belief in the superiority of the friends of the people over the people.

A regular attendee of these conferences was William Henry Pratt, the founder of the Carlisle Indian Industrial School, which, at the time, was considered the premier institution for teaching Indigenous youth. It was presented to the world as a model for how this population should be educated. At the Friends of the Indian conferences, Pratt was considered one of the most progressive and imaginative participants. The fact that his school was denying the culture of hundreds of children and creating an environment that produced endless trauma for these children and generations after them was not considered. After all, Pratt was the person first attributed with using the word *racism*. Yes, racism—the word that is defined as bias, discrimination, or antagonism against someone of a different race—was first used by the person who used the school he started as a way to discriminate against Native Americans in the most racist ways possible, including physical violence. The bitter irony is that the person who first used the word *racism* was himself a racist, even though he was framed by society as a person who was doing good. This signals the true nature of how the system of education creates frenemies. They gather to support each other and their projects/initiatives and nonprofits and always appear to be providing something of benefit to those who are less advantaged. All the while, they are maintaining a larger system or structure designed to bring about the demise of those they profess to care about. I have heard people who are brutal to Black children in their pedagogy justify their flawed approach by saying that those who want to intervene on behalf of the young people are promoting White supremacy. They will throw around equity phrases as a cover to hide behind, even though their statements follow no logic. They argue that they have "high expectations" but do not articulate that what they mean is high expectations to be like excellent sheep. They celebrate when children cut their hair and are more respectable, as though some goal of "looking appropriate" is an indicator of learning. They create horrific working conditions for educators who then carry their mistreatment and put it onto students. Yet they argue that because they care about students, any opposition to their model serves to support White supremacist practices. This is the prototypical frenemy.

On February 8, 2000, the album *Let's Get Free* by the hip-hop group Dead Prez was released. The album, referenced through this text, was a powerful blend of Afrocentric ideology, classic hip-hop production, and fiery lyricism that was groundbreaking in an era when most hip-hop artists were consumed with rapping about materialism and making a leap from the urban music charts to Top 40 radio. The album opens with a song that sets the pace for the entire project and introduces the listener to one of the most poignant breakdowns of the frenemy concept I have found. It starts with a piano riff that slowly introduces the howl of a wolf, more sounds, and then a classic thumping hip-hop beat. Instead of having rappers share their lyrics on the track, Dead Prez has the Pan-Africanist speaker Omali Yeshitela (the same man who pulled the racist painting from city hall in St. Petersburg) share a folktale about hunters in the Arctic. While I used that narrative to explain a point earlier, I want to connect it here to an Inuit folktale about hunting wolves. In this tale, instead of using a blade, hunters remove the baleen from whales' mouths, soak it until it becomes flexible, and sharpen its ends. The baleen is then folded into a densely packed and compact accordion shape made flat. This shape is maintained by wrapping fine sinew from caribou or other similar organic material, like thread, around it. The hunters then wrap the compressed plates in fat or caribou meat and leave them for wolves to eat. Hungry wolves see the feast left for them. Once the meat is swallowed, the wolves' own natural digestive juices slowly break down the sinew/thread that hold the plates together. Eventually, the plates unravel in a wolf's stomach and kill the animal.

The theme to consider across this narrative is that the hunter presents sustenance, or the appearance of it, to the wolf in a way that seems as though his intention is to feed the wolf. Even if the wolf does not know which hunter left the food, it will eat. If the wolf sees the hunter place the food where it is available to eat, the wolf may falsely believe that this hunter is an ally or that the hunter is harmless. The wolf believes that anyone who leaves me food must not have the intention to harm me. This is especially the case if I am hungry. Somehow a desire to eat may outweigh my instinct for self-preservation. In reality, the hunter is the enemy of the wolf. When the wolf eats what the hunter offers, the wolf dies from the inside out. When young people with hunger to learn enter schools where information is provided to them but wrapped in narratives of success and acceptance, they consume the learning, but it eventually unravels within them. These are the folks who lose their energy and end up as cookies holding up white filling. The entire dynamic between the hunter and the wolf is designed to take away the wolf's energy or life source. The goal of education for most young people and particularly for Black youth is to rob them of their energy and magic.

Many who claim to be interested in improving schools for youth of color employ theoretical frameworks and philosophies that obscure how curriculum harms. They often present sharp baleen covered by narratives of care, which young folks consume until they lose their energy. Fundamental educational theories like constructivism are presented in schools of education as essential for effective teaching but are misused and/or misinterpreted. For example, constructivism is a theory that suggests that people construct their own knowledge by experiencing life and reflecting on those experiences. However, if the educator does not see value in young people's experiences or does not recognize the community conditions that frame their experiences and build their knowledge, their teaching cannot capture the imagination of the student and will inevitably cause a sort of ratchet resistance. Teachers armed with theory that institutions convinced them was infallible enact practices steeped in colonial mentalities and imperialist philosophies that unravel and destroy them in the classroom. *Colonial mentalities* are ways of thinking that are about controlling or exerting power, and *imperialist philosophies* refer to the adherence to rules, or a set of norms, that are implemented by force. In other words, educators see the classroom and those within it as always needing to be controlled, and they see their teaching as having to control by some kind of force. Consider practices like SLANT, which has grown in popularity in urban schools over the last decade. SLANT is an acronym for sit up, lean forward, ask and answer questions, nod your head, and track the speaker. It was first published in a teaching strategies workbook and has since become a protocol that is blindly accepted in many urban schools. In a SLANT-focused class, young folks present as obedient and attentive to the teacher, and this is seen as an indicator of good teaching and good learning. Educators who are trained to believe that strategies like SLANT are essential for effective teaching will inevitably force students to adopt those approaches, and students whose ways of engaging in the world do not align with this approach will naturally reject it. The teachers will then assume that the problem (not getting the response they desire or expect) lies not with the strategy but with the student who resists it. The expectation that students need to appear to be attentive even if their teacher does not connect with them is baffling. A disengaging and culturally incompetent teacher who expects students to SLANT despite the poor instruction and then reprimands them for not responding according to the formula should expect a ratchet and oppositional response to the poor pedagogy.

Instead, because of the reliance on strategies, the teacher starts thinking, "If amazing teaching techniques from experts cannot make them better, these students must be particularly problematic." This is where terms like *superpredator*, which has been used to describe urban youth of color, come from. In the 1990s, political scientist John DiIulio conducted a study on crimes committed by juvenile offenders and predicted that the rate of these crimes—particularly those committed by Black youth—would continue to rise sharply. He was joined by criminologist James Fox who made extreme statements about a new generation of mostly Black boys who would murder and rape with reckless abandon, and he referred to them as *superpredators*. The Decepts, for example, were called superpredators. In 1996, Hillary Clinton infamously used the term in an attempt to appear tough on crime. As a result, she reinforced the notion that certain young people were prone to predatory behavior and unredeemable. The predictions about the superpredators to come were later proven to be incorrect. In fact, it was shown that the initial study had little merit and that crimes committed by the so-called superpredator population actually decreased significantly at the time DiIulio predicted they would rise. Despite the flawed predictions and their statistically unfounded claims, the nation held on to the superpredator name and who they saw as an exemplar of it. The word *superpredator* fed the perception society had of Black males. Furthermore, blaming Black men for the crimes committed in response to poor conditions in their communities (that went unaddressed by elected officials and other stakeholders) absolved the system of taking any responsibility to address the young people's basic needs related to factors like mental health and education. As a result of this seeing/naming of Black youth as something other than who they are, society sees them as superpredators and not human beings whose basic needs are not being met in schools and beyond. Today, while it may no longer be socially acceptable to call young people superpredators, when young people express their ratchet in response to the poor structures of schools, educators still call them unteachable and still see them as less than who they are.

Consider that a majority of the theories for improving education, teacher preparation, school leadership, and sociology of education were constructed/formulated in an era when Black people, by law, were not supposed to be educated. This means that the frameworks we are employing for teaching youth of color were designed without consideration for how young folks of color should be taught or how the circumstances in which they are currently embedded impact their learning. These theories and ideas were constructed at a time when certain young people were seen as intellectually inferior, even before they could prove who they were. How then can researchers and educators use these formulations as the foundation of work that is supposed to affirm the brilliance of Black babies? I argue that they cannot. Enemy-constructed structures with friendly discourse only breed frenemies, and frenemies are more dangerous than enemies because their words lull us into letting down our defenses so our enemies can steal our energy. We have let institutions off the hook for their part in maintaining the inequities they so eloquently speak out against in their mission statements and public narratives. Many institutions that advocate for social justice and equal opportunity operate within a paradigm that devalues the ways of knowing and being for youth of color and forces them to eat food that unravels when consumed—hemorrhaging their energy. You cannot have equity in your "progressive" school that serves Black kids if your definition of equity is being like White folks. This is especially the case when actual

White folks aren't like what you imagine them to be. You aren't preparing students to compete with the real world if you are comparing them to some fictional White appropriateness that doesn't actually exist. I've been to schools across the world. Ain't no White schools I've seen where the children aren't free to question. Those children are not forced to slant their bodies toward teachers and nod silently while their sense of self is stripped from the curriculum. Generally speaking, White folks wouldn't subject their children to that type of cruelty. The reality is that what we have based our ideas of equity (a desire to be equal) on is imagined. If you visited the most progressive White schools, you would find that they do not employ strategies that condone complicity. Enemies of Black communities have convinced frenemies who work with young folks that their job is to make the youth feast on the curriculum they are handed without considering that once ingested it will unravel and eventually immobilize them.

When I make the types of assertions mentioned in the previous paragraph, there is always a group of people who wonder how this came to be for Black children. They ask me questions like, "Under which administration did this start?" and "Who put these structures in place?" There is some assumption that the current state of education is a new or newish phenomenon. My answers always point back to the education of First Nations people—not just in the United States, but across the world. Erasing student realities from curriculum, standards, textbooks, and approaches to instruction simply because of who they are has been occurring since long before those who perpetuate the inequity we currently see in schools were born. Those who are marginalized in today's schools are not children of/from a lost generation who have issues that we have never seen before. When we frame them this way, we erase the fact that this has happened before, and that it is still happening and will continue to happen until we gather our ratchet and push back. We must recognize that youth in today's schools are new victims of the same oppression. Schools are part of an age-old system that presents itself as the site for making life better while, in actuality, it functions to make those within it feel less than. We must begin asking how schools can profess to be interested in social justice when their students cannot voice dissatisfaction with their schooling. How can a student feel brilliant in a school when its curriculum persistently sends messages about students' worthlessness? When there is a misalignment between the words and actions of those who work with our children, we must learn to listen to our innate sensitivity to the hypocrisy and call out frenemies. In "Feel It in the Air," rapper Beanie Sigel describes the feeling of knowing when you are in the presence of the frenemy: "I read between the lines of your eyes and your brows. Your handshake ain't matching your smile."[8] This is a sensitivity that is sharper in young people. They express it when they are around teachers and school leaders who don't see students for who they are. Students react to it by expressing a raw aversion to anything school leaders and teachers present. They are loud in class. They don't listen. They refuse to be obedient to those they sense are not there for them, and we penalize them for investing their energy on being seen—on being ratchet.

CHAPTER 10

TOWARD HEALING

A Cure for Impostor Syndrome

A wise man once said, you can't heal what you don't reveal.

College graduation ceremonies are beautiful. At Ivy League institutions, they are spellbinding. I've attended ceremonies at Brown, Columbia, Harvard, University of Pennsylvania, and Yale and have marveled at the majesty of the ceremonies and the events that surround them. The department parties, the honors ceremonies, the student and celebrity speakers, and the dinners at nearby restaurants all create a phenomenal spectacle. Each graduation has its own unique combination of tradition and attention to detail that would make any person watching the pageantry want to be in the shoes of those graduating. The students proudly walk the grounds of their institutions as banners that have flown for hundreds of years decorate the sky. They march in elaborate gowns and receive their degrees. While all graduations have a similar feel and all graduates exhibit a sense of pride, the look on the faces of graduating students of color at Ivy League institutions carries something uniquely different. These are students who are marching proudly across the stages of institutions that at some point in history would not admit them. The success of these students resonates with me in a unique way because in my role as a faculty member at one of these institutions, I have heard so many of them agonize over microaggressions committed by both faculty members and fellow students. During office hours, phone calls, and chance meetings in hallways, I have witnessed them wrestle with self-doubt as a result of these experiences. I have shared my own experiences with the same phenomena and wished I could tell them that the feeling is just par for the course in navigating higher education and that there is redemption on the other side of graduation—but sometimes there isn't.

When I hear the rousing welcome of the graduates into the club of alma mater and the cheers from friends and family that say to the graduates that they are finally among the "best and brightest," this brings a deep smile to my face. Unfortunately, my joy fades as I remember what life looks like on the other side of the ceremony for far too many. Those who have been convinced that this day, the moment when a piece of paper is handed to them, marks the beginning of their acceptance into a more perfect and more accepting world will soon discover that such a world doesn't truly exist. The narrative around struggling through school to have a better life is one that I, and many other educators whose hearts are in the right place, have had a part in disseminating and perpetuating. We have learned that one of our chief roles as educators is to convince students that they should withstand the challenges of schooling so they can have a better life afterwards. Education has become defined as a set of exercises in delaying gratification or withstanding a life without joy or pleasure for the sake of having those things later. We tell this story because we want to believe it. It was told to us when we were in school, and even though many never experienced the joy that was promised when we completed the process, we keep telling the story. There are millions of people who withstood traumatic experiences in schools because they were told it would pay off later but who ended up broken (doubting themselves and questioning their intelligence) and expecting to be healed from their brokenness with careers and wealth that either never come or when it comes, brings no joy and no mechanism for healing the damage to the self that schools caused.

Others leave school with what I previously described as educational Stockholm syndrome in which they develop feelings of affinity for the system that stole them away from their ratchet selves. Victims of schooling who have been snatched away from their authentic selves and forced into institutions designed to break them down psychologically and emotionally still feel connected to these institutions and end up looking for jobs or taking on roles that give them the same feelings they had in school because it is what they have grown accustomed to. That feeling of brokenness is all they think they deserve and all they think other folks deserve as well. Folks still believe that schools are functioning for the greater good and will "pay off" because a narrative to the contrary is too heartbreaking to consider. Graduating, even if the process to get there is damaging to a sense of self, is framed as a necessary prerequisite to greater opportunities and a brighter life because it is too hurtful to imagine that there is no other side to a life someone who does not love you has designed for you. For Black folks in particular, the notion that suffering at the hands of White-controlled institutions (like slavery or schooling) is a prerequisite to a better afterlife have been part of stories told since the first enslaved Africans arrived on these shores. If you listen to your masters, even if they beat you, you will make it to judgment day and then heaven. If you obey your teachers and follow the school rules, you will make it to graduation, a good job, and a better life. Because this narrative has been ingrained into the psyche for generations, segments of the population believe that experiencing harm (including microaggressions and self-doubt) at the hands of an institution not designed for them is to be withstood because it is a path toward a more glorious future. Graduation day then becomes the threshold before redemption because it has been presented as the time when those who have harmed you will finally recognize you and give you a degree that will unlock a better and brighter future. It is not that students who have fought for access and resources in education all of a sudden start to trust people who have intentionally and unintentionally harmed them; it is that they have been convinced that the world is better after graduation because their hope has been attached to a brighter future they have earned through their previous struggles. The graduation ceremony is supposed to be the celebratory event that signals admission into this new world. However, after graduation, many students realize the hypocrisy of the institutions they attended and that a college degree cannot heal the brokenness they feel.

In the midst of the perfectly scripted magic of the graduation ceremony, the most truthful part is when the graduates' names are called and the students walk proudly across the stage to receive their diploma and are handed a piece of paper that is not the diploma they earned but a prop. The diploma you are given on graduation day, which is sold as a passport to being valued and respected by society, is counterfeit. Many students don't get the real one until they have paid the university any monies/fees the institution says they owe. After receiving their actual diploma, they realize it is more of a brochure advertising a better life than a passport that grants access to the future they were sold on. Beneath the graduation spectacle are emotions that have not been faced and a brokenness that has not been healed.

A few years ago, the institution where I work started a tradition of a separate graduation ceremony for first-generation college students. It was a wonderful idea that recognizes the challenges of those who may not have had the social networks or family models to navigate higher education and who persisted anyway. First-generation college students attend the larger graduation ceremonies for all students but are also invited to this more intimate ceremony that honors the fact that they are part of a special group who made it to a milestone that no one else in their family had achieved. A speaker at the graduation a few years ago remarked that "what these graduates have done is change the trajectory of their lives, the lives of their families, and those of generations to come."

At the third first-generation graduation ceremony, Black and Brown students who had recently earned master's and doctoral degrees and their friends and families filled the auditorium. The friends and families had been seated first and then, after an announcement came blaring through the speakers, students, whom many would argue represent the best that their communities had to offer, filed into the auditorium. They were dressed in their powder-blue regalia and black caps and beamed with pride as their loved ones cheered for them as they entered. During the event, a number of students were given the opportunity to address their fellow graduates and their families. Each speech was personal and deeply emotional. Some students shared the challenges of growing up in poverty, and others described the sacrifices their families made for them to get their education. As always, these narratives resonated with me, but then I started noticing an interesting theme in each of the speeches. Students were not just telling tales of their struggles and what it took to get on the graduation stage; they were all telling stories about their experiences in schools. I heard many different narratives about how it felt to be the only one in classes who didn't feel smart and how students and even faculty questioned their abilities. These were incredibly capable Black and Brown graduates from one of the most prestigious institutions in the world expressing self-doubt and feelings of inadequacy at a moment that is supposed to be the pinnacle of their academic accomplishments. Somehow, even after their "greatest accomplishment," they felt less than. This phenomenon is what many psychologists and physicians have identified as *impostor syndrome*.

Impostor syndrome is mostly experienced by high-functioning people from historically marginalized groups in academic and professional spaces that were not necessarily designed for them.[1] It causes brilliant people to become paralyzed by what they perceive to be their deficiencies, even when these deficiencies don't really exist. I suggest that it is one of the most pervasive aftereffects of the erasure of the ratchet and authentic self because one's academic identity becomes built on a false persona. By this, I mean that after the ratchet self and core identity get erased, the person who remains is an empty shell of the real person. This shell then navigates institutions, hopes they get told they are smart, and keeps on "succeeding" until graduation. The students at graduation are the ones who have withstood the loss of their ratchet selves, spent their lives performing brilliance as defined by an institution, and suffered assaults to who they are, as schools demonize people who look like them. At graduation, they truly believe that redemption will eventually come. However, it never will because these individuals will always see themselves as less than and undeserving. Dena Simmons has brilliantly articulated how students of color experience impostor syndrome when they attend White boarding schools and other settings that do not center their experiences.[2] I suggest that impostor syndrome extends into the workplace and throughout the lifespan in a more widespread and traumatizing way than those who have never experienced it can imagine. It is a loss of self, coupled with unfulfilled promises of wholeness and a never-ending pursuit of redemption.

Impostor syndrome causes folks to question their existence and to see themselves as inadequate. Conversely, it causes them to see value, worth, and intelligence in everyone other than themselves. They feel like impostors because they see others as being better than them and cannot fathom that a better version of themselves is within them. Without the recognition of their own excellence, they will always judge themselves through the lens of the perceived excellence of others. In a previous chapter, I discussed the experiences of excellent sheep and the ways that society judges all others based on their experiences. Here, I want to emphasize that the reverse is essential: not only must there be a recognition of the genius that is embedded in the ratchetness of those from marginalized communities, but they should be seen as the benchmark of genius. What I am suggesting here is a role reversal of sorts in order to highlight the distinct areas of superiority that folks who inhabit subaltern positions (those who have been sociopolitically pushed outside of the power structure) have. I am calling for consideration of arenas like moral superiority, which folks from communities of color consistently outperform their counterparts in. I am calling for an expectation that all folks within schools meet the high moral benchmarks that Black folks like

Stacey Abrams achieve in terms of overcoming brokenness and still committing oneself to the greater good. Without an intentionally ratchetdemic approach to teaching and celebrating contemporary heroes who look like them, youth will always pursue acceptance from a dominant group who lacks the genius that Black youth already possess. The goal here is not just valuing the ratchetness in ourselves and in young people; it is ensuring that there is an acknowledgment of a ratchetdemic advantage. A ratchet understanding of the world formed by challenge-induced resilience, poverty-shaped creativity, and hip-hop-informed power with words far surpassing whatever a person who has not experienced lack or struggle can ever possess—and it must be held as a standard. Academic knowledge or "book smarts" can be gained by simply spending time with whatever there is to be studied or learned. Ancestral resilience and experiential knowledge that shape outlook and vision are not as easily attainable. They are what makes someone academic and intellectual. The issue we currently have is that we have allowed powerful experiences to be framed as imperfections, and we've allowed folks without such experiences to claim their lack of them as an advantage. With a more expansive view of what is required to be smart or intelligent, it becomes clear that those who have been identified as such are lacking much while those who have been positioned as outside the tradition of intelligence, or smartness, are actually closest to it. Pedagogically, the ratchetdemic educator who highlights this truth for young people and celebrates them for their expression of ratchet brilliance changes the way they look at themselves and the world. An effortless, witty comeback; the ability to construct or decode text in the form of rap lyrics or other prose with ease; and creativity birthed from lacking material resources are each forms of brilliance that must be named and identified as such. Most importantly, leveraging them to attain book knowledge is EVERYTHING!

Young people who have worked with ratchetdemic educators and start seeing the possibility of merging their ratchet and academic selves develop natural gifts in magical ways. Even if what they hold is misidentified by the world as valueless, they see themselves as intelligent and worthy of love. They begin to live and learn in a world that they construct where there is no desire for validation and/or complicity from folks who refuse to see their genius. They see value in who they are and then pursue academic knowledge for the sake of learning. Having young people reach this point must be the goal of schooling. There is no need for instilling empty hope that comes from living for the purpose of possibly being legitimized by those who oppress you. There is a level of self-confidence that comes from operating in one's genius that surpasses whatever fleeting version one gets at a graduation ceremony. Every day feels like graduation when one operates from a place of freedom and can always be one's authentic self. I suggest that many who have "made it" to heights that many like them have not are saddled by impostor syndrome, because they tossed their ratchet away when it appeared like an imperfection. They're credentialed but broken because they lost their ratchet and are afraid to go looking for it. They have trained themselves to move through schools and offices in a way that is not threatening to those in charge. They only speak when spoken to, never question authority, keep eye contact, memorize what they are told to memorize, spew it back out when tested, don't express too much emotion, don't dress too colorfully or appear too stylish, speak at a certain volume, and distance themselves from others who look like them. They follow these rules with a desire for being close to power without recognizing that what they are chasing is weaker than what they already have or what they once had. In reality, those who we have been told they are excellent are the true impostors, because they are framing themselves to be perfect when they are fundamentally incomplete. They have no ratchet to draw from or their forms of ratchet are deficient in comparison to what folks who continually experience real life possess.

My point here is not to dismiss the emotional and psychological impact of experiencing impostor syndrome. The feelings that come from experiencing it are legitimate. However, it is important to remember that feeling like an impostor is often rooted in not recognizing that historically marginalized folks have always operated on a higher moral and intellectual plane than the rest of the world. What has been described as hood rules—which include giving and expecting respect, not being or acting like someone you're not, minding your business, and representing "your people" well—are basic rules of engagement in urban America that are not part of how schools operate. Folks who are accustomed to hood rules have to bend themselves to the world's idea of morality and genius, even though they have been framed as having to reach up for it. Michelle Obama's proclamation that when they go low, we go high presents a challenge for the ratchetdemic. Because we are already high. When they go low, just standing as we are is going high. The challenge is having to always bend down to those who are less than you and, in too many instances, getting stuck being bent or breaking in the process. When we consider ratchetdemic ways of being in the world, we begin to stand in our worth and start seeing that institutions stand on their power because without it they don't have much else. Once you are in the rooms they have not designed for you, but you have earned your right to be in them, know that it is because you have not only what they have but also what they can never get. Your ratchetness unleashes the ultimate genius that reveals the real impostors. Do not deny your ratchet self when you have a seat at the table. Many times, your expression of it, mixed with showing your command of what systems expect, is what magnifies both your genius and their deficien cies. Once teachers recognize this and model it for students, teaching and learning become more about residing in genius than being maligned by an invisible force that tells students of color that they are never good enough.

Teaching well requires healing from both impostor syndrome and any hang-ups about what we have allowed others to identify as imperfections. This includes everything from feelings about our overall worthiness to feelings about how we look. Any piece of ourselves that we fail to face and accept will impact our ability to be free and, consequently, our ability to teach and learn. Owning your ratchetdemic self is not just about holding on to an unpolished or hood identity. It is also about developing an appreciation for your full self. For folks of color this involves the very challenging and often ignored work of loving our complexions, the size and shape of our bodies and noses, and even the texture of our hair. An acceptance of all of this is preparation for teaching. When we are looking at White standards of beauty to gauge our attractiveness, it is impossible to challenge Whiteness as it relates to intelligence. We can never reach a sense of fully accepting who we are as thinkers and academics when we are still uncomfortable about how we look and don't see the magic in how ratchetdemic folks do seemingly insignificant but magical things like blend more traditional styles with more aesthetically rich community-rooted ones. There is magic in natural Black hair in locs and Afros being worn by teachers and academics in formal institutions. There is stylistic superiority in the right pair of kicks paired with a suit or blazer.

My argument for ratchetdemic approaches to being in the world includes an appreciation of our physical attributes and a recognition of the subconscious damage we do to ourselves by not accepting those forms of beauty, art, and style. We have all heard of the great Black thinkers of our time and even comedians highlight the irony in folks of color dying their hair or bleaching their skin to look more White, while White folks who have not been blessed with melanin spend endless hours at tanning salons or in the sun in an attempt to get their skin darker. Each group of people is in search of a perfection that doesn't exist because the closest one can ever get to perfect is recognizing and appreciating their own beauty. When I share my thoughts on loving who you are and accepting what you look like as well as what you culturally have to offer, I am often looked at like this is outside the scope of teaching and learning. What I want educators to understand is that if you don't love yourself, you can't love anyone else, and love is the engine that drives good teaching. Finding and loving the ratchetdemic in you is the most essential part of teaching.

During my first year of teaching, I was assigned to teach math and science in a middle school in the Bronx. On paper, I was well equipped to teach there. I was young, energetic, well-credentialed, and from the same community where I was teaching. However, when I got in the classroom, I struggled. I had a bout of self-doubt about my ability to teach and was trying to be what I thought a good teacher was. I thought that this required discipline, endless rules, and a hyper-structured classroom. This ended up leading to student resentment and my inevitable ineffectiveness. Over the course of the school year, I had one or two days when I felt like I was really reaching the students. On one of those days, I was teaching a lesson on ratio and proportion and stumbled into a connection to forensic science and crime solving. Somehow, I wrapped the lesson into the solving of a crime that had recently happened in the neighborhood, and I had gotten the students' attention. I retold the news story that they all knew about already and then transitioned into how crimes like these get solved. Slowly, I made a connection to the videotape evidence from the crime and how scientists can determine the height of the person who committed the crime and other data about the perpetrator using ratio and proportion. I hooked them. I had hit pedagogical pay dirt.

I skillfully transitioned into a set of word problems. These are word problems that would not have been attempted if I didn't set them up with my cultural relevance and pedagogical dexterity. It was magical. The entire class of thirty was working on their word problems. I breathed deeply. I was actually doing this. I was *teaching*. I had left the lesson plan, paid attention to my intuition, and brought in something all the students had recently either experienced or heard of. The students responded by paying attention in a way they had not before, and my self-confidence grew. This felt like graduation. As soon as I breathed in this new sense of self as teacher, a student who had not been able to witness my last twenty minutes of teaching genius because he was late walked in from the hallway. When he walked in, his peers were working individually on math problems. He scanned the room, seemed to take in the rare peace in the classroom and purpose in his peers and decided to disrupt it. He announced himself loudly with "What's good, y'all?" and proceeded to walk over to his classmates and give a succession of handshakes and loud greetings. Those he walked over to were distracted, and everyone saw the humor in the situation and started laughing. I stood in front of the class completely despondent. My first good day was ruined. I looked at him angrily, and he responded with a look of falsified innocence as he shrugged his shoulders and said, "What? I just walked in." I immediately felt a wave of emotion that was a mix of anger, frustration, and disappointment. Perhaps I wasn't as good at teaching as I thought just a few minutes ago because I didn't know how to handle this situation. The student's raw and ratchet response revealed something powerful in me and my belief in my role as a teacher. I felt like an impostor. I wondered what it was that I had to offer the students. The moment of quiet I had when all the students were working on an assignment was a glimmer of hope that I could possibly be good enough to teach. When that student walked in and disrupted the silence, it highlighted my self-doubt, even though I was not yet willing to admit that it existed.

My first verbal reaction to him saying "I just walked in" came as a rapid-fire set of questions sent with ill intent and expected to paralyze him into compliance. It was a model I had seen from other teachers and that I had experienced as a student. I shouted, "WHY ARE YOU LATE? YOU NEED A PASS! YOU ARE DISRUPTING MY LESSON," and then, "WHY DON'T YOU JUST GO BACK WHERE YOU CAME FROM?" The first question and statements were initially ignored but as soon as the last one left my lips, I realized it struck a nerve as he looked up from giving his friend a handshake and glared at me. I responded by doubling down on my question, "AS YOU CAN SEE, THE CLASS WAS FINALLY WORKING BEFORE YOU WALKED IN. JUST GO BACK WHEREVER YOU CAME FROM!" That last statement was meant in reference to wherever he came from before he walked into my class that day, but he interpreted it differently. He responded, "Where I came from? I'm Mexican, you want me to go back to Mexico?" I immediately fumbled together a series of words about how I loved Mexican people and had Mexican friends, which caused me in that moment to appear biased. This is what not knowing yourself or being uncomfortable in your ratchet self does. It highlights the bias within you and moves you to lead with it. If we had a more ratchetdemic classroom, a lateness would not have been seen as a disruption to the lesson. We would have flowed anyway. If I was comfortable with who I was or even who I used to be at his age, I would've known that his intention was not to disrupt but to be seen. His loud "What's good, y'all?" would have warranted an equally loud "What's good?" and then a continuing on with the lesson. In many ways, he reminded me of myself at that age.

When I was a teenager, I was known as Chris with the long hair. My hair was part of my identity. Most days it was braided into neat cornrows, and on those days when I wanted a natural boost of confidence, I would wear it out and let it dance on the nape of my neck as I played basketball. My long hair was my infallible ego boost until I turned about twenty, and I noticed my hair thinning just a tad at my temples. It wasn't something anyone else had noticed or mentioned, but I noticed it, and it impacted me. I would look at my slowly receding hairline in the mirror and wish my hair was back. A few years later, as I began my teaching career in the Bronx, I kept my braids even though my hairline traveled further north. No one ever mentioned it, so it was something that I only worried about when I was alone. My long hair was part of my identity, and I held on to it because it gave me the small bit of confidence I needed to enter into a profession in which my confidence was constantly under assault by administrators who believed so little in my ability to teach that everything they handed me to teach was completely scripted. This day was different. I followed my intuition, left the script, and was having a successful lesson when, all of a sudden, everything that I thought was working well was being compromised by this one student.

I looked at the class and it seemed that one student had found a way to rally them all against me, even though, just minutes before, we were having what I thought was an amazing class. Now they were responding to his every move, laughing at his antics, and looking at me with disdain when I rambled on about him going back to where he came from. I assessed the situation and decided that if he was going to disrupt me, I'd call the school safety officers to remove him from the class. I walked to the telephone at the front and declared, "I am calling security." As I picked up the phone to make the call, the student walked up behind me. As I grabbed the phone, he grabbed my arm. In response, I flung my hand back and told him to back away from me. To ensure that I was clear, I chose to speak to him in a way that would ensure that he understood I was being serious. I repeated slowly, "Fam, fall back. You need to fall back." The whole class was watching the exchange intently as I told him one last time to fall back. There was an odd silence in the room for a second that seemed like an eternity, and then he finally responded with, "Fall back? Like your hairline." An *ooh* erupted from the class as students giggled and then laughed hysterically. It took me a moment to catch the wit within the insult. No one had ever publicly mentioned my receding hairline. I was mortified. I quickly bounced back with, "No, fall back like your grades if you don't get started on this work." He smiled. I returned the smile. No school officers were called, and no other major disruptions happened. We saw each other for who we were. We undid the tensions from earlier because in that moment I matched his ratchet. The class laughed at us both as I massaged my hairline in front of them, and we returned to learning.

When that day passed, the energy in my classroom was a little different. I was a bit more of myself. I had a long way to go to be effective, but I was on the path toward being a better teacher. I am not suggesting that this response would have worked the same way for other teachers. I am saying that in that moment, he and I had an exchange with our authentic selves that had not happened previously. He was a younger version of me. I had played the dozens (where community members from shared social environments tease each other in good fun for entertainment and to sharpen each other's wit) a thousand times before. This was all in good fun, and I knew

how to play that game. There was no need for me to perform the role
of the angry teacher who called security. My ratchet and hood self
knew that calling the officer was a violation of hood rules. He did
not have to perform being the thug kid who would put his hands on
a teacher. In that moment, we eliminated the need to battle versions
of ourselves that the institution scripted for us. He just wanted to be
seen, and I just wanted to be a good teacher. Being ourselves allowed
us to see that. Not operating from a place of fullness or truth about all
that you are will always manifest as feeling less than when you enter
into spaces not designed for you. However, if you own and love all of
who you are, it doesn't matter if a space was designed for you because
you operate within it knowing all that you bring to it makes it better.
You no longer exist to try to fit into spaces; you exist to transform
them. The alternative to not operating in your full self is a perpetual
frustration.

The frustration with not being able to express yourself is the tension that exists when you have to hide who you are or dim your light
for the comfort of an institution or individuals within it. It is captured
in the ever-present struggle the ratchetdemic educator faces when
someone in the school building tells them that they are being too
friendly with students and in the scrutiny they receive for bringing
their out-of-school talents into the school. To get beyond that tension
and ensuing frustration, they must trust in who they are and what they
have to offer the world. This allows one to embrace a radical vulnerability that is at the root of being ratchetdemic. Owning how you look
and talk, facing your fears about being inferior, and then recognizing
the uniqueness of your particular ways of looking, talking, and being
in the world are how you claim power, even in the face of institutions
and their agents who try to make you feel inadequate.

UNAPOLOGETIC: TOWARD A THEORY OF RATCHET HUMILITY

There are educators who have taken up the charge to teach and be
ratchetdemic and who have transformed the lives of their students by

becoming more authentic versions of themselves and transforming the way they teach. Once they are their true selves in the classroom, they hold a magic that propels them beyond the institutions they are in and the positions they hold and into a certain divine position. They move with a regal spirit that intimidates a lot of the adults around them who work in the same building but do not operate with purpose. These types of teachers are often more preoccupied with connecting with students and spend less time trying to force relationships with other teachers. This is particularly the case if their colleagues are not aligned with the teacher's mission of creating learning spaces where students feel whole and are able to express themselves freely as they learn.

One major critique that other teachers will have of these ratchetdemic educators is that they are arrogant or lack humility. "She doesn't want to spend time with the other teachers. She is so arrogant." "Look at how he just walks around like he runs the school." As mentioned earlier, haters will always have something to say to distract from the mission of the ratchetdemic educator. However, when trying to disparage the educator is not enough, haters will question the educators' humility and attack them at a deeply personal level. This form of attack on the ratchetdemic educator is particularly hurtful because the work of teaching and being ratchetdemic is full of professional sacrifices and is guided by a spirit of service. It is for this reason that the field of education must critically look at humility and the way it has been weaponized against teachers who refuse to be silent puppets of standards, empty rules, and curriculum. The ratchetdemic educator refuses to be victimized by someone else's perverse notion of humility. As we work toward being more humble in our roles as listeners and practitioners, it is essential to understand that performing subservience is not the same thing as humility. Understand that folks will weaponize humility to keep radical educators subservient to institutional norms. They will expect you to get along with folks whose mission is counter to yours and use humility as the reason why you should blindly follow people who are against your mission.

Humility is not about refraining from ruffling feathers or being timid about speaking about what you and folks who look like you have done or are doing. It is appreciating the gift you have to do what you are doing for a living and recognizing that anybody else with the same combination of luck, opportunity, and circumstance could be doing it as well. For the ratchetdemic, if there is pride, it is pride in the fact that all who are like you have infinite potential and opportunity to be exceptional. It is speaking up for yourself and demanding to be seen because your visibility as your ratchet self elevates the larger mission of creating classrooms where the genius of young people is welcomed in its purest and most unadulterated forms. Young folks must understand that keeping their head and shoulders down and not speaking back when they are offended or dismissed betrays the ratchetdemic genius that they hold within. When they are not fully seen, or when their ratchet selves are being suppressed, the response is not to give those who enforce the status quo the pleasure of seeing their anger. It is choosing to continue operating with unapologetic expressions of one's ratchetdemic self—with pure conviction, truth, and intelligence.

We are all complex beings who are a combination of all our previous experiences. The person others see every day is simply a shell that we have both voluntarily and involuntarily constructed to make others more comfortable. Who we truly are is so complex and layered that the senses cannot grasp it. Because of the inability of people to fully grasp all of who we are, we go to extreme measures and oftentimes undergo severe trauma for the sake of shrinking ourselves into tiny morsels that are digestible to the unsophisticated. This is particularly the case for those who have been given positions of leadership within institutions but have had to subject themselves to subservience under those who "gave them the opportunity" to lead. For these people, the position of power or leadership they hold is attached to the consistent reminder that they need to be less than or hide pieces of themselves in order to keep it. The challenge for these folks is to remember that they have a responsibility to fulfill. In the words of Toni Morrison, "When you get these jobs that you have been so brilliantly prepared for, just remember that your real job is that if you are free, you need to free someone else. If you have some power, then your job is to empower someone else."[3]

CHAPTER 11

THE GET BACK

In this book thus far, I have made a number of arguments about why teachers and students must operate by knowing and being themselves and seeing themselves as intelligent and worthy of love. I argue that knowledge of self is the ultimate wealth, and navigating structures not designed for you to be succcesful requires tapping into that wealth to activate the hope, stamina, and conviction to overcome the assault on working in your genius and expressing your gifts. A powerful example of this pursuance of self-worth in the face of incredible odds—and the labor it requires to retain one's self-worth within an institution/industry that fails to recognize you yet seeks to destroy you—is the story of Dapper Dan.

In 1944, Daniel Day was born in Harlem, New York, to a family who struggled financially but was rich in the desire to not let their circumstances define them. After pursuing a number of careers, and not finding much success in any of them, he realized that his true passion was in fashion. In the mid-1980s, Dapper Dan, as he came to be known, opened a luxury clothing store in Harlem, New York. Before long, he began to cater to a financially well-off clientele who included drug dealers, athletes, and entertainers. These were people who had some financial resources but were not welcome in most high-end designer stores. Besides, the luxury design houses did not make products that fit the bodies and style of Black folks. The clothes from traditional designers lacked flair and the type of details that mattered to folks from the hood who wanted to flaunt their newfound wealth and showcase their style.

Dapper Dan knew that designer brands like Fendi, Gucci, and Louis Vuitton had immense appeal, not because of their quality or style but because of what they signified—success and a high-class lifestyle. Their brand recognition made them valuable, and he recognized that if he could maximize this appeal in a style that matched the needs of his clientele, he would have a successful business. He decided to source some leather and find a way to print designer logos on the leather to create his own materials. He made prints that had luxury brand logos all over them and would often blow up the size of the logos to make them more visible. He would make hats, shirts, jackets, and even car accessories that carried the names of the top designers and transform them into styles that the original designers would have never imagined. His pieces were uniquely made for his clients and had a certain flair that the fashion world had never seen. Before long, everyone who was in the know would go to Dapper Dan's store. Famous Black athletes and entertainers like Mike Tyson and LL Cool J would wear designs that were Dapper Dan's reimagining of the famous logos. The world began to take notice, and his designs were internationally recognized. Once the brands found out that their logos were being used, they connected with law enforcement and eventually the FBI raided Dapper Dan's store. They seized everything he had amassed since he started his career in fashion. In one fell swoop, they shut down his business and livelihood. He was left with absolutely nothing.

For decades, Dapper Dan "went underground," traveling from city to city trying to reestablish himself, with very little success. In 2017, a lifetime after he was driven from his business and was financially ruined, he found himself still in Harlem, looking for an opportunity to reclaim his past glory. That same year, Louis Vuitton started making outfits that featured an enlarged logo that harkened back to Dapper Dan's clothes. Dan's interpretation of the logo was about making it be larger than life and hypervisible. Across the world, at a fashion show in Florence, Gucci presented a "new" line of designer clothes. Most of the outfits on the models also seemed to harken back to Dapper Dan and his designs. One outfit in particular caused an enormous stir. It was a jacket made from a mix of materials. It had enlarged shoulders and slim sleeves and was an exact replica of a jacket Dapper Dan had made years ago. Before long, an image of the "new" Gucci jacket side by side with a photo of Dapper Dan's jacket had started making the rounds on social media. Olympic track star Diane Dixon, who was the woman in the now famous photo of Dapper Dan's jacket, attested to the fact that it was her in the jacket and that the picture was taken in 1988. She was a fan of Dapper Dan's work and had forged a relationship with him after she won an Olympic gold medal in 1984. Following an endless stream of tweets and Instagram posts about cultural appropriation and the need for companies like Gucci to pay homage to creatives like Dapper Dan, Gucci reached out to him and offered him a position with their company. News outlets from *People* to the *New York Times* covered the story. This was a man whose genius had led to an all-out assault on everything he had built. There was no attempt by the fashion houses to see his creativity and talent. They never considered compromising with him. Their sole intention, when they saw his talent, was to shut him down. Years later he was inspiring their style, and they were replicating designs he had created. They also worked with him to open a Dapper Dan Gucci store in Harlem where he creates exclusive designs with material sourced by Gucci. The collaboration between Dapper Dan and Gucci is unprecedented in the fashion industry. He operates his own store that bears his name and consults with the company on their designs. They provide him with their fabrics and he creates what he sees and wants. He has emerged as one of the few self-taught tailors in an overwhelmingly White fashion industry to create a new model for partnership that opens up the space for other Black entrepreneurs to showcase their talent.

In 2017, shortly after the company started collaborating with Dapper Dan, there was a controversy when Gucci designers created a black turtleneck sweater that covered the lower half of the face and had a cutout, framed in red, for the mouth. The sweater eerily resembled blackface (a racist tradition in which White folks would wear makeup to depict Black folks in the most heinous ways possible). Gucci's turtleneck was seen by many to be deeply offensive, and there was a windfall of articles and social media posts that made it clear that the company had to be held responsible for its racism. In response, Gucci quickly removed the sweater from its shelves, but for Dan and other Black folks, that was not enough to erase the offense. Dan responded by holding Gucci to account and pushing them to make significant changes to how they do business. As the controversy made its rounds on social media, Dapper Dan made a social media post that read, "I am a Black man before I am a brand. . . . There is no excuse nor apology that can erase this kind of insult. The CEO of Gucci has agreed to come from Italy to Harlem this week to meet with me, along with members of the community and other industry leaders. There cannot be inclusivity without accountability. I will hold everyone accountable."[1] The end result was a fund and scholarship to support diversity and inclusion in fashion, support for a number of nonprofits, and the creation of a council of community members to keep the organization accountable.

What is fascinating about how this scenario has played out is that Dapper Dan, after a career in which the fashion industry ruined him, had the responsibility and power to hold the company accountable for its racist actions. For Dapper Dan and the clients he had before he partnered with the luxury brand, the big fashion houses and their logos had an exclusive power that they wanted to have access to. His Blackness, his Harlem roots, and his lack of formal training were gifts. In an industry that dismissed him, he held the gift. He could have created his own brand and logo, but he knew that whatever he created, no matter how good it was, would not be seen as having the same value as the established brands.

The narrative of Dan's life in fashion is a powerful metaphor for the relationship a lot of folks of color who are socioeconomically disadvantaged have with schools and formal education. They see the value and power that education garners, they want to be a part of it, but they are well aware that the system is not designed for them to be successful. It is not that they don't see the value of education; it is that they don't have access to power within it.

Dapper Dan had to get access to the power the fashion houses held and combine that with his natural talents. He knew he had something valuable to offer that would become recognized if it could be merged with the "brand name." He knew that by merging his talent with the luxury logos, his talent would be recognized for what it is. That's when he decided to buy machines that print on leather to make his own designer fabric.

The point here is that Dapper Dan was successful at bringing two worlds together because he knew that what he had to offer was valuable, despite how it was seen by the fashion industry. The industry didn't have the foresight to identify his talent. Instead of initially embracing or learning from him, they dismissed him and what he was doing. They predetermined that he was worthless, even though Black folks saw his worth. The issue was never the talent he possessed; it was that he had the audacity to have the talent and the ingenuity to be better than them at their own game. This is the case with Black youth and urban education. They are smarter than their teachers, more innovative and creative than their counterparts, and generate ways of sharing information through music and art that schools have not even figured out yet.

When Dan's store in Harlem was shut down in the 1980s, the fashion houses would never admit that there was anything special about Dan's street-savvy designs. They were dismissed as too street, too raw, too ratchet. However, years later, as they recreated his ideas, it became clear that what they claimed to be too ratchet was actually ahead of its time. This is the way schools view Black children. They are too loud and too expressive for some, but they are sharing the future of education that schools have not yet seen.

In education, the advanced degree is like the designer fabric/logos that Dapper Dan coveted. He needed the logos not because they were any better than what he created but because of the stature they afforded those who wore them. Like Dapper Dan, young people have to understand that they can use the machines at their disposal to create their own version of the designer brand. By this, I mean that on their own, they can garner the same knowledge that schools profess to offer. In this season, more than ever before, young people can develop their own version of the established brand and be legitimized. They can be ratchet and pursue academic knowledge and certifications online. I don't want to dismiss the power the brand holds (he still needed their logos), but that power doesn't determine the value of what he created and the talent he has. I do want to make clear here that the ultimate goal isn't just about making your own version of the brand but about changing and infiltrating the system/structure that produced the original version to become an equal partner with the institution and still retaining your ratchetness. This happens by leaning into and trusting that the intellectual acumen that is expressed when one is ratchetdemic will always have value. Dan's designs were always going to transform the fashion industry because they came from a ratchet place. The loudness of the colors, the size of the logos, the detail of the designs were better than what the formally trained designers were doing. They inevitably had to come to him and create the opportunity for him to hold them accountable for their actions. He held a superiority to them by virtue of who he was.

Audre Lorde once stated that "the master's tools will never dismantle the master's house."[2] I wholeheartedly agree. However, my thought is that in education our work is not to destroy the master's house but to reimagine it—to claim it as our own with all the power and privilege it holds and then take it over—and utilize the power held within the institution to reimagine and repurpose it.

A reimagined and repurposed education shows young people that they can get the highest of grades and still wear clothing that represents who they are. They can be loud and smart. Street and luxury. They need to know that there is nothing scarier to a school-educated person with nothing else of substance to offer than showing them you have the same knowledge they have *and* your own natural flair. This is what made Dapper Dan so popular in his community but also made his presence so threatening to the status quo that they had no choice but to work with him. He found a way to get the power of the logo and still create his own designs. We must teach young people to be ratchet but also academic. Don't lose your hood identity, and still be academically excellent.

In the age of the internet, anyone can gain institutional knowledge about anything and use that knowledge to transform existing areas of study or bodies of work. Educators have a responsibility to teach young people to understand this truth. If what is produced reflects genius, it will travel across the world, and the little systems that attempted to devalue it will seek it out and desire to partner with it. The establishment will initially attempt to take away or discredit all that you have worked for and attempt to send you underground, but real genius cannot be confined. Genius, especially in the case of our young people, is the combination of experiences in communities, natural talent, and ancestral intuition. It cannot be permanently contained.

In the moments when Dapper Dan's genius was denied—when he was unable to express his art because the institution shut down his store and took away his livelihood—I am sure he experienced a loss of faith in his abilities. The same is true for ratchetdemic folks. When doubt in their gifts starts to emerge, the impostor syndrome creeps in. It is then that the ratchetdemic person has to trust in the gifts they have and be who they authentically are. This is the only way for them to be successful, and that success is about making a difference in the world. When one is operating in their authentic truth, the community recognizes who they are and what they are in the world. Community members will advocate for them and ensure that they get the position and recognition they deserve. The community that rallied around Dapper Dan when his ideas were adopted by Gucci led to his current partnership with the company. Like with Dapper Dan, this community support comes with community expectations.

This means that there is some responsibility that the ratchetdemic person has to ensure that the system is reimagined when they are operating within or in partnership with it. The community expects the ratchetdemic educator to call out the institution for its missteps in addressing their needs and to ensure that changes are implemented to reimagine the institution moving forward.

Ratchetdemic educators cannot be silent partners who stand in the background as decisions are being made for and about communities. They cannot be the person in the room who is the generator of good ideas but silent when it is time to discuss their implementation. Being ratchetdemic is to sit at the helm of the table, push the institution forward unapologetically, and ensure that the work being done is honest about meeting the needs of the most marginalized. The role of the ratchetdemic person is to highlight that a lot of "new," "revolutionary," and "progressive" initiatives in schools are not radical and involve systems adopting community-generated terminology but producing the same old cycle of failure and oppression. Approaches to instruction and engagement that folks of color have enacted daily until they were "discovered" and then trotted out like Dapper Dan's old design on the Gucci runway have to be brought to the fore and exposed for being fabrications and not improvements. Being ratchetdemic highlights the hypocrisy in socioemotional learning being advocated by institutions that don't value the ways Black youth express emotion. It reveals the hypocrisy in institutions touting cultural relevance when they have a perverse view of the culture of Black youth. The fact that terms like *socioemotional learning* and *cultural relevance* are used to pacify the public into watered-down versions of how folks engage within communities—and framed as innovations for communities who created the ideas to begin with—must be highlighted. With a radical honesty and unabashed authenticity, this is what ratchetdemic folks do.

It is not acceptable that folks are forced to adopt approaches to instruction that are weaker in potency than what they have envisioned or required for themselves and then are demonized for rejecting them. Just as we are not moved by folks tossing around phrases like *socioemotional learning* and *culturally relevant pedagogy*, we are not lulled to sleep by the hidden flaws in project-based learning, design thinking, critical listening, and advanced literacies because we have always taught within our communities with a keen awareness of the emotional comfort of learners in Black churches. We have always used an iterative process that runs from empathy to ideating and testing to solve real-life problems like not having heat or dealing with broken elevators in high-rise apartment complexes. We have always listened deeply and thoughtfully and asked questions after our elders and preachers spoke. We understand the need to develop different ways of communicating for different members of our community and develop different literacies for different street corners and neighborhoods. Ratchetdemic educators are more concerned about what good teaching looks like than what new education terms sound like.

Ideas, perspectives, and insights that are generated by ratchetdemic folks will always find a way to be expressed in the world. Dan's designs were going to make their way into the world on the level they were supposed to, when it was their season. It makes no difference how long the idea has been made dormant by the powers that be. It makes no difference whether society views the person who generates the idea as foolish or stupid. Good work will find a way into the world and change it. My experiences using hip-hop in education and facilitating hip-hop-rooted rap battles in science classrooms have transformed the learning experiences of a number of young people despite critiques from folks within schools and in academia who cannot see the power of hip-hop culture in the classroom even as they claim to be proponents of culturally relevant pedagogy. The issues we currently have in education are twofold. First, we have the powerful ideas/practices generated by ratchetdemic folks being watered down, repackaged, implemented in schools, and then used as an excuse to not engage in the more radical and ratchetdemic pedagogy they were rooted in. The second issue is with the dismissal of those who are the generators/initiators of ideas in a world that has removed the potency of those ideas and, consequently, the impact of those who created them. How do we acknowledge the collateral effects of folks being consistently broken down for being creatives and innovators? What happens when youth are being fed versions of their own culture that don't reflect their lived experience within it? What happens when the conditions we force them to live under break their spirit?

UNCLE TRUTH

He was tall and had deep entrancing eyes and an incredible presence. He was about fifteen years older than me but was somehow effortlessly in tune with everything that mattered to a fifteen-year-old. He knew the lyrics to all the songs that I secretly listened to, but he was still able to introduce me to songs I wouldn't have listened to otherwise. From him, I learned about the Last Poets and the Watts Prophets without having to be lectured on the history of Black music or the struggle for liberation. My favorite thing about him was that he knew all the latest slang and how to use it appropriately. He knew that *swag* was not a gift bag at the end of a conference and that *drip* had nothing to do with a faucet. He knew how young folks could make words evolve and take on meaning, and he was confident enough in who he was as a man of color and where he was in age to move with the times without losing any sense of self. He was my favorite uncle, and he was the ultimate cool. He would've been an amazing teacher.

Over the course of my life, he has been a touchstone to keep me in sync with the heartbeat of the hood as I navigate the pretentiousness of academia. Being the incredibly self-assured person he is, the advice he gave always amounted to a reminder to be myself and a reassurance that I have what it takes to be successful in whatever world I become a part of because of where and how I was raised. He had this amazing ability to see past pretense and pierce right to the core of any issue. Unfortunately, at one point in his life, in a story that can only be described as differing viewpoints on the same scenario, he was arrested and spent a few years in prison. I did not see him at all during his incarceration. My parents forbade me from visiting him. Their reasoning was partly due to how much I adored him and a fear that seeing him in jail would somehow glorify that place in my mind.

Months after his release from prison, I reached out to my uncle to take him out for a meal in celebration of his "new beginning." It was an invitation that I am sure he had received from others. Every person who comes out of jail receives invitations to meals that are surrounded with the language of new beginnings and the "start of a new life." It is part of the rules of engagement in the urban communities where I have lived and worked. I find it ironic that the same language that is used when someone is released from prison is also used when someone graduates from school. This is a "fresh start," the "beginning of the rest of your life," and "a chance to make something of yourself in the world." Each phrase about new beginnings is said without doing anything about the fact that telling someone they are physically free while putting them through a process where they are psychologically bound is not freedom, but manipulation. In the case of my uncle, and for many others who have become entangled with the criminal (in)justice or school cultural theft system, after a release from prison or a graduation, they are returning to the same circumstances that led them into the system to begin with. Only now, they have to contend with deep psychological and emotional wounds that come from the time they have served.

For our meal, I chose a restaurant in a nice part of town. It was one of those places with a beautiful extended awning and outdoor seating. We walked in, were guided by the hostess to a table, and settled into seats that faced the street. Well-dressed people walked up and down the sidewalk in front of us as we scanned the menu and decided on what we wanted. Once the waitress got to our table, we ordered our food and had a conversation about the many times that he taught me to love and speak up for myself. I told him that his words helped me to be strong and be free. He smiled deeply as I told stories of how I had taken his words and philosophies and applied them to aspects of my life.

Before long, the waitress placed our plates of food in front of us. She placed mine on the table first, and I commented on how beautiful the dish looked. I breathed in its scent, looked at my uncle, and watched as she placed his dish on the table. The second his plate touched the table, he cowered over the plate, covered it with his left hand, and ate at such an incredible pace and speed that passersby stopped and watched. It happened so quickly and without warning that I didn't say a word. Here we sat at this outdoor space with no roof above us being catered to by the most inviting smile, but my uncle had been so harmed by incarceration that he was still incarcerated. In his mind, he was still protecting his meal from the threat of someone taking it. He scarfed it down quickly to ensure that he got a chance to eat. Despite the smile on his face, he had been broken. Some may have viewed his eating without regard for those around him as an extension of him being unapologetic. He may even have been called ratchet. The reality is that in some scenarios this raw expression is an indicator of deep pain.

The point here is that even powerful folks who have developed confidence around their ratchet identity can be broken by a system that incarcerates them physically, mentally, or emotionally. These people will inevitably be dealing with the long-term consequences of this brokenness even after they leave the institutions that imposed the violence. When they express the collateral effects of the trauma they have undergone, they become a spectacle. Folks on the street will look on and be disgusted by the behavior they see without any consideration for what led to that behavior. Whether we are talking about jails or schools, the phenomenon is the same. People who show us their pain are seen as inconvenient interruptions to our normalcy even though they are reflections of who we are and what we do to each other.

The truth is, we were told our whole lives to love ourselves by folks who either never learned to love themselves or had that love for themselves beat out of them. They taught us with a beauty and strength that we came to discover was fragility, complicity, and hurt.

Now, to operate fully in the world, we must reveal our hurt, understand the ways that it has burrowed deep within us, and heal.

I have met parents who can't walk into their child's school for fear of being triggered and reminded of their own failures and shortcomings when they were in school and who do not possess the language to articulate what they are feeling. When I have met with them in their homes and asked why they don't come to their child's school, all they can say is that school isn't for them. I have heard parents say, "The teachers ain't trying to hear what I'm saying. I've tried to help him with the schoolwork, but I can't get into that building." These adults are describing their experiences in a system that was never designed to make them feel intelligent or valuable and which was successful in making them feel less than as evident by these parents' responses. Oftentimes, bad experiences within formal education reflect how schools have been designed to uphold White norms at the expense of Black lives and Black success. There are parents of children whose grandparents and great-grandparents were the descendants of slaves who experienced their own traumas around teaching and learning. I argue that there are generational traumas at play that come from going through experiences within institutions that many are struggling with but never mention because they don't have the language to articulate it. My uncle was going through severe trauma. Parents who cannot bring themselves to walk into schools that they send their children to are going through it as well. This trauma has to be named, understood, and addressed through a ratchedemic approach to teaching and learning that serves as a path toward healing.

CHAPTER 12

RESTITUTION OVER RESCUE MISSIONS

Despite the arguments laid out in this book about the need for embracing a ratchetdemic approach to being a better school leader/ teacher/student/person, many will choose to dismiss the arguments made thus far in favor of having things remain as they are. They will find justifications for why complicity is necessary for survival. One such argument will be that young people need to pass standardized exams, and the only way for them to do this is to follow the curriculum. Others will argue that they have been teaching for X number of years and have been successful enough so they cannot fathom doing things differently. Many more will resist doing the work necessary to find their ratchet self because of the personal discomfort associated with embarking on this journey. When this type of hesitation exists, particularly among Black educators, even in the midst of a global movement to decenter Whiteness and give value to Black lives, it is because the teacher has never experienced full citizenship and simply cannot understand what they have lost for their entire life. A teacher who has no value for self and who has been denied full citizenship cannot grasp the fact that the true purpose of teaching is to prepare young people to become full citizens of the world—with inalienable rights (of the body, to be fully actualized, and to all things that human beings deserve). I understand that those who read this text may opt not to disrupt the status quo. I also recognize that there are moments when subtlety may be the preferred approach to addressing flaws in the schooling system that we have all been a part of and, in many cases, benefited from. However, I also think we must recognize that we are living in unprecedented times that require boldness and bravery. Subtlety is preparation for a lifetime of complicity, and those who are confined by it tend to victimize others in the same way they're victimized, simply because they don't know any other way. The highest seat in the nation has recently been occupied by a person who didn't follow subtlety or any established norms of appropriateness. He was unapologetic about ignoring established rules for respectful engagement, used profanity to describe people from developing countries, and sent messages through social media riddled with misspellings and poor sentence structure. This lack of appropriateness and subtlety was expressed in pursuit of an agenda hell-bent on the denial of full citizenship or humanity of those who society has positioned as less than for reasons that range from their race, ethnicity, gender, sexuality, and political affiliation. The protection from retribution he was offered for driving divisiveness can only be counteracted with an unapologetic pursuit of healing and wholeness not contained by subtlety or appropriateness.

Choosing to be ratchetdemic is choosing to challenge respectability and what those who have power cherish the most—their power and the security it affords them. Being ratchetdemic is choosing to no longer be agreeable with your discomfort or the oppression of children through pedagogies that rob them of their genius, even in its most raw and unpolished forms. Most importantly, it is the restoration of the rights of the body to those who have been positioned as undeserving of them. By "the rights of the body," I refer to seven rights articulated within Buddhist tradition. These are identified most clearly in the book *Eastern Body, Western Mind*, which, although not directly related to education, can serve as a guide for teaching and learning. The seven rights of the body identify what has been denied to students when they are robbed of the opportunity to be ratchetdemic.[1] These rights—to be here, to feel, to act, to love, to speak, to see, and to know—are at the essence of teaching and learning. Educators who anchor their teaching in the restoration of these rights to young people use their pedagogy as protest against the ways that emotional and psychological violence against young people has been normalized in schools.

The right to be here is the first and most fundamental right of the body. In education, it must be modified to the right to be here as you are. For that right to be granted, young people must feel as though their presence in the classroom, in whatever way they choose to express it, is always welcome. Ratchetdemic teaching begins by recognizing that students—especially Black students, who typically feel unwelcome in schools—have the right to be there. Their comfort and agency are compromised by the norms of the institution. Consequently, they feel as though school is not for them. This denial of the right to be here affects not just their comfort in the physical classroom but their ability to learn. The restoration of this right is a fundamental component of working with young people to become ratchetdemic. It is accomplished in the classroom by explicitly stating when students walk into the school and/or the classroom for the first time that the entire enterprise of schooling is about them. Students must be told they have a right to be there, and they must be reminded that school is not about anything other than ensuring that they are whole and learning. This is where statements like, "This is your school," "This is your classroom," and "I work for you" become essential until it is understood by students that because of divine rights they have been born with, wherever their feet tread is a space they have a right to take up and are welcome.

The second right—the right to feel—is about ensuring that students have the space to express their emotions and the vocabulary to name what they are feeling. Human beings are born with the right to feel. It is an essential right to return to young people because in schools students are only afforded a very limited range of emotions. In the eyes of teachers, Black youth (in particular) can be only angry or agreeable. A number of actions that are indictors of a bevy of emotions are attributed to anger and addressed as though they are rooted in negative intentions. If Black or Brown students are curious or unclear with instructions, they are perceived as angry and questioning authority. If they are frustrated, sad, or pensive, they are perceived as angry. In fact, for too many students anything other than blind complicity is read as anger and confronted with the wrath of the institution and its operatives. The work of the educator then becomes working with young people to name their emotions—sharing the language that helps them to identify what and how they are feeling—while creating the space for these emotions to be felt and expressed without demonizing young people. This right also involves creating classroom spaces where young people can share their emotions about what is going on in the world without judgment and have a teacher who can model how to work through these emotions.

The third right that must be restored to students in order for them to have the ideal learning space and be fully actualized is the right to act. Once students are afforded the right to feel, they must also have the right to act on how they feel. Being able to name how you feel must be accompanied by having the space to act on those emotions in order to feel free. As long as the act does not violate the rights of someone else, acting on an emotion is a way to feel affirmed and confirm the right to be present and take up space. In classrooms, creating space and time for the physical expression of emotions is essential. A moment in the class to scream and a corner in the class to move demonstrates a value for the students' full self.

The fourth right of the body is the right to love and also be loved. This right is about agape love—the love of others for the good of humanity and betterment of society—and also about opening up the space for students to express a love for the people and things in their world that have significance to them even if they lack value in schools. The love of music, sports, and cultural artifacts and figures must be allowed in the classroom. The love of people and the space to express that love is also important. The work of ratchetdemic educators is to ensure that they teach about and with the artifacts and people that students love. Pedagogically, the right to love recognizes that there is no more compelling emotion than love, and there is no place where love is more needed than in learning. Activating the love young people have for phenomena that are perceived to be nonacademic in classrooms—and loving them enough to be creative and uncomfortable in uncovering the connections between those phenomena and academic content—transforms the nature of teaching and learning and restores a lost right to students.

The fifth right of the body is the right to speak. This right involves creating space where the voice of the student is not compromised or distorted in the pursuit of learning or being "better educated." The right to speak is about being welcome to speak in one's own tongue, dialect, or accent and honoring that right even if and when the discourse of power is different. The right to speak is not just about having voice but speaking truth to power. The ratchetdemic educator creates pathways and platforms for young people to speak about issues in the school, the community, and society to those who hold positions of power and authority. This is not about providing a voice to students. It is about amplifying their voices and providing them with access to those who hold power so that their voices can be heard. The right to speak requires creating curriculum that provides opportunities for young people to speak both within and beyond the classroom.

The sixth right is the right to see. It involves the recognition that students have the right to see things from a different perspective than the teacher or the school. The right to see is the right to have and express inner visions in the tradition of Stevie Wonder—a deep and reflective excavation of self as it relates to society and an expression of one's vision of the world based on one's reality. To allow young people to see things differently and then allow their visions to come to life in the classroom restores a faith in their own visions of the world and provides the classroom and the school with new approaches to transforming education to meet the needs of young people. The educator must consistently challenge students to envision the classroom and the world differently. The right to see is about activating the imagination and creating a classroom with young people that is closest to where they are most free to learn.

The seventh and final right is the right to know. In the classroom, this right is connected to the fact that schools deny Black children the right to know about themselves, their history, their legacy, and the causes for the inequities they live under. The right to know is compromised by the low expectations that teachers hold of students and the belief that students are not prepared to know about the inequities of the world or ill equipped to understand what is perceived to be rigorous academic content. The right to know is also the right to be challenged academically and to have all the information needed to understand the world shared with you. I argue that once all the other rights of the body have been provided, youth thrive when they have the right to know because their full selves are affirmed and free to accept and pursue knowledge.

Many will misconstrue the provision of the rights of the body in pursuit of being ratchetdemic as intentionally undermining established norms simply for the sake of being disagreeable. Some will read all I have written so far and misconstrue this as a lack of value for formal education. Neither is the case. This is not about unbridled anger or undervaluing education. It is about love—love of self, love of students, love for the community one comes from, love for one's ancestors, and, most importantly, a love for education. If one learns from this work to be disagreeable, it is because something within them deems it necessary. If what has been learned is how the system of education replicates systems designed to break those already pushed to the margins, then my hope is that this information inspires action.

The ultimate goal of the work is to hammer down particular points about contemporary education and provide new lenses through narratives that drive us to be who we need to be for students and inspire them to be what they need to be to become their best selves. I am setting those who read this on the course to "good trouble" in the tradition of the late John Lewis. As I push to pursue this goal, it would be irresponsible of me to not make it clear that this work—this presentation of being ratchetdemic and unapologetic—will illicit anger and be misread as intentionally antagonistic. I have been denied promotions and professional opportunities for being too honest and vocal about the landscape of contemporary education and too unorthodox in my approach to life and work. I have received what was framed as "critique" that was hatred and racism when speaking about the pursuit of freedom for teachers and students.

For years, I moved solely with passion and had no idea that it was not smart to proceed without strategy. I came to discover that the worst thing a person who holds no power within an institution can do is challenge its norms alone and expect to survive fully whole. To fight for your rights and the rights of others is lonely in an education system that is rooted in the silencing of those who challenge the status quo. Given this fact, I suggest that before one enters into any space where they will be students or employees, they must first understand who holds power within that space and who does not. The person who is most vocal about a particular policy is not necessarily the person making the decisions, and the person who says the right things is not necessarily the person who believes them. To be ratchetdemic requires that educators operate with wisdom. Educators must have a general wherewithal about the political landscape in the contexts where they are embedded. They must understand what type of constraints there are to doing good work and who their allies are in that space. Ratchetdemic folks must be deliberate about testing the strength of their allies through innocuous daily banter on current events to allow folks to reveal themselves. This is essential because nothing brings power together more forcefully than a threat to it, but nothing challenges power more effectively than a multidimensional and cross-cultural push against it. You have to know who your people are and who they aren't if you want to effect lasting change.

Once it's clear who is and who isn't for you in positions of power and your connections within the institution are established, it is the work of ratchetdemic folks to form coalitions with other folks who have also been marginalized by the system and denied their rights of the body. This next phase is about working with them to find footing within the institution—to declare themselves full citizens with unalienable rights within any space they occupy so they may reform it into what it should be. These coalitions may be with students, administrators, fellow teachers, parents, custodial workers, community members, and networks beyond the building where the teacher works. An example of such a multidimensional and democratic community is the hundreds of educators, parents, community members, and students who are part of the HipHopEd community and who gather weekly on Twitter to have conversations about the intersections of hip-hop and education. These are folks who work across the country in a number of different roles but who are all committed to ensuring that members of the community have access to advice, resources, and social connections that support them in the pursuit of good trouble in transforming school for the benefit of students. In that digital space, community members work to ensure that all participants know and argue for their rights in their local communities.

The largest challenge for educators in doing this work is moving beyond themselves and the elitism, which is a function of the systems they work in, and connecting with folks who are not defined by what the traditional academic holds so dear. This work of forging connections in and with the hood helps you to find your humility and your ratchet. Being with folks who are not going to be easily convinced of your newfound truth and wokeness challenges you to be as close to truth as possible. Committing to fellowship with people who in many instances have been burned by academics, schools, and individual teachers and had their rights of the body denied before allows you to experience the implications of maintaining the status quo. You've got to prove yourself to those whose chief skill is to reveal whether your newfound truth is a function of a ratchet role identity or a core self revealed. In other words, you've got to get your ratchet tested. To get your ratchet tested, you've got to be in communities and work to form coalitions across boundaries. You've got to give yourself the grace to have your own rights of the body affirmed before working to give them to others. Otherwise, the pursuit of the rights for others becomes about being a part of a rescue mission and not restitution.

I am often asked how one can form coalitions across boundaries with folks one doesn't know. How do you just show up to a community space? How do you give back to folks you don't know? The answer is you just do. Introduce yourself, explain where you come from, share what you represent, and demonstrate a willingness to learn. Be clear that what you are doing is for the benefit of the children; don't be afraid to share what you want to do better; and recognize that others can support you in your endeavors because they have skills, experience, and knowledge that surpass your own. Does the bus driver know what you are working on with your students? Do the paraprofessionals feel like they are an active part of the lessons you are designing? Do you celebrate your students' academic successes with everyone (beyond the classroom and the school) who will listen? Do you go to the concert, church, mosque, barbershop, corner store, cookout, or birthday celebration to share your work and ask for help to be better at your work? When you get there, is your message consistent about reimagining schooling to reflect the genius of the community? Our silence about our work and inability to ask for help are part of the way that we lose our voice. You can't do work for communities if it's only about you. You must forge connections with folks in communities, and you cannot forge connections with folks if you have not shared your passion for the work with them in the most humble yet raw, unapologetic, and consistent way possible. If you speak your truth, your people will find you, and they will support you. Even if your ratchet ain't their ratchet, real will always recognize real. Folks will share their passions with you, and you have a responsibility to support them. When you share your passions with them, they will do the same for you because they know it is about their betterment and the benefit of their children. This is the only way that we can create a multilayered assault on the status quo. When power cannot identify what direction the pushback comes from and sees it coming from places it never imagined, power begins to erode and, over time, is forced to restore rights to those for whom it is their birthright.

With that being said, those who are threatened by the ratchet-demic identity are quick to challenge the academic ability of the ratchetdemic person. You will be the subject of harsh critique, including of your academic credentials/ability. You must persist in your mission. When you bring folks who have never been a part of the educational discourse into the schools, those in power will make them feel unwelcome and label them as angry when they speak their truths. The newcomers will be denied the right to feel. They will be asked to leave places when they act in ways deemed inappropriate. Those in power will limit what the newcomers can say or do. They will not be treated with love and will not be allowed to love. Their rights will be denied in the same way they've been denied throughout their lives, but it will be more intense because it will be concentrated and enacted in the moment. You must stand for and with them and understand and explain that this is an expected result and no worse than anything that has come before. This is why Black folks have always been either implicitly or explicitly told by folks who supposedly love them that they have to be twice as good as the average White person to get half as far. Unfortunately, that adage has also grown to mean be twice as good or work twice as hard to be half as free. I suggest that we are automatically more than twice as good when we are ratchetdemic and free.

Bringing our community partners to the sites of their oppression (schools) means ensuring that they are equipped with statistics, legislation, and policy briefs about what is happening in their schools and their community. When their other rights are being denied, they must be armed with the right to know. When you bring folks to speak, let them speak and be informed as they do so. Much in the same vein, when the ratchetdemic educator enters the classroom, you must be an expert in every aspect of your craft and be well aware of the ideas, language, and theories that you are going to be assessed by. You must also give as much of yourself to knowing about (the roots and intent of) the pedagogy you employ as you do to the enactment of it. You must know more about the rubric measuring your effectiveness than the person who is using it, and you must also move far away from the rubric, or assessment, tool if it is damaging to your spirit, your intuition, or your pedagogy. A message like this is easy to receive but often gets read through the lens of how hard it is and how unfair it is to have to do more. Yes, it is unfair that we must give so much and do so much just to allow young people to have the conditions they need to learn and the rights they need to be free. However, if we do not do the work, the system remains as it is. Being twice as good or knowing twice as much is not a burden or detriment. It is a gift. The gift of a legacy to create and a future to contribute to is something we must learn to love and approach with joy.

For far too many of us, education has become a system that convinces us to accept and almost welcome suffering. Teachers learn to live unfulfilled and joyless lives and students learn to withstand classrooms instead of thriving within them. Progress, for the teacher and the student, has become about accepting violence and suffering and passing these on to others. There is physical, emotional, psychological, and spiritual violence woven into the structure of schools and manifested through everything from instruction to curriculum. The only options many teachers and students have been given is accepting the way things are (sitting with suffering) or hoping for a kinder suffering or more gentle denial of their rights. Given this reality, teaching must be about a refusal to exist in suffering and a refusal to impose suffering on others. Ratchetdemic teaching is about healing. It is about refusing to enact violence, accept violence, or sit with suffering, because it is about pursuing the joy that comes with connecting to the true self in a way that burns away the structures and systems that impose suffering by existing on a plane that lies beyond it even when within it. To be ratchetdemic is to reclaim one's rights in a system and world that has denied them. Ratchetdemic teaching is the pursuit of love—loving all of you and all of the souls that teaching brings to your path. It is a love without condition, manipulation, or control. This love is about claiming and creating contexts for naming and sharing rights and high expectations. It is rooted in the unconditional acceptance of self and others. This ratchetdemic love is captured in the mantra below that I wrote and recite to myself daily on my path to reimagining academic excellence. I have had the gift of hearing teachers and students across the country recite it as they pursue this same goal for themselves and their students. My hope is that it also becomes a mantra for you.

I will not hide my ratchet self to make a broken system powerful.
I will not be made to be less than because I choose to be myself.
I will not judge brilliance by how I think it looks or sounds.
I will take up space where I have been previously denied.
I will be genius and I will be free.
I will be equally as ratchet as academic.
Oreo no more.
Ratchetdemic.

DISCUSSION
QUESTIONS

CHAPTER 1

THEME: Identity Development

1. Who are you? How would you describe your multiple identities to your colleagues and/or students?
2. What are the most salient parts of your personal identity (political and social values, community affiliation, sports team preference, critical life experience, education, etc.)?
3. What are the most salient parts of your social identity (race, ethnicity, sexual orientation, religion, socioeconomic class, etc.)?
4. Are there any aspects of your identity that you have not considered until today?
5. Which aspects of your personal or social identities feel especially meaningful to you and why?
6. In your opinion/experience, how does society/the world view you?
7. What part(s) of your personal identity would you want to exhibit more and share with your school community? What actionable steps can you take to do this?
8. What is your purpose as it relates to education, your school, your students, and the school community?

CHAPTER 2

THEME: Personal Identity as It Relates to Oppressive Systems

1. In this chapter, Emdin discusses how educators can at times actively protect Whiteness while believing that they are supporting Black and Brown students. Describe one time when you protected Whiteness/established institutional norms.

2. What caused you to make that decision, consciously or unconsciously, to protect Whiteness/established institutional norms that did not make sense to students?

3. How have your students been impacted by the consequences of you choosing to protect or uphold Whiteness/Eurocentric systems/traditions?

4. In what ways can you create opportunities for students to critique and challenge systems and structures within your school and/or classroom space?

5. What can you do within your position as an educator to create opportunities for students to critique and challenge systems and structures?

CHAPTER 3

THEME: Using Identity and Pedagogy as Tools for Effective Instruction

1. What effective pedagogical practices do you contribute to your school community?
   a. How do you know your pedagogy is effective?
   b. What is your pedagogy's impact?

2. Through your pedagogy or within your school space, how can you create space for students, particularly students from underrepresented backgrounds, to express their authentic identities?

3. Emdin shares, "For Black women, who undergo a distinct form of oppression and violence, describing their ratchet forms of resistance as vulgar and violent is an attempt to

disarm them from the beautifully complex weapons and tools they have created from the shards of a shattered societal image"(p. 70). How can your school/classroom create a space for Black women and girls to be self-actualized?

    a. What are practical steps that your school community can take to create an intentional space for Black women and girls to self-actualize and authentically express themselves?

4. The ratchet that you embody is a response to oppressive structures as well as self-expression. What is your ratchet?

    a. How is it expressed?

    b. How is it received by society?

CHAPTER 4

THEME: Identifying and Becoming Ratchet

1. Emdin describes core identity as the aspect of who people are and what they are most invested in; it is the truest self. Through your pedagogy, how can you uncover students' core identities?

    a. What biases does society have about Black youth?

    b. How have these biases been revealed/demonstrated in your school community?

2. What can you do within your classroom and as a school community to challenge societal biases against Black youth?

3. In your opinion, what does it mean to be a ratchetdemic educator?

4. What steps can you take to become ratchetdemic?

CHAPTER 5

THEME: Positionality

1. In your opinion, what policies, rules, procedures, or guidelines within your school should be reconsidered in support of Black lives?

2. Emdin defines an "elevator" as an individual or group of people whose goal is to challenge you to see things from a different vantage point. Who are the elevators in your crew?

    a. What do you need from elevators to support the development of your consciousness?

3. Emdin defines "haters" as people who have a singular goal of disrupting the work of those who are operating successfully in their mission to transform a circumstance or institution. What is an effective way of engaging with a hater?

    a. What might this look like?

    b. Where have you experienced haters?

4. Emdin defines a "sucka" as a person who is opposed to the fundamental ideas behind this book: that all young people have the potential for academic excellence and that all young people (particularly those from historically marginalized and oppressed populations) possess a genius that educators do not create but that they must bring forth and enhance because it already exists. What is an effective way of engaging with a "sucka"?

    a. What might this look like?

5. Reflect on times when you have been an "elevator," "hater," and "sucka."

    a. What has been the impact?

    b. What would you do differently today?

CHAPTER 6

THEME: Understanding the Context of Schooling and Conditioning of Black Youth

1. Emdin states, "Creating ratchetdemic classrooms is about ensuring youth are seen, not judging them for what they initially present, treating them like they have value, and making them comfortable" (p. 122). What can you do within your classroom space to ensure that students are valued?

    a. What are ways to encourage students to value the content of your course?

2. In your experience, how do schools condition students? How would you reimagine schools and educational services for your population of students? What would teaching and learning look like?

   a. What classroom norms do you imagine?

   b. What would parent and community engagement look like?

3. Emdin states, "Schooling, which places young folks in metaphorical cages and inhibits them from being free, is a contemporary form of historical phenomena like slavery" (p. 136). How will you ensure that students are experiencing freedom and joy within your classroom space?

CHAPTER 7

THEME: On Excellence

1. Emdin states, "Maintaining the narrative that Black folks are less than is one of the chief ways that White mediocrity maintains itself" (p. 146). In what ways does Black excellence manifest itself in your school community?

   a. What are some specific examples?

   b. How can you amplify instances of Black excellence for the school community to witness?

2. Emdin shares that schools must be redesigned in order to disrupt educational systems that uphold standards of Whiteness and discourage expressions of Blackness. In order to do this, Emdin suggests that "Excellent sheep must offload their privileges, reveal their imperfections, acknowledge their undeveloped ratchetness, recognize the more complex and layered ratchetness of young people, and most importantly, create contexts to allow for the leveraging of both the teacher's and student's ratchetness to construct a ratchetdemic pedagogy" (p. 149). What can you do to help your school community be open to the redesign and disruption of educational systems?

CHAPTER 8

THEME: Interrupting and Healing

1. Research that promotes effective strategies that support cultural relevance, responsiveness, and competence in teaching and learning, such as culturally responsive pedagogy and multicultural education, became popular in the 1990s. In your opinion, why do teachers and schools continue to struggle to engage students while utilizing their culture?

2. What does enacting a pedagogy that has roots in and carries a legacy of social justice and equity look like within your context?

3. For the people who are at the epicenter of targeted oppression, not only are they fighting to heal, but they are constantly being retraumatized by those outside of their culture profiting from their wounds without giving voice to their realities. How can you stop/reduce this cycle of targeted oppression?

4. Emdin states, "Soul wounds are created by assaults on culture that result from the policing of cultural expressions. The wounds are inflicted by teaching, teachers, and schools that claim to love culture but see it as superficial" (p. 162). How can you create the space for healing within your classroom/school space?

CHAPTER 9

THEME: Witnessing and Dismantling

1. As an educator, how can you position yourself to bear witness and understand the inequities that young people are dealing with and face daily?

2. The chapter describes educational theories and frameworks that were developed pre-emancipation as enemy-constructed structures with friendly discourse. Identify some examples of

these theories. How may we move beyond basing our teaching on these theories?

    a. As a school, how can you interrogate teaching practices, frameworks, and philosophies to ensure that they are not inflicting harm on students?

3. Is your school responsible for upholding and maintaining inequalities against Black and Brown youth?

4. How can we be critical of policies, procedures, and pedagogies that oppress Black and Brown youth?

    a. What are the necessary steps to dismantle these oppressive policies, procedures, and pedagogies?

CHAPTER 10

THEME: On Impostor Syndrome and Genius

1. Emdin writes, "Impostor syndrome causes folks to question their existence and to see themselves as inadequate. Conversely, it causes them to see value, worth, and intelligence in everyone other than themselves" (p. 194).

    a. When have you experienced impostor syndrome? How did you overcome it? How have you healed from it?

    b. Have you witnessed your students experiencing impostor syndrome? How can you help students overcome impostor syndrome?

    c. How can you teach students to understand that their ratchetness is a skill that no one else possesses?

2. What do celebrations of your school community look like?

    a. Are students' cultures taken into account and represented within these celebrations?

    b. How can you empower students and use their support to plan future celebrations?

3. How can you authentically highlight and celebrate the genius of your students within your school community?

    a. How can you celebrate youth for their expression of ratchet brilliance?

4. What do you need as an educator to teach from a place that promotes joy and liberation?

CHAPTER 11

THEME: On Your Role and Community

1. As an educator, you are inherently a part of a system that has historically marginalized Black and Brown youth. As a part of this system, how can you use your position to generate positive change for students and the communities you serve?
2. What do you understand your role to be as a ratchetdemic educator?
3. How can your school invite community members to heal from oppressive educational experiences?

CHAPTER 12

THEME: Beyond the Book

1. Do you choose to be ratchetdemic? Why?
2. How has this text inspired you as an educator?
3. How has this text shifted your perspective on teaching and learning?
4. What did you take away from this text?

NOTES

INTRODUCTION

1. Quoted in bell hooks, *Teaching to Transgress: Education as the Practice of Freedom* (New York: Routledge, 1994), 15, https://aud.ac.in/uploads/1/admission/admissions2019/Reading_3_MA_Education_SES.pdf.

2. James Baldwin, from 1961 interview, available in *James Baldwin: The Last Interview* (Brooklyn, NY: Melville House Books, 2014).

3. Evelyn Brooks Higginbotham, *Righteous Discontent: The Women's Movement in the Black Baptist Church, 1880–1920* (Cambridge, MA: Harvard University Press, 1993).

4. Larry Chang, ed., *Wisdom for the Soul: Five Millennia of Prescriptions for Spiritual Healing* (Washington, DC: Gnosophia Publishers, 2006), 111.

5. Katherine M. Charron, *Freedom's Teacher: The Life of Septima Clark* (Chapel Hill: University of North Carolina Press, 2009).

6. Martin Luther King Jr., *Strength to Love* (1963) (Boston: Beacon Press, 2019).

7. Patricia Hill Collins, *Black Feminist Thought: Knowledge, Consciousness, and the Politics of Empowerment* (New York: Routledge, 2002).

8. Nikki Giovanni, *A Dialogue: James Baldwin and Nikki Giovanni* (New York: Lippincott, 1973).

CHAPTER 1: DR. WHITE

1. Johann G. Fichte, *The Vocation of Man* (1800), http://www.sophia-project.org/uploads/1/3/9/5/13955288/fichte_vocation.pdf.

2. Christopher Emdin, *For White Folks Who Teach in the Hood . . . and the Rest of Y'all Too: Reality Pedagogy and Urban Education* (Boston: Beacon Press, 2016).

CHAPTER 2: OREO

1. Chadwick Boseman, *The Shop*, HBO, season 3, episode 1, https://www.hbo.com/video/the-shop/seasons/season-3/episodes/episode-1/videos/having-direction.

2. S. Fordham, "Beyond Capital High: On Dual Citizenship and the Strange Career of 'Acting White,'" *Anthropology & Education Quarterly* 39, no. 3 (2008): 227–46; J. U. Ogbu, "Collective Identity and the Burden of 'Acting White' in Black History, Community, and Education," *Urban Review* 36, no. 1 (2004): 1–35.

3. Janet Cornelius, "'We Slipped and Learned to Read': Slave Accounts of the Literacy Process, 1830–1865," *Phylon* 44, no. 3 (1983): 171–86.

4. Kristin Appenbrink, "America's Favorite Cookie Is (Not Surprisingly) the Oreo," Kitchn, 2015, https://www.thekitchn.com/americas-favorite-cookie-is-not-surprisingly-the-oreo-food-news-216291.

5. Barack Obama, nomination acceptance speech, Democratic National Convention, Chicago, 2012; Donald Trump, *The America We Deserve* (Los Angeles: Renaissance Books, 2000).

6. Lauretta Charlton, "Study Examines Why Black Americans Remain Scarce in Executive Suites," *New York Times*, December 9, 2019, https://www.nytimes.com/2019/12/09/us/black-in-corporate-america-report.html.

CHAPTER 3: RATCHET AS TOOL

1. L. Boosie, "Do Tha Ratchet," *United We Stand, Divided We Fall*, Lava House Records, 2004.

2. N. E. Brown and L. Young, "Ratchet Politics: Moving Beyond Black Women's Bodies to Indict Institutions and Structures," Academia.edu, 2015, https://www.academia.edu/10365778.

3. T. A. Pickens, "Shoving Aside the Politics of Respectability: Black Women, Reality TV, and the Ratchet Performance," *Women & Performance: A Journal of Feminist Theory* 25, no. 1 (2015): 41–58.

4. Thomas L. Webber, *Deep Like the Rivers: Education in the Slave Quarter Community, 1831–1865* (New York: W. W. Norton, 1978).

CHAPTER 4: RATCHET AS BEING AND FREEING

1. Webber, *Deep Like the Rivers*.

2. K. Bales and R. Soodalter, *The Slave Next Door: Human Trafficking and Slavery in America Today* (Berkeley: University of California Press, 2010).

3. S. M. Collins, "Black Mobility in White Corporations: Up the Corporate Ladder but Out on a Limb," *Social Problems* 44, no. 1 (1997): 55–67.

4. W. C. Rhoden, *Forty Million Dollar Slaves* (New York: Three Rivers Press, 2007).

5. Jonathan H. Turner, *The Problem of Emotions in Societies* (New York: Routledge, 2012).

6. Turner, *The Problem of Emotions*.

7. Turner, *The Problem of Emotions*.

8. Turner, *The Problem of Emotions*.

9. Webber, *Deep Like the Rivers.*

10. R. A. Bauer and A. H. Bauer, "Day to Day Resistance to Slavery," *Journal of Negro History* 27, no. 4 (1942): 388–419.

11. "The Fox and the Grapes," Aesop's Fables, trans. Aphra Behn, https://aesopsfables.wordpress.com/the-fox-the-grapes, accessed December 9, 2020.

12. James Baldwin, "A Talk to Teachers"; originally published in *The Saturday Review*, December 21, 1963.

CHAPTER 5: ELEVATORS, HATERS, AND SUCKAS

1. Peyton L. Jones, "Struggle in the Sunshine City: The Movement for Racial Equality in St. Petersburg Florida 1955–1968," master's thesis, University of South Florida, 2010, available at https://scholarcommons.usf.edu/etd/1672.

2. Enoch Douglas Davis, *On the Bethel Trail* (St. Petersburg, FL: Valkyrie Press, 1979).

3. Jones, "Struggle in the Sunshine City."

4. Omali Yeshitela, speech at Malcolm X commemoration, Tampa, Florida, May 19, 1977.

5. E. Fischbein, "Intuition and Proof," *For the Learning of Mathematics* 3, no. 2 (1982): 9–24; L. B. Orlandi and P. Pierce, "Analysis or Intuition? Reframing the Decision-Making Styles Debate in Technological Settings," *Management Decision* 58, no. 1 (2020).

6. D. Cruickshank, *Maxine Greene: The Importance of Personal Reflection*, Edutopia, 2008, http://edutopia.org/maxine-greene.

CHAPTER 6: CAGES AND CONDITIONING

1. J. DeGruy, "Post Traumatic Slave Syndrome," *Dr. Joy DeGruy* (blog), https://www.joydegruy.com/post-traumatic-slave-syndrome, accessed December 9, 2020.

2. L. Geddes, "Fear of a Smell Can Be Passed Down Several Generations," *NewScientist*, December 1, 2013, https://www.newscientist.com/article/dn24677-fear-of-a-smell-can-be-passed-down-several-generations.

CHAPTER 7: CLONES

1. W. Deresiewicz, *Excellent Sheep: The Miseducation of the American Elite and the Way to a Meaningful Life* (New York: Simon & Schuster, 2015).

2. F. Gardaphé, "We Weren't Always White: Race and Ethnicity in Italian American Literature," *Lit: Literature Interpretation Theory* 13, no. 3 (2002): 185–99.

3. B. Bourke, "Experiences of Black Students in Multiple Cultural Spaces at a Predominantly White Institution," *Journal of Diversity in Higher Education* 3, no. 2 (2010): 126–35.

4. Deresiewicz, *Excellent Sheep*, 22.

5. M. Kaufman, "There's a Black Sheep in Every Family Fold," *New York Times*, November 23, 1988, https://www.nytimes.com/1988/11/23/garden/there-s-a-black-sheep-in-every-family-fold.html.

6. Malcolm Gladwell, *David and Goliath: Underdogs, Misfits, and the Art of Battling Giants* (New York: Little, Brown, 2013).

CHAPTER 8: SOUL WOUNDS AND WHITE GAUZE

1. Dead Prez, "They School," *Let's Get Free*, Apple Music, 2000.

2. Nas, "One Love," *Illmatic*, Columbia, 1994.

3. Biggie Smalls, "Juicy," *Born to Die*, Bad Boy Records, 1994.

4. DaBaby, "Under the Sun," *Revenge of the Dreamers III*, Dreamville Records, 2019.

5. J. A. Banks, "Multicultural Education: Development, Dimensions, and Challenges," *Phi Delta Kappan* 75, no. 1 (1993): 22–28.

6. Banks, "Multicultural Education," 22.

7. Tanya A. Christian, "Legal Ruling May Force Georgia Gov. to Reveal How He 'Stole' Election from Stacey Abrams," *Essence*, February 11, 2020, https://www.essence.com/news/politics/governor-brian-kemp-voter-purge-methodology.

8. E. L. Green and K. Benner, "Louisiana School Made Headlines for Sending Black Kids to Elite Colleges. Here's the Reality," *New York Times*, November 30, 2018, https://www.nytimes.com/2018/11/30/us/tm-landry-college-prep-black-students.html.

9. E. Duran, J. Firehammer, and J. Gonzalez, "Liberation Psychology as the Path toward Healing Cultural Soul Wounds," *Journal of Counseling and Development* 86, no. 3 (July 2008).

CHAPTER 9: FRENEMIES AND ENERGY

1. W. E. B. Du Bois, "A Negro Schoolmaster in the New South," in *The Teacher in American Society: A Critical Anthology*, ed. Eugene F. Provenzo Jr. (Los Angeles: Sage, 2011), 49.

2. Michele Foster, *Black Teachers on Teaching* (New York: New Press, 1997), 2.

3. "African American Teachers in Kansas," Kansas Historical Society (1953), https://www.kshs.org/kansapedia/african-american-teachers-in-kansas/11995, accessed December 9, 2020.

4. Du Bois, "A Negro Schoolmaster," 49.

5. Du Bois, "A Negro Schoolmaster," 49.

6. F. P. Prucha, *Documents of United States Indian Policy* (Lincoln: University of Nebraska Press, 2000), 161.

7. Prucha, *Documents*, 161.

8. B. Sigel, "Feel It in the Air," Roc-A-Fella Records, 2004.

CHAPTER 10: TOWARD HEALING

1. T. E. Dancy and M. C. Brown, "The Mentoring and Induction of Educators of Color: Addressing the Impostor Syndrome in Academe," *Journal of School Leadership* 21, no. 4 (2011): 607–34.

2. Dena Simmons, "How Students of Color Confront Imposter Syndrome," November 2015, TED video, https://www.ted.com/talks/dena_simmons_how_students_of_color_confront_impostor_syndrome.

3. Toni Morrison, "The Truest Eye," interview by Pam Houston, O, *The Oprah Magazine*, November 2003, https://www.oprah.com/omagazine/toni-morrison-talks-love/all.

CHAPTER 11: THE GET BACK

1. Alyssa Vingan Klein, "Internal Memo from Gucci CEO Shows He's Taking the Blackface Scandal Very, Very Seriously," *Fashionista*, February 11, 2019, https://fashionista.com/2019/02/gucci-blackface-sweater-ceo-marco-bizzarri-statement.

2. Audre Lorde, "The Master's Tools Will Never Dismantle the Master's House," in *Sister Outsider: Essays and Speeches* (Berkeley: Crossing Press, 2007), 110–14.

CHAPTER 12: RESTITUTION OVER RESCUE MISSIONS

1. Anodea Judith, *Eastern Body, Western Mind: Psychology and the Chakra System as a Path to the Self* (New York: Random House, 2004).

INDEX

Abrams, Stacey, 195
academic achievement: affluence
	and, 132; conformity and, 4,
	18, 29, 49, 86; ratchetness
	combined with, 133, 212–13;
	as synonym for proximity to
	White ideals, 149–50; valuing
	of students and, 123; White
	and Black, 145–49
academic rigor, 30, 122–24
acceptance, 19–20, 194–95,
	197–203
to act, 223
acting White, 38–41
affirmation, 30, 64, 117, 118, 155,
	225
affluence, and reality pedagogy,
	126–32, 134–35
African Internationalism,
	166–162
Afro-Caribbeans, 47
agape love, 223–24
agency, 3
agnosia, cultural, 168–69
Aldridge, Derrick, 170
Alim, H. Samy, 159
Americanism, 100–101
anger, 222–23
antirespectability, 8
archaeology of the self, 17
athletes, professional, 74, 76

authenticity, 5, 15, 17, 195–96.
	See also identity
Autobots, 59–60

Baldwin, James, 8–9, 93, 95
behavior management, 43–44
"better self" model, 17–20
bias, 127–28
Black Americans: classism and,
	146–47; cultural acceptance,
	81–82; Oreos, 38–41; power
	and, 3–4, 221, 224, 226–27,
	229
Black feminist thought, 8
Blackness, 4; acceptable versions
	of, 47–48, 148, 236; demon-
	izing, 45, 115; erasing, 50;
	Oreos and, 38–42; perceptions
	of, 78, 83–84, 97; performing,
	97; understanding and accep-
	tance, 92–95
black sheep, 146–52
Black women, 5, 68–70, 233–34
Boosie (Lil Boosie), 67, 68–69, 70
Brooklyn Technical High School,
	60–61
Brown, Nadia, 68–69

Carlisle Indian Industrial School,
	181–82
chaos, 6